Conflict and effective demand
in economic growth

Conflict and effective demand in economic growth

PETER SKOTT

Institute of Economics
University of Aarhus

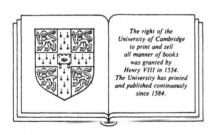

The right of the
University of Cambridge
to print and sell
all manner of books
was granted by
Henry VIII in 1534.
The University has printed
and published continuously
since 1584.

CAMBRIDGE UNIVERSITY PRESS

Cambridge
New York   Port Chester
Melbourne   Sydney

CAMBRIDGE UNIVERSITY PRESS
Cambridge, New York, Melbourne, Madrid, Cape Town, Singapore, São Paulo

Cambridge University Press
The Edinburgh Building, Cambridge CB2 8RU, UK

Published in the United States of America by Cambridge University Press, New York

www.cambridge.org
Information on this title: www.cambridge.org/9780521365963

© Cambridge University Press 1989

First published 1989
This digitally printed version 2008

A catalogue record for this publication is available from the British Library

ISBN 978-0-521-36596-3 hardback
ISBN 978-0-521-06631-0 paperback

Contents

Guide to text notation

Carets, $\hat{\ }$, and dots, $\dot{\ }$, are used to represent proportional growth rates (logarithmic derivatives) and time derivatives, respectively; i.e. $\hat{x} = (dx/dt)(1/x)$, $\dot{x} = dx/dt$. Subscripts are used to denote partial derivatives; if, for instance, $I/Y = f(u, \pi)$ then $\partial(I/Y)/\partial u = \partial f/\partial u = f_u$.

For ease of reference, the most important variables used in chapters 4–8 are listed below. Symbols which are used only within a few pages are not listed, and in the survey chapter, chapter 3, it has not always been possible to follow the same notation. The subscript i denotes a firm specific variable, and a star * is used to indicate an equilibrium value or a desired value of a variable.

C = consumption in real terms
I = gross investment in real terms
K = capital stock in real terms
L = labour
M = stock of money (= amount of bank deposits = amount of bank loans)
N = number of securities issued by firms
P = gross profits
S = gross saving in real terms
W = total wage bill
Y = gross output in real terms

e = employment rate
g_w = warranted growth rate
i = nominal rate of interest on bank loans and bank deposits
n = rate of growth of the labour supply in efficiency units
p = price of output
q = Tobin's q
r = real rate of interest on bank loans and bank deposits
s_p = corporate retention rate
u = rate of utilisation of capital

v = price of securities
w = money-wage rate

α = ratio of the value of securities to profits net of depreciation and real interest payments
β = ratio of total nominal income to bank deposits (demand for money). The parameters α and β describe households' saving and portfolio behaviour
δ = rate of depreciation of capital
γ = inverse of the own-price elasticity of conjectured demand
ι = cost of finance
λ = output–labour ratio
π = share of gross profits in gross income
ρ = elasticity of a firm's conjectured demand price with respect to the price of rival firms
σ = output–capital ratio at full-capacity utilisation

$f(u,\,\pi) = I/Y$ = investment function
$h(\pi,\,e) = \hat{Y}$ = output-expansion function

Acknowledgements

Many colleagues and friends have helped me in the writing of this book. I should like to thank, in particular, Paul Auerbach and Meghnad Desai. They both read the entire manuscript and their detailed suggestions have greatly improved the final version. Discussions with Victoria Chick have influenced the treatment of financial issues, and comments and criticisms from David Soskice, Malcolm Sawyer and especially Bob Rowthorn led to substantial changes in chapter 8. I have also benefited from numerous discussions with colleagues at the University of Aarhus as well as at the University of Copenhagen and University College London. The research was made possible by a Research Fellowship at the University of Copenhagen, and large parts of the book were written while I was an Honorary Fellow at University College London. Finally, I wish to thank Margaret C. Last, Francis Brooke and Patrick McCartan. Margaret C. Last has been a superb subeditor and Francis Brooke and Patrick McCartan have been patient and encouraging throughout the preparation of this book.

CHAPTER 1

Introduction

Economic growth and cyclical movement are issues of central importance and public concern. They are also areas of immense controversy. Does capitalism have strong tendencies toward steady growth at full employment? Are the causes of fluctuations in output and employment to be found outside the economic system or are they intrinsic to the system? These questions are fundamental to economic and political decision-making, and it is the search for answers to these questions which motivates this analysis.

Most of modern radical economics is based on a vision of class conflict and Keynesian market failures, and in this respect the present book is no exception. But there will be no attempt here at exegetical reconstruction and little direct reference to the 'masters': Marx, Keynes and Kalecki. Furthermore, although the fundamental ideas are rooted in the traditions of Marx and Keynes, I shall draw on developments and techniques from mainstream economics. The theory to be presented retains basic insights from Marx and Keynes, but it differs from existing formulations of their theories in important ways and some common criticisms of post-Keynesian and neo-Marxian theory are examined explicitly.

The book is addressed not only to a neo-Marxian and post-Keynesian audience but to economists of a more orthodox persuasion as well. The differences between the 'visions' of rival schools of thought are profound, and in my view the heterodox framework presented here offers an appealing and fruitful approach to the study of capitalist market economies. Nevertheless, it would be a mistake to exaggerate the differences and incompatibilities between different approaches. In the past, heterodox economists have often been able to draw on work from mainstream economics and vice versa. Nor is orthodox theory monolithic, and the apparent strength of the neoclassical tradition may reflect primarily the perceived lack of a credible alternative. With this book I hope to show that an alternative post-Keynesian and neo-Marxian synthesis can be given precise formulation. The alternative framework can address a range of questions which have normally been ignored within the radical tradition, and it provides a coherent explanation of many of the stylised facts of capitalist economies.

The structure of the book is as follows. Chapter 2 examines some methodological issues. It argues that the frequent criticisms of 'equilibrium' and 'equilibrium economics' are misguided. All logically consistent economic theories have equilibria. One may criticise particular theories and particular equilibria but it is impossible to develop an economic theory without equilibrium. The chapter also discusses the optimisation assumption in neoclassical economics and, especially, the use of profit maximisation in the derivation of firms' production and investment decisions. Profit maximisation may be a useful analytical device, but the dogmatic emphasis in general-equilibrium theory on optimisation and disaggregation should be rejected: it makes it virtually impossible to approach dynamic issues in a satisfactory way.

Chapter 3 gives a brief survey of some important contributions to the post-Keynesian and neo-Marxian literature. The main purpose of the chapter is to motivate the analysis in later chapters and to situate this analysis within the wider tradition: some central issues are raised and it is indicated how the standard analyses of these issues suffer from important shortcomings.

Chapters 4–6 contain the analytical core of the book. The basic assumptions are presented in chapter 4. It is assumed that firms (attempt to) maximise profits, and the resultant production decisions are analysed in detail. The economy, however, is not always in Keynesian short-run equilibrium: firms' (short-term) demand expectations may not be fulfilled and the speed of adjustment of output is finite. The difference between actual and expected levels of demand is an important determinant of production decisions, but changes in production and employment are also influenced by labour-market conditions. The rate of unemployment – the size of the reserve army of labour – determines the strength of workers *vis-à-vis* capital, and the rate of expansion of production and of employment is inversely related to workers' strength.

With respect to consumption and saving, it is assumed that there is a desired relation between stocks of financial assets and current flows of income. The average saving rate thus is not exogenously given nor is it determined as a simple weighted average of the saving propensities of different classes or income categories. The explicit inclusion of financial stocks offers a more reasonable description of household behaviour than traditional Keynesian formulations based on flows alone. In addition, it facilitates the analysis of financial constraints on firms' investment. The influence, for instance, of Tobin's q on investment and the desired capital–output ratio can be examined explicitly.

The analysis of the model in chapter 5 falls in two parts. I first adopt the standard short-run assumption that investment is exogenously given. At any moment the level of output is predetermined, and accommodating variations in the distribution of income are needed in order to establish ultra-short-run equilibrium between saving and investment. In the short term, however, output adjusts and a multiplier relation between investment and output is obtained.

In the long run, investment ceases to be exogenous, and I consider the polar case of steady growth where the capital–output ratio is at the desired level. Under reasonable assumptions there is a unique steady-growth path (the warranted path) and the steady-growth rate is equal to the growth of the labour force: the warranted and natural growth rates coincide. The effects on the growth path of changes in key behavioural parameters are examined, and in most cases the effects conform to intuitive expectations. An increase in workers' militancy, for instance, raises the rate of unemployment: as workers become more militant, a larger reserve army of unemployed is required in order to maintain discipline. Two additional results should be noted. The normal Keynesian paradox of thrift needs to be modified. A change in households' desired ratio of financial assets to income has both saving and valuation effects: it will affect Tobin's q and thus firms' investment decisions as well as the average saving propensity, and the net effect on growth may be ambiguous. Secondly, the rate of inflation – and the specification of the Phillips curve – turns out to be irrelevant to the determination of the steady-growth path. This result, however, is sensitive to the precise specification of the model.

Chapter 6 abandons the assumptions that either investment is exogenous (in the short run) or the capital–output ratio becomes fully flexible and equal to the value which firms consider optimal (in the long run). A detailed analysis of investment decisions is of interest in itself, and it is also needed in order to examine the dynamic properties of the economy. In deriving the investment function, I assume profit maximisation but depart from the standard approach which postulates convex adjustment costs. Instead, the inflexibilities of investment are represented by an investment lag as well as indivisibilities in individual investment programmes.

Having derived the investment function, the chapter examines the dynamic behaviour of the economy as a whole. The steady-growth path turns out to be locally asymptotically unstable and Harrod's instability result thus survives. Variations in the reserve army of labour, however, have class-struggle effects on production and these effects transform the divergent movements into cyclical fluctuations around the steady-growth path.

Chapter 7 discusses some monetary and financial aspects of the model and examines the effects of changes in some of the assumptions. It is shown, first, why households cannot 'call the tune' with respect to long-run saving, investment and growth. Household behaviour may determine the financial valuation of firms, but this is not sufficient to control firms' production and investment decisions.

The chapter also comments on recent Keynesian debates about the role of finance and saving in the investment process and examines the effects of alternative specifications of firms' financial behaviour. Finally, it looks more closely at the question of 'money wage neutrality': assumptions in chapters 4–6 imply that the level of money wages and prices, as well as the rate of inflation, is irrelevant to the determination of relative prices and quantities. These results, however, depend on the twin assumptions that there is no outside money and that real interest rates on bank loans remain constant over time. I now relax these assumptions and examine two alternative specifications: the monetarist case, where the money supply grows at an exogenously given rate, and the case of constant nominal interest rates.

In chapter 8 I address distributional questions. Class conflict and the relative strength of workers *vis-à-vis* capitalists are key concepts in Marxian distribution theory. Recently, however, Marglin (1984a) has argued that the introduction of conflict-based distribution mechanisms into a Keynesian model will create an overdetermined system. The overdeterminacy arises from the assumption that actual income shares are equal to 'target shares'. This assumption is questionable. It would seem to be an essential aspect of class conflict that the rival claims of workers and capitalists are incompatible and that actual income shares are determined by the relative strength of the classes. But how is relative strength determined, and is there any way in which workers can influence *real* wages? The answer depends on how pricing decisions are made, and the chapter concludes with a discussion of one very influential answer to this question. Theories of monopoly capital – probably the dominant school of radical economics – suggest that there has been a trend decline in the degree of competition in advanced capitalist economies and that this decline has led to increasing price–cost margins, stagnation, falling capital utilisation and falling profitability. I examine this argument and its implications for the present theory.

Chapter 9, finally, discusses some of the results and limitations of the theory.

CHAPTER 2

Methodological issues

2.1 INTRODUCTION

The general perspective of the theory offered here differs from that of
many previous formulations in the post-Keynesian and neo-Marxian
literature in at least three ways. The first difference is the presentation of a
'unified' theory of a pure capitalist economy. The theory is unified in the
sense that it covers a range of issues not normally analysed within the same
analytical framework. Trade-cycle fluctuations are usually examined
separately from monetary issues; the analysis of long-term growth is
normally carried out in the context of a special long-run model which
leaves out many of the concerns of short-term models. Taylor (1983), for
instance, presents a number of different models each designed to illumi-
nate a particular set of problems, and in Marglin's (1984a) attempt at a
synthesis of Marx and Keynes the emphasis is on long-term growth while
short-run issues as well as monetary and financial aspects receive little
attention. In contrast, the present book attempts to deal with these and
other issues within a single unified framework.

Secondly, stability issues feature prominently in the analysis. In spite of
the manifest fluctuations in economic activity in all advanced capitalist
countries, a concern with the stability of the steady-growth path has been
largely absent in post-Keynesian and neo-Marxian growth theory. The
present work brings stability back on to the stage. The long-term path of
the economy emerges as a sequence of (ultra)-short-run equilibria. A
steady-growth path with a constant rate of growth does exist but Harrod
was right: the warranted path is unstable.

The third difference concerns the analysis of behavioural relations.
Good macroeconomic theory should have a microeconomic dimension:
there should be a correspondence between macroeconomic outcomes and
microeconomic behaviour. Production and investment decisions, in particular, play a crucial role in both Marxian and Keynesian theory, and the
behavioural relations which describe these decisions should be modelled

very carefully. There is a wide consensus that firms aim to make as much profit as possible, and in this book investment and production decisions will be related explicitly to the profit-maximising behaviour of individual firms.

The remainder of this chapter comments in greater detail on these three differences and on the relation of the present theory to orthodox economics.

2.2 A UNIFIED THEORY

The aim is to develop a coherent and reasonably comprehensive theory of a closed capitalist economy. There are obvious dangers in this unified approach. It is illusory to believe that one universally applicable model can be found which is suitable for all problems. Theory must be adapted to the specific question at hand, and generality is not to be desired for its own sake.

The present theory applies to capitalist economies but it is more specific than that. In order to analyse a range of different issues, it has been necessary to introduce many simplifying assumptions: otherwise the model would have become analytically intractable. These assumptions have been chosen on the basis of their empirical plausibility. It turns out, for instance, that some results depend on the value of parameters which describe firms' financial behaviour, and instead of maintaining a general model (and a range of different possible regimes) I concentrate on the regime which in the light of available evidence appears most relevant.

The simplifications can be challenged, and alternative specifications are possible. The theory certainly does not include all possible specifications as special cases. Generality in this sense always comes at a high cost – perfect generality signals nothing but perfect vacuity. Without substantive and challengeable assumptions there can be no substantive conclusions. A unified theory covering a range of issues does, however, accentuate the need for simplifying assumptions. If one wants to paint a broad canvas then one may have to compromise on the level of detail.

A unified theory will need to be supplemented by detailed analyses of specific areas. But the different models should belong to the same theoretical universe, and it is important to examine the general outline of that universe. Thus, the analysis of long-run equilibria only makes sense if one believes that the economy will actually converge or fluctuate around the long-run equilibrium configuration; the model used to analyse monetary issues should be consistent with the views developed on the analysis of trade-cycle fluctuations; and so on. The specification of one relatively comprehensive model permits the development of partial models which are informed by a coherent overall vision of how the economy works.

The simultaneous consideration of a number of different factors may also help to narrow down the range of possible outcomes. One of the most important reasons for doing theory is precisely that by increasing our understanding of the economy, we may limit the set of outcomes which a priori seems possible. If, for instance, one looks only at the product market then the long-term rate of growth appears to depend upon the state of thrift and animal spirits, and a catalogue of possible scenarios can be drawn up. We may have a golden age of continuous (near) full employment where the growth rate of employment equals the rate of growth of the labour force. Alternatively, the rate of growth of employment may fall short of or exceed the rate of growth of the labour force, and this gives rise to limping golden ages. Taking into account possible constraints on long-term growth as well as the possibility that initial conditions may fail to permit steady growth, the list of mythical ages is further expanded to include a leaden age as well as galloping and creeping platinum ages (Robinson, 1962). But are all these scenarios equally plausible? The neoclassics have not thought so. They have argued that Joan Robinson – and the post-Keynesians in general – ignores important equilibrating forces such as relative factor prices and the choice of technique. Marxians likewise have felt that too little attention has been given to the influence of the size of the reserve army of labour on the conditions of production and realisation of surplus value. In the end one may not agree with these criticisms, but the implications of including these and other factors in the model should be examined.

2.3 INSTABILITY AND THE NOTION OF EQUILIBRIUM

There can be no doubt that the notion of equilibrium occupies a central position in orthodox economics, and heterodox economists have often focused their criticisms of orthodoxy on exactly this point. Myrdal, Kaldor and Kornai are among the prominent critics of 'equilibrium economics' but new schools within the orthodox tradition have also announced the end of equilibrium: some years ago, for instance, Barro and Grossman (1976) (among others) saw a need to go beyond equilibrium theory and employ new disequilibrium methods. Hahn, on the other hand, has repeatedly come to the defence of equilibrium economics.

The analysis below confirms the Harrodian instability of the warranted growth path, and this result could be seen as another argument 'against equilibrium'. I shall argue, however, that to be against equilibrium is to be against theory in general, and the debate for and against equilibrium therefore has not been helpful. There are important differences of opinion between the protagonists, but focusing on equilibrium only serves to obscure these differences.

There is fundamental disagreement over the formulation of appropriate equilibrium conditions, but it is a basic premise of all scientific endeavour that the object under investigation possesses some sort of 'regularity'. The purpose of scientific work is to uncover the regularities and represent them as fully and adequately as possible. This representation takes the form of theories (sets of statements and hypotheses about regularities in the scientific object), and a theory defines a set of equilibria.

In the Arrow–Debreu theory of general equilibrium, for instance, it is assumed that consumers have well-defined preference orderings which – in conjunction with budget constraints and initial conditions – determine their behaviour, i.e. their trading activities. The budget constraints state that prices are parametrically given and that the value of purchases must not exceed the value of sales. Firms also face given prices, and production activities are chosen such as to maximise profits subject to constraints defined by exogenous and well-behaved production possibility sets. The theory thus (i) postulates a set of regularities regarding the determination of production and trading decisions and (ii) predicts that, for any given set of initial endowments, production possibility sets and preference orderings, prices will be such that the desired actions of all agents become mutually compatible. Price vectors which satisfy this consistency requirement are called 'equilibrium prices', and the associated consumption, production and trading activities of individual agents constitute the 'equilibrium' behaviour of agents.

Analogously, a simple Keynesian textbook model may assume that the desired level of total investment is a historically given constant, that the desired level of consumption is functionally related to income and that total income is equal to the sum of investment and consumption. The regularities posited by this theory concern the predetermined character of investment and the fixed relation between desired consumption and income. The theory predicts that total income will be such that investment and consumption may both attain the desired levels, and these predicted levels are termed equilibrium levels.

In general, any non-vacuous and internally consistent theory will describe a number of regularities and define a non-empty set of outcomes satisfying the regularities. This set of consistent outcomes constitutes the equilibria of the theory. A proof of the existence of equilibrium therefore is simply a check on the logical consistency of the theory. A theory without equilibrium (in the sense I use the term) is logically false.

One implication of this notion of equilibrium should be noted. Stability questions concern what happens outside equilibrium, and all implications of the theory are summed up in the set of equilibria. The stability of equilibria associated with any given theory can therefore only be investigated with reference to a more general theory which includes the original theory as a special case and which contains the original set of equilibria as a subset of its own set of equilibria. In other words, the most general theory cannot, as a matter of logic, be tested for stability: the analysis of stability is predicated on the existence of an even more general theory. Stability analysis is a test of the relevance of the associated theory, and for the most general theory the only possible test is a direct and empirically based assessment of its usefulness in the applications for which it is intended.

In the present book the most general equilibrium will be the 'ultra-short-run equilibrium'. By assumption, the economy is always in ultra-short-run equilibrium, and, although arguments will be advanced to support this approach, there will be no formal stability analysis of ultra-short-run equilibria. In contrast, the stability of more restrictive equilibria, e.g. steady-growth equilibria, can and will be examined formally within the framework of the general theory.

An analogy may help to clarify the argument. A theory without equilibrium corresponds to a self-contradictory null hypothesis in statistical theory, e.g. $H_0: X \sim N(\alpha, \sigma^2)$ with $\alpha \in \varnothing$. Economic theorists, furthermore, may investigate the stability properties of an equilibrium associated with a theory T_1 with respect to a more general theory T_0. This stability test finds a parallel in the statistical testing of a special hypothesis H_1 against the more general hypothesis H_0. In both cases one examines whether the description provided by a simple special hypothesis is (almost) as good as that afforded by a more general hypothesis. If the equilibrium of T_1 is stable under the assumptions of T_0 then the predictions of T_1 should be almost as accurate as those of T_0. Stability of the warranted growth path, for instance, suggests that the average growth rate of the economy will be (approximately) equal to the warranted rate. Stability thus enables one to focus on the simple theory (at least for some purposes and assuming a rapid speed of convergence). The stability test is the theorist's way of testing a relatively stringent hypothesis against a more general theory.

'Equilibrium' is a purely methodological concept on a par with 'theory'. But any particular equilibrium carries with it the ontological implications of the associated theory. The real question underlying the debate about equilibrium concerns the adequacy of specific theories or theoretical approaches with respect to some specified class of issues. Kaldor (1972), for instance, accused 'equilibrium economics' of irrelevance with respect to an understanding of the growth process of modern capitalist economies. But his critique was directed at Walrasian economic theory, not theory in general or 'equilibrium' in general.

The theory developed in this book does not break with equilibrium methodology. It does, however, address some dynamic issues which are often ignored, and the general framework is decidedly non-Walrasian.

2.4 WALRASIAN GENERAL EQUILIBRIUM

By general consent, general-equilibrium theory is at the centre of orthodox economics. It is the 'hard core' of a research programme. According to Weintraub (1979), it 'is a metatheory, or an investigative logic, which . . . is used to construct all economic theories' (p. 73) and it is 'rooted . . . in the very structural unities of science itself. To attack general equilibrium in economics is to *simultaneously* deny homeostatic reasoning to psychologists and morphogenic analysis to the biologist' (p. 72). These are strong statements, but, unless one defines general-equilibrium theory so broadly that the concept becomes void of content, I find the statements absolutely false.

Walrasian and neo-Walrasian general-equilibrium economics defines a particular vision of how the economy works. It may be difficult to describe the vision precisely, but some fundamental characteristics of the general-equilibrium approach can be identified.

The most striking aspect is probably the emphasis on choice-theoretic foundations. Agents are assumed to be rational in the sense that the economic behaviour of each individual agent is determined by a preference ordering and a set of well-defined constraints on the choice set. The emphasis on choice-theoretic foundations carries with it the desire for a great degree of disaggregation in the specification of economic agents. It may sometimes – for instance in applied work – be necessary to deal with aggregated groups of agents. Economic theory, however, is founded on the rational behaviour of individual decision-makers, and a completely disaggregated framework represents the ideal vehicle for theoretical work. Theories which cannot be 'generalised' to incorporate any number of agents are viewed with great scepticism.[1] The choice sets of agents are given as subsets of the commodity space, and the emphasis on choice-theoretic foundations therefore also leads to a concern with commodity-

[1] Tobin's criticism of Kaldor's distribution theory represents a clear-cut and rather polemical example of this attitude: 'If Mr Kaldor is going to transform the Keynesian theory of employment into a Keynesian theory of distribution, should he not aspire to a *General* Theory of Distribution? For all the flaws that Mr Kaldor detects in it, neoclassical theory is general; it will divide up national product among 3 or 101 factors as well or as badly as between 2. Mr Kaldor's substitute should not do less' (Tobin, 1960, p. 119).

space generality: theories should – in principle – be general enough to include any number of commodities.

2.5 CHOICE-THEORETIC FOUNDATIONS

The methodological individualism embedded in orthodox economic theory has been a frequent target of criticism, but some of the criticism is wide of the mark. The view that social and economic phenomena should be analysed in terms of the interrelations between the actions of rational individuals does not require an extreme notion of ahistorical individuals with preferences that are independent of social influence and institutions.[2] A much weaker form of methodological individualism will suffice.

General-equilibrium theory does not necessarily deny or devalue the influence of (holistic) sociological and historical factors on the behaviour of agents. But it does imply that the influence of these factors is mediated through individual behaviour and can be analysed indirectly through the effects on the preferences and initial endowments of the individual agents comprising the general-equilibrium model. For general-equilibrium theory the important point is that the preferences of individual agents remain constant over time. If this condition is met, the formation of preferences themselves can be left outside the domain of economic theory.[3]

The stability over time of preferences is, however, questionable. The preferences of individuals exhibit considerable change of time. Furthermore, the preferences of different individuals are likely to be strongly interdependent.[4] From a macroeconomic perspective, one important manifestation of this instability and interdependence is changes in worker

---

[2] Lucas (1981), however, comes close to stating just that: 'The time pattern of hours that an individual supplies to the market is something that, in a very clear sense, he *chooses* . . . there is no question that social convention and institutional structures affect these patterns, but conventions and institutions do not simply come out of the blue. On the contrary, institutions and customs are designed precisely in order to aid in matching preferences and opportunities satisfactorily' (p. 4).

Lucas seems unaware of the problems involved in the infinite regress – individual behaviour being affected by institutions being affected by individual behaviour etc. – which could equally well support a holistic 'methodological institutionalism'.

[3] This does not imply that it is wise to neglect institutional and historical analysis. Morishima (1984) is a recent critique of general-equilibrium theory along these lines. See also Kornai (1971).

[4] A simple and well-known game-theoretic example may illustrate this. In the so-called 'battle of the sexes', the stereotypical husband would like to go to a football game while the wife prefers a ballet. If no agreement is reached they will either have to go separately or stay at home, and the husband (wife) rates these alternatives below a joint outing to the ballet (football game). In other words, the commodity preferences – the preferences over ballet versus ball game – of one spouse depend on the decisions of the other. See Skott (1986) for further discussion of these issues.

militancy, France 1968 being perhaps the most prominent example from the post-war period. For present purposes, however, the main point is that changeable and interdependent preferences make it futile to strive for full generality and disaggregation in the study of interrelations between individual decision-makers. Instead, a conscious and judicious choice of representative agents is needed, the appropriate choice as well as the degree of disaggregation being dependent on the object of the particular enquiry. No good purpose is served by pretending that – at least in principle – this choice can be avoided by a 'general theory'.

Simple notions of microeconomic foundations are thus untenable. It is impossible to escape aggregation and the use of representative agents, but this does not imply that microeconomic decision-making can be ignored. The need to look carefully at microeconomic decisions is particularly acute with respect to firms' production and investment decisions.

There is widespread agreement among economists from (almost) all traditions that firms aim to make profits, but consensus on the main objective conceals major differences between competing schools of thought. In neoclassical theory the profit criterion is translated into profit *maximisation*. Firms, like all other agents, maximise their objective function, in this case the amount of pure profits, subject to a set of constraints. This procedure has been met by sustained criticism from post-Keynesians, neo-Marxians and institutionalists alike. The thrust of their argument has been that any emphasis on rigorous maximisation will obscure the main issues and make the analysis degenerate into empty formalism.

The maximisation cannot, so the post-Keynesians argue, take into account the fundamental uncertainty which surrounds all long-term decision-making and, in particular, the investment decision. This problem, the neo-Marxians add, is intrinsic to capitalist systems since the anarchy of the market must necessarily be a source of uncertainty and instability, and, furthermore, the formalisation glosses over many conceptual problems including the origin of profits in surplus value and the exploitation of workers in production. Institutionalists and behaviourists like Simon, finally, stress the general complexity of decision problems as well as the fact that firms are made up of many different individuals with different interests and different views about the environment and the constraints facing the firm. This, they suggest, invalidates the notion of maximisation and, instead, decision-making is better conceived in terms of satisficing: decisions are reached in accordance with a set of routines and only if outcomes fall short of aspiration levels will there be an attempt to reassess and improve the routines.

It is generally recognised, also by general-equilibrium theorists, that economic agents face computational and informational limitations, but the implications of these limitations are often overlooked. Hahn (1984), for instance, accepts that 'knowledge and computation are themselves objects of choice and that seems to leave the theory dangling by its bootstraps' (p. 7). But he then goes on to argue that imperfect information and computational limitations merely lead to 'a somewhat richer model of rational choice than the one of the textbook' (p. 7): a consumer, for instance, will spend time and effort on gathering further information 'when he believes the gain from search large enough' (p. 8). Hahn thus suggests that the simplified maximisation problem which determines the agent's day-to-day behaviour is itself rationally determined by a higher-level optimisation programme: the simplified programme is chosen such that the (expected) marginal improvement in the optimal solution from a relaxation in simplifying constraints is precisely offset by increased search and computation costs. This is not convincing.

In a truistic sense each agent does what he thinks he prefers to do given the constraints.[5] Hahn wants to translate this into constrained maximisation. He accepts that because of computational and informational constraints the translation requires the imposition of simplifying constraints, but he then suggests that the simplifying constraints are themselves 'rationally determined'. If, however, the simplifying constraints were themselves rationally determined by 'high-level maximisation' then the solution to the simplified problem would also solve the original complex problem (which takes into account all informational and computational limitations). Simplifying constraints cannot be both necessary and rational. If they are rational then the solutions to the simplified and the full optimisation programmes coincide, and the full solution can in fact be calculated. If, on the other hand, simplifying constraints are necessary then the full solution is, by assumption, unknown and the known solution to the simplified problem will only coincide with the full solution by sheer fluke.[6]

The choice-theoretic foundations of general-equilibrium theory are thus based on a decomposition of the overall decision of individual agents into an unexplained (and 'irrational') choice of simplified maximisation programmes and a subsequent 'rational' decision, conditional on the chosen maximisation programme. The first step is usually left in the dark and, when this step is acknowledged, it is implied that somehow the step

---

[5] But it may be misleading to identify preference with personal welfare. See Sen (1979) for a discussion of the importance of 'commitment' in determining choice. For present purposes, however, the influence of commitment on choice can be ignored.

[6] The criticism of 'rational simplification' can also be cast in terms of an infinite regress: if the complete optimisation programme is insoluble, then the higher-order programme which is used to determine the simplifying constraints must itself include simplifying constraints.

can be carried out rationally in a way analogous to the optimisation of the second step; the foundation in rational choice can therefore be pronounced the hallmark of scientific work in economics. The complexity of actual choice may render the existing, highly simplified models of economic behaviour unsatisfactory. But, according to this approach, models which to any layman might look rather arbitrary and uninteresting can be justified as steps towards a complete analysis of the full decision problem. The specific simplifications of the analytical model need little or no justification in terms of direct relevance *vis-à-vis* actual choice situations: the limitations on rational decision-making are seen as (temporary) shortcomings of analytical economics and not as intrinsic to actual decision-making.

The reaction to the classic study by Hall and Hitch (1939) on pricing is an example of how the maximisation paradigm has misled the profession. Hall and Hitch presented data showing a widespread use of mark-up pricing – industrial firms appeared to change prices in proportion to variations in average variable cost – and this finding has been widely seen as evidence of a trend away from competitive pricing. However,

The Hall and Hitch study was far from being a confirmation of the development of imperfectly competitive practices from an earlier period in which firms 'competitively' set price equal to marginal cost. It was in fact a documentation of the partial progress that had been made up to that date in Britain towards the creation and diffusion of accounting procedures which contained even a minimum level of uniformity and comparability between firms. For the first time, there was the possibility of even a modicum of resemblance to the 'rational' cost and revenue calculations outlined in neoclassical theory.   (Auerbach, 1988, p. 109)

The maximisation models took for granted a level of information and a human infrastructure which simply were not there. A slow process had gradually given managers the tools and skills to act in a way which approximated the assumptions of the theorists but, unaware of this process, the theorists completely misinterpreted the evidence of remaining 'imperfections' when it came to their attention.[7]

How could mistakes of this kind be avoided? At a general level, the answer seems obvious: less emphasis on rigorous models of rational behaviour and a greater concern with actual business behaviour will be needed. There is nothing wrong with formalisation and rigorous analysis as such, but a rigorous analysis of uninteresting questions is simply rigorously uninteresting.

[7] One need not go back to the thirties to find examples of striking departures in actual business practice from 'rational' profit-maximising behaviour. Recently, Carsberg and Hope (1976) found that 63 out of a sample of 103 large UK firms discount real cash flows using a money discount rate. A number of other examples are discussed in Wadhwani (1987).

Does this mean that maximisation should be banished from economic theory? The answer is no. Profit maximisation may be acceptable as a purely analytical device. Any theory must by necessity focus on a rather narrow set of factors and, in particular, a relatively simple specification of the perceived environment of firms. The world is immensely complex but the model universe must be simple, and *in the context of the model* it may involve no loss to identify profit-seeking behaviour with the maximisation of profits subject to a given set of – perceived and actual – constraints.

A purely analytical use of maximisation does, however, have important implications. Profit-seeking behaviour may be equivalent to profit maximisation within a simple model universe, but model and reality must not be conflated in the interpretation of results. Concepts of optimality and efficiency figure prominently in neoclassical economics. But if the constraints on maximisation reflect (the model-builder's views on) the skills and routines of agents then optimality will be conditional on historically given routines, expectations and perceptions. The routines are not themselves founded on rational behaviour, and informational and computational limitations also contaminate expectations and perceptions with an element of arbitrariness.

This conditionality weakens the concept of optimality and makes it almost meaningless. If the beliefs of decision-makers fail to reflect their objective situation then it is possible that the imposition of additional constraints – by, for instance, a political authority – may improve the welfare of all agents in the economy. Behavioural routines, furthermore, will depend on actual outcomes and thus should not be taken as constant in the thought experiments which form the basis of any definition of optimality: if a satisficing agent were to experience a significant drop in income then changes in routines and operation procedures are likely.

It should be noted, finally, that – keeping in mind the distinction between complex reality and simplified theory – there can be no a priori reason to assume that the views and expectations of individuals in the model should conform with the objective structure posited by the model. More specifically, there is no reason to assume that agents have perfect foresight (or rational expectations). Nor is there any reason to suppose that all agents share the same views and expectations. The model does not describe how agents would behave if they had inhabited the simple and transparent model universe. On the contrary, it gives a simple and abstract picture of how the model-builder believes that agents behave in a very complex world. As an empirical matter, it is possible that everybody in the real world may share the same view, and that the model-builder simply articulates this common vision of how the economy works. But this is an empirical proposition, not something one could deduce from first principles, and as an empirical proposition it is contradicted by the evidence.

In conclusion, one should be careful with the interpretation of models based on optimisation, and there is no reason why macroeconomic theories must necessarily be based on profit maximisation (even if one believes that firms are guided exclusively by the profit motive). Agents who cannot be completely rational must ultimately be content with 'satisficing'. This may involve periods of routine behaviour, punctuated by abrupt changes in routine, when aspiration levels fail to be met. The conditional rationality of simplified optimisation is one possible form of routine behaviour, but there are no compelling reasons to rule out other possible forms a priori. Yet it is on these a priori grounds that the need for choice-theoretic foundations has been widely accepted. Provided one bears in mind these caveats, however, there are no strong objections against the use of profit maximisation as a purely analytical device, and in the present book the macroeconomic relations describing output and investment will be related explicitly to the profit-maximising behaviour at the firm level.

2.6 SIMULTANEOUS EQUILIBRIUM

In addition to the emphasis on choice-theoretic foundations, Walrasian general-equilibrium theory is characterised by an equilibrium concept involving the simultaneous consistency of the desired actions of all agents. In the simple Arrow–Debreu model, prices are given parametrically, and agents will never be restricted in their trading by quantity constraints. In other general-equilibrium models, quantity constraints of various forms may occur, and the interpretation of 'desired actions' will depend on the constraints imposed by the particular model. But, in all versions of the theory, there is a sharp contrast between on the one hand the great efforts to achieve generality and disaggregation in the commodity and agent spaces and on the other hand the almost total neglect of essential aspects of time.

Hahn (1973) links the notion of equilibrium explicitly with possible 'terminal states of economic processes' (p. 16). He argues that the complexity of dynamic processes and our ignorance of these processes are such that they make a general dynamic analysis impossible. The concentration on simultaneous equilibria in general-equilibrium theory is therefore dictated by necessity: the analysis of economic systems in 'terminal states' is all we can hope to master, and these systems are adequately described by the simultaneous general-equilibrium models. An economic system which reproduces itself over and over again in a set sequential pattern – possibly with some increases in scale – can be reduced to a synchronised process in logical time without any real loss.

Hahn's argument is powerful[8] but one would not lightly postulate this sort of stationariness with respect to a historical period and an economic system which are first and foremost characterised by a process of unprecedented structural shifts and unbalanced growth. Can we not do better?

In his attempt to justify the simultaneous equilibrium notion, Hahn (1973) has in fact unwittingly provided evidence that dynamic analysis is both possible and necessary. He argues that 'in an economy with unemployed resources an excess of intended investment over intended savings is used to predict that incomes will not persist at their present level and indeed they are likely to rise' (p. 9). He claims that the conclusion is derived from a 'weak causal claim' aided by a knowledge of 'the most general features of actual processes'. But the weak causal claim – that 'no plausible sequence of economic states will terminate, if it does so at all, in a state which is not an equilibrium' (p. 7) – does not enable him to draw any conclusions whatsoever about the future levels of income. The conclusion that incomes will change and most likely rise is based entirely on the unspecified (non-equilibrium) knowledge of 'the most general features of actual processes'. The example thus shows not the usefulness of the general-equilibrium approach but on the contrary its impotence. The implicit dynamic theory which Hahn relies on needs to be made explicit. It needs to be analysed and developed, and an emphasis on agent and commodity generality is unlikely to be helpful in this task.

There is a trade-off between progress on the sequential front and generality in other spheres. In order to achieve disaggregation in the time dimension a higher degree of aggregation in the commodity and agent spaces will be necessary. General-equilibrium theory has focused on a corner solution: the obsession with commodity and agent generality goes hand in hand with a neglect of essential aspects of time and the passage of time. In contrast, dynamic issues are central to the analysis in the ensuing chapters, and we shall therefore have to conduct the analysis at a relatively high level of agent and commodity aggregation.

[8] In fact a similar argument has been advanced by some post-Keynesian writers; see, for example, Eichner and Kregel (1975), p 1296.

CHAPTER 3

A survey of some post-Keynesian and neo-Marxian ideas

3.1 INTRODUCTION

The majority of economists and policy-makers in our time appear to believe that markets can solve most economic problems efficaciously. The theories of Keynes and Marx are either considered old-fashioned and simplistic, or (in the former case) they are adapted and modified beyond recognition. In my view the traditions of Keynes and Marx have much to tell us about contemporary economic events but in this review the emphasis will be on shortcomings rather than achievements. The criticisms, however, call into question neither the importance of the writings in general nor their central influence on my own approach.

3.2 HARROD

The publication in 1939 of Harrod's 'An essay in dynamic theory' marked the birth of modern growth theory. Keynes had published the *General Theory* three years earlier and Harrod was deeply influenced by the new ideas. He felt, however, that the *General Theory* was too static and that a more dynamic approach was needed.

In the *General Theory*, Keynes focused on the relation between current investment and current demand (and output). The stock of capital goods as well as the time path of output up to the present period were seen as historically given, but the analysis did not include these predetermined variables explicitly: the *rates of increase* of the capital stock and of the different categories of demand were not considered. Modifications of the analysis in this direction may seem like modest steps. After all, if the Keynesian analysis determines current investment and output, and if past levels of output as well as the capital stock are predetermined, then the analysis can be restated as a relation between the growth rate of the capital stock and the growth rate of output. This recasting of Keynes's theory is at the centre of Harrod's analysis and the change in perspective immediately opened up a new range of questions.

The dynamic perspective enabled Harrod to derive several startling results. He showed that a steady-growth path (the warranted growth path) exists, but his theory contains no mechanism to ensure the equality between the warranted growth rate and the growth rate of the labour force (the natural growth rate). The static Keynesian problem of involuntary unemployment thus has a dynamic counterpart: there is no reason to expect that the growth rate of employment will be in line with the growth rate of the labour force. In addition, the economy will face a second problem: the warranted growth path is, Harrod argued, likely to be unstable.

The basic argument in support of these conclusions is simple. Assume that there is a given constant technique represented by a constant (maximum) technical output–capital ratio, σ, and assume further that utilisation rates, u, are at their normal level, the latter assumption being reasonable for an economy in steady growth. The output–capital ratio is then constant, $Y/K = u\sigma$, and, if the average saving propensity is s, then the Keynesian equilibrium condition, $S = I$, implies that the growth rate of the economy is given by

$$g_w = \frac{I}{K} = \frac{S}{K} = \frac{sY}{K} = su\sigma \qquad (3.1)$$

Equation (3.1) describes the warranted growth rate. It is fully determined by the variables, s, u and σ, and, unless one of these three variables adjusts appropriately, the warranted rate will not be equal to the rate of growth of the labour force except by a happy coincidence.[1]

Harrod acknowledged the logical possibility of accommodating changes in the saving rate or the output–capital ratio but saw no reason to expect any such adjustments. The choice of technique, for instance, would depend on the relative costs of inputs and in particular on the rate of interest, but 'the rate of interest and the MARC [the minimum acceptable rate of return on capital] do not often have a big effect on the method chosen' and an attempt to derive a rate of interest 'which brought the warranted growth rate into equality with the natural growth rate . . . really makes no sense' (Harrod, 1973, pp. 172–3).

The validity of equation (3.1) is not restricted to steady growth paths. If

[1] An earlier generation of economists might have rejected the assumption of an exogenous natural rate of growth. Instead, population growth could be determined by per capita income and this would open another possible adjustment mechanism. Harrod (1973, pp. 25–6) rejected the relevance of the Malthusian argument for the present era and expressed doubts concerning its validity in earlier periods. The Malthus view, however, has played no part in recent debates.

g_w denotes the actual rate of capital accumulation and σ is the actual output–capital ratio then (3.1) is a simple restatement of the equilibrium condition for the product market, $I = S$. Outside warranted growth, however, the interpretation of the equation changes.[2] The output–capital ratio will not always be at its normal level so, while the steady growth value of g_w is determined by exogenous values of s, u and σ, causality is reversed in any short period. In the short run, the rate of investment (the rate of accumulation of capital) is the exogenous variable which determines the rate of output (the output–capital ratio) and a priori there is no presumption that firms will choose investment levels which conform with the requirements of warranted growth. Or will they? If one traces out a sequence of short-run equilibria will it then approach the steady-growth path? According to Harrod the answer is no. The warranted growth path is likely to be unstable.

The argument for instability of the warranted path depends upon the properties of the investment function. The rate of investment is subject to many influences and some of these are difficult to pin down analytically (for instance long-term expectations, uncertainty and 'animal spirits'). Nevertheless, it is uncontroversial that firms' investment decisions will be influenced by the level of demand and, in particular, by the utilisation rate of the existing capital stock. In other words, changes in demand will have an accelerator effect on investment.[3]

The accelerator effect would, Harrod thought, have profound implications. If the rate of utilisation of capital were to rise above the desired level, then this would (eventually) lead firms to expand their investment plans. Any such increase in investment would have multiplier effects on output and thereby exacerbate the initial disequilibrium: utilisation rates would rise *pari passu* with the increase in output. The resulting instability of the warranted path might not be of the knife-edge type often attributed to Harrod. Indeed, he has explicitly repudiated the knife-edge metaphor and instead described the instability as being akin to 'a ball on a grassy slope' (Harrod, 1973, p. 33). But, in any case, instability of the warranted growth path and the discrepancy between warranted and natural growth rates were serious problems which in Harrod's view could only be overcome through determined policy intervention.

[2] Implicitly it is assumed here that the warranted growth rate is constant: warranted growth is identified with steady growth. This identification is only valid as a special case. Harrod defined the warranted rate at any moment and independently of initial conditions. A warranted rate is a rate of accumulation with generates a level of demand such that in retrospect firms feel that they chose exactly the right rate of investment (Harrod, 1973, pp. 17–18). For present purposes, there is no loss involved in focusing on the special case of steady growth.

[3] Harrod had already combined multiplier and accelerator analysis in 1936 in *The Trade Cycle: an Essay*.

3.3 THE NEOCLASSICAL SOLUTION

The profession's faith in markets and their efficacy is, however, strong and the post-war era has seen powerful attempts to recast Keynes's analysis as a special case within a wider neoclassical framework, the special case arising due to the imposition of wage and price rigidities[4] and/or resulting from the neglect of real-balance effects. When, in the 1950s, the neoclassical economists turned to growth theory, it came as no surprise that they viewed Harrod's analysis with great scepticism. The very simplicity of the Harrodian argument invited objections. Had he not (like Keynes) ignored important variables which may help to generate steady growth at full employment?

The favoured neoclassical solution to Harrod's first problem – the inequality between warranted and natural rates – has been to introduce a variable output–capital ratio as the accommodating variable (Solow, 1956; Swan, 1956). The warranted growth rate depends, as shown by equation (3.1), on the output–capital ratio and a discrepancy between warranted and natural growth rates would, it was argued, cause endogenous changes in this ratio.

The argument is simple but it depends on strong assumptions: it is assumed at the outset that there is full employment. Keynesian problems of effective demand are thus ruled out, and the rate of investment is determined by full-employment saving.[5] If the purpose is to examine the robustness of Harrod's conclusions then the full-employment assumption seems surprising: if there is permanent full employment and the labour force grows at some exogenous rate, n, then it is hard to imagine how the growth rate of production could differ from n in the long run (in the absence of technical progress). Furthermore, instability of the growth path, Harrod's second problem, finds no place in a model which assumes continuous full employment and which has no room for an independent investment function. By imposing full employment, the neoclassical economists had effectively assumed away most of the problems which worried Harrod.

The simple Solow–Swan model (and subsequent elaborations and extensions) thus has not answered the two questions posed by Harrod. Instead, it performs a more limited task: it demonstrates that, by introduc-

[4] The interpretation based on rigid wages and prices has no foundation in Keynes's writing. Unfortunately, in Leijonhufvud's words, 'today's economics profession, taken as a whole, simply does not care enough about the truth or falsehood of statements of this doctrine–historical kind to enforce reasonable scholarly standards' (Leijonhufvud, 1986, p. 23).

[5] The disappearance from neoclassical analysis of independent investment decisions is not confined to the simple Solow (1956) model. See Bliss (1975), pp. 309–12, for a discussion of investment in neoclassical models.

ing a variable output–capital ratio, it becomes possible to tell a logically consistent story involving permanent full employment. In the Solow–Swan model, the actual growth rate of the capital stock equals the warranted rate (as determined by the saving propensity and the predetermined full-employment value of $u\sigma$) and, if, say, the warranted rate exceeds the natural rate, then the continuous decrease in the labour–capital ratio (and hence in the output–capital ratio) will automatically cause a gradual decline in the warranted rate. This decline continues as long as the output–capital ratio exceeds the level which equalises the warranted rate to the (exogenously given) natural rate of growth.

Is this a reasonable story? Harrod did not think so. Limits on the range of variability of the output–capital ratio may prevent the adjustment, and, even if there were sufficient technical variability, relative input prices may not adjust so as to induce firms to choose the appropriate technique. These issues will be dealt with in greater detail in chapter 5, but another, and perhaps better-known, critique of the neoclassical story also deserves comment.

The capital controversy occupied many of the best minds in economics for more than a decade.[6] In the end, there was general agreement that aggregation of capital into a one-dimensional measure is impossible except under extremely restrictive conditions. Aggregation problems, however, do not just apply to capital: output and labour are subject to similar problems. From this one could conclude that any one-sector model will be inadequate, based as it must be on unwarranted and illegitimate aggregation. No doubt, this sort of reasoning provides part of the explanation for the proliferation in the 1960s and early 1970s of two-sector and multi-sector growth models. But the reasoning is not compelling. No theory stands in one-to-one correspondence with the real world and it is not at all obvious that adding more sectors will produce extra insights: the more one complicates a theory in one direction, the greater the simplifications needed in other areas in order to make the theory tractable. If the Cambridge (UK) criticism of Solow-type parables had amounted to nothing more than a general condemnation of aggregation, it would have been hard to take it seriously.

What about the more specific aggregation criticisms? It may have taken a long time and great effort to persuade the profession that capital reswitching and reversing could occur. Yet, in retrospect, the result looks less devastating than it first appeared. In Joan Robinson's words, '[t]he long wrangle about "measuring capital" has been a great deal of fuss over a secondary question. The real source of trouble is the confusion between

[6] See Harcourt (1972) for a survey of the debate.

comparisons of equilibrium positions and the history of a process of accumulation' (Robinson, 1974, quoted from Robinson, 1978, p. 135). A pseudo-production function

can be used only for comparisons of supposed steady state economies, not for analysing a process of accumulation changing the value of capital per man. A similar difficulty arises in arguing from Walrasian general equilibrium ... A change in demand ruptures the equilibrium, disappoints expectations – some for the better and some for the worse – and requires investment in one kind of stock and disinvestment in others. Here also, further developments can be analysed only in Keynesian terms.   (Robinson, 1978, p. 123)

The whole question of aggregation which figured so prominently during the debate was thus in large part irrelevant. Aggregation issues were raised by Cambridge (UK) economists because the conceptual problems involved in the notion of aggregate capital were regarded as symptomatic of deeper problems with the static notion of equilibrium. Neoclassical theorists on the other hand were all too keen to discuss technical aggregation problems: they could point to full-fledged general-equilibrium models as evidence that they had shown far greater concern over aggregational issues than had their critics. Furthermore, the Walrasian framework was obviously immune to the accusations of circularity and logical inconsistency arising from the use of aggregate capital. The neoclassical economists failed to notice that the general-equilibrium model was far from unaffected by the real issues of equilibrium and time. Seen in this light, Hahn's observation that the harshest critics of the use of neoclassical production functions often themselves work with highly aggregate models is less paradoxical than it first appears (Hahn, 1973, p. 35).

3.4 KALDOR

It was not only the neoclassical economists who found Harrod's problems disturbing. Kaldor, one of the leading post-Keynesians, has produced full-employment models which in Samuelson's view are worthy of a Jean-Baptiste Say (Samuelson, 1964, p. 345). Kaldor's position, however, is not difficult to understand considering his strong dislike of abstract theorising for its own sake. Theory should help us understand the 'stylised facts', and in the 1950s and early 1960s Kaldor – together with most observers – thought that steady growth at full employment was a reasonable approximation to actual trends in advanced economies. Keynesian theory, consequently, ought to be able to explain such a condition.

Kaldor developed his growth and distribution theory in a series of papers published in the late 1950s and early 1960s.[7] The following model, based on Kaldor (1957), summarises the essential characteristics of the theory:

$$\frac{S}{K} = \sigma(\alpha + \beta\pi); \quad \alpha \geq 0, \quad \beta > 0 \tag{3.2}$$

$$\frac{I}{K} = \sigma(\alpha' + \beta'\sigma\pi) - 1; \quad \alpha' > 0, \quad \beta' \geq 0 \tag{3.3}$$

$$\frac{I}{K} = \frac{S}{K} = \hat{K} \tag{3.4}$$

$$\hat{Y} = \alpha'' + \beta''\hat{K}; \quad \alpha'' \geq 0, \quad 1 > \beta'' \geq 0 \tag{3.5}$$

where σ and π are the output–capital ratio and the share of profits in income respectively; α, α', α'', β, β', β'' are non-negative parameters and a caret is used to denote growth rates (logarithmic derivatives). In addition to the parameter restrictions given in (3.2)–(3.5), it is assumed that

$$\beta > \beta'\sigma \tag{3.6}$$

$$\alpha'\sigma - 1 > \alpha\sigma \tag{3.7}$$

With these assumptions, it can be shown that the economy will converge to a steady-growth path with constant distributive shares and a constant output–capital ratio.[8]

The rationale behind the model is as follows. By assumption there is full employment of labour, and at any moment the levels of output and capital as well as the money-wage bill are predetermined. With a given level of output, both saving and investment are functions of the share of profits in income, the share of profits being itself an increasing function of the price of output. The equilibrium condition for the product market, equation (3.4), thus serves to determine the distribution of income (the price of output), and using (3.2) or (3.3) the rate of accumulation can be found as a function of the predetermined output–capital ratio. The growth rate of the output–capital ratio is now determined by the technical-progress function and, given the restrictions on the value of β'', this ratio is declining (increasing) when the rate of capital accumulation is greater than (less

---

[7] Kaldor (1956, 1957, 1959, 1961), Kaldor and Mirrlees (1962). Unfortunately, the later papers are flawed. The famous Kaldor–Mirrlees model for instance does not even have an independent investment function: the level of investment is passively determined by the amount of saving (see Skott, 1989b). The early prototype model, Kaldor (1957), thus remains the best exposition of Kaldor's growth and distribution theory.

[8] The model has been comprehensively analysed by Champernowne (1971), who also noted that empirically the restriction (3.7) seems strong.

than) $\alpha''/(1 - \beta'')$. Since the rate of capital accumulation is positively related to the output–capital ratio, it follows that the rate of accumulation will converge to its unique steady growth value, $\hat{K}^* = \alpha''/(1 - \beta'')$.

As a Keynesian theory of growth and distribution, Kaldor's model has several shortcomings,[9] but undoubtedly the most puzzling aspect of the model is the full-employment assumption. Even if one were to assume that somehow the warranted and natural growth rates are equalised in the long run, it is still not clear why a Keynesian model should produce continuous full employment at all times. Kaldor provides no explanation of how full employment is achieved, but within the logic of the model there appears to be only one possible explanation: variations in nominal wage rates induce firms to expand employment exactly in line with the growth of the labour force. Such a hypothesis, however, is extremely un-Keynesian: the main theoretical message of the *General Theory* is precisely the impossibility of eliminating involuntary unemployment and securing full employment through variations in nominal wages.[10]

Consider next the role of the saving function. In place of a single average saving propensity, s, Kaldor introduces differential saving propensities, s_w and s_p, applicable to wage and profit income respectively (β in equation (3.2) is equal to $s_p - s_w$). It is this 'semi-classical' saving function which permits a (post-)Keynesian determination of the distribution of income: variations in the distribution of income may adjust the average rate of saving so as to bring it into equality with any given share of investment in output.[11]

Kaldor claimed that the saving function and the post-Keynesian distribution mechanism make the warranted rate adjust to the natural rate and thus allow full-employment growth.[12] Similar views have subsequently been repeated by many other writers (see, for example, Jones, 1975, p. 148). The claim is not, however, correct. To see its falsity, assume first that there is a given technique and that utilisation rates are at their 'normal' level. These assumptions assure that the capital–output ratio is constant and that both saving and investment are functionally related to the share of profits. The slope of the saving function exceeds the slope of

---

[9] The criticisms are developed more fully in Skott (1989b), chapters 7 and 8.

[10] Kaldor's full-employment 'proof' in Kaldor (1959) and (1961) does not establish the full employment of labour but (at best) the (near) full employment (utilisation) of capital in steady growth; see Skott (1989b), chapter 8.

[11] The distribution mechanism is similar to Marshallian ultra-short-run pricing: with given supply, the price of output (distribution of income) adjusts so as to clear the market. In a macroeconomic context, Keynes used the distribution mechanism in the *Treatise on Money* (1930). Hahn (1972), which was written in 1951, also relied on this mechanism, and similar views can be found among the classics; see, for example, the discussion of Malthus in Costabile and Rowthorn (1985).

[12] See, for instance, Kaldor (1957), p. 611.

the investment function and the intersection between the two schedules determines the distribution of income as well as the warranted growth rate. The warranted rate is unique and only by pure chance will it be equal to the natural rate. The differential saving function has not provided an extra degree of freedom; or, more accurately, the extra degree of freedom has been swallowed up by the Kaldorian distribution mechanism and the introduction of an explicit investment function. In Kaldor's model, the equalisation of warranted and natural growth rates requires a variable capital–output ratio as well as differential saving rates.

It may be reasonable to abandon the simple Harrodian assumption of given technique and fixed utilisation rate, but the way Kaldor relaxes the assumption is questionable. In order to establish the stability of the equilibrium for the product market, it is assumed that saving is more sensitive than investment to variations in profits (see inequality (3.6)). Although in itself this assumption may be plausible, problems arise when the assumption is combined with other aspects of the model.

The fluctuations in distribution reflect unanticipated changes in demand (and a given predetermined output level), and these changes should influence the desired production levels: if demand is lower than anticipated (and profits are low) then firms will most likely want to contract production and employment and, conversely, if profitability (demand) is unexpectedly buoyant, they will want to expand. This feedback from profitability (demand) to production is ruled out by the full-employment assumption. The level of output is determined by the assumption of continuous full employment and variations in demand are reflected exclusively in the share of profits. In Kaldor's model, a strong influence of output on the desired capital stock thus does not represent an accelerator mechanism. A plausible short-run stability condition (relative insensitivity of investment to changes in profitability) has been combined with an assumption of full employment and as a result, the factors which might destabilise the steady-growth path have effectively been cut out: the accelerator has been undermined.

The absence of accelerator effects on investment is perhaps best seen by noting that the desired rate of capital accumulation can be positive even in a permanent state of zero profits (cf. the investment function, equation (3.3), and the parameter restriction, (3.7)). Autonomous and unexplained investment thus drives the model, and this property is neither satisfactory nor in accordance with the views expressed by Kaldor himself.[13] Further-

[13] Kaldor (1957) argues that 'the continued growth in output capacity presupposes in turn a belief (which must be grounded, and can only be grounded, in past experience) in the

more, the equalisation of the warranted and natural rates of growth is brought about through accommodating variations in the output–capital ratio. Not only does Kaldor therefore follow the neoclassical economists in assuming full employment, but the mechanism which equalises warranted and natural growth rates is also similar.[14] The difference between Kaldor's model and the neoclassical one is that Kaldor introduces an explicit investment function which serves to determine the distribution of income. The neoclassical model, on the other hand, leaves out the investment function and uses marginal-productivity conditions to determine distribution.

To summarise, Kaldor's 1957 model is unsatisfactory for a number of reasons: (i) there is no convincing mechanism to ensure full employment, (ii) autonomous investment drives the model, and (iii) accommodating variations in the output–capital ratio serves to adjust the warranted rate to the natural rate of growth.

3.5 PASINETTI

Pasinetti (1962) has raised an additional criticism of Kaldor's model and, more specifically, the saving function. In Kaldor's version, the saving propensities attach to income *categories* (profits and wages) rather than to different *classes* (capitalists and workers). According to Pasinetti, this involves a logical error. Kaldor has, he argues, overlooked an important implication of workers' saving.

When workers save, they will gradually become owners of a part of the capital stock. As a result, they will receive profit income as well as wages, and one would expect them to apply the same saving rate to both categories of income. If this is the case, however, then the average saving rate out of profits becomes a weighted average of the saving propensities of workers and capitalists with weights depending upon the distribution of ownership. A respecification of the saving function along these lines may at first sight appear to complicate matters but it will in fact, Pasinetti argues, simplify the analysis as well as strengthen the post-Keynesian case.

Consider a simple model. If workers do not save and capitalists save all profits, then the equilibrium condition, $I = S$, must imply that profits are equal to total investment and hence that the rate of profits equals the rate of accumulation. Keynesians view investment as the active variable and saving as passive, and it therefore follows that accumulation determines

continued growth in markets' (p. 600). See also Kaldor's (1951) critique of the role of autonomous investment in Hicks's (1950) model of the trade cycle.

[14] And, as noted by Black (1962), the linear technical-progress function in Kaldor's model is formally equivalent to a Cobb–Douglas production function.

the rate of profit (or, if investment is influenced by profitability, that animal spirits – the form and position of the investment function – determine profitability). With the more general Kaldorian saving function, the relation between profits and investment needs modification. If workers save then distribution will still be related to accumulation, but the technique of production (the capital–output ratio) will also influence distributive shares; to see this, simply substitute equation (3.4) into (3.2).

Pasinetti suggested that one could do better than that. Using the amended class-based saving function, the introduction of workers' saving will have no effect at all on the long-run relation between profitability and growth. The reason is as follows. In long-run equilibrium, the share of capital owned by workers is constant. The growth rate of workers' capital, the growth rate of capital owned by capitalists and the overall growth rate of the capital stock must all be equal, and since the growth rate of capitalists' capital stock is given by $g_c = s_c \sigma\pi$, where s_c is the saving propensity of capitalists and $\sigma\pi$ is the rate of profits, it follows that $g = g_w = g_c = s_c \sigma\pi$, or $\sigma\pi = g/s_c$. A simple linear relation between the rate of profits and the rate of accumulation has been restored.

Pasinetti's paper sparked off a major debate. In his model the rate of profits must be equal to the rate of accumulation divided by the saving propensity of capitalists. Profitability thus appears to be determined entirely by factors under the direct control of capitalists, and this result, furthermore, is independent of the choice of technique. Both of these aspects run against the grain of neoclassical analysis so a reply was predictable.

Meade (1965) and Samuelson and Modigliani (1966) pointed out that Pasinetti's argument relies on the survival of a class of pure capitalists in long-run equilibrium. This premise, they argued, cannot be taken for granted: in the simple case, for instance, where both capitalists and workers have the same saving propensity, the growth rate of workers' capital must exceed that of capital owned by pure capitalists. Depending on relative saving propensities (and on the properties of the production function), the pure capitalist class may thus cease to exist in long-run equilibrium. Samuelson and Modigliani suggested that, judging by empirical data on saving propensities, this was indeed the most likely long-run configuration. Contributions from Pasinetti and Robinson challenged this assessment, and to this day papers appear which in one way or another try to ensure that the pure capitalist class will never die out.[15] I used to find this a very important issue but confess that it now fails to excite me.

---

[15] An obvious extension is to assume that workers are discriminated against and that they do not get the same return on their capital as capitalists; see Fazi and Salvadori (1981, 1985)

The Pasinetti equilibrium is not just a long-run equilibrium; it is by its very nature a *very* long-run equilibrium: the convergence of the distribution of the ownership capital to its steady-state value is an extremely slow process, and it seems somewhat irrelevant whether or not the class of pure capitalists would be eliminated eventually if the process were to be allowed to run its course without changes in any of the parameters. The shape of the long-run saving function may also for other reasons be less important than is sometimes believed: it does not, for instance, affect the stability of the warranted growth path nor does it have any bearing on the equality between warranted and natural growth rates. Finally, I do not find Pasinetti's critique of Kaldor's specification convincing. Kaldor's response to Samuelson and Modigliani, and in particular the appendix containing the 'neo-Pasinetti theorem', not only answers Samuelson and Modigliani's point, it also addresses Pasinetti's original criticism. Kaldor sets up a simple model showing that no inconsistency is involved in the specification of saving propensities which are specific to income categories rather than to classes and that, furthermore, Pasinetti, as well as Samuelson and Modigliani, has failed to take into account the distinction between real and financial assets.

3.6 THE NEO-PASINETTI THEOREM

Kaldor (1966) states his disagreement with Pasinetti with regard to the causes of differential saving propensities. No logical slip, he argues, is involved in ignoring the effects of workers' saving on ownership rights in firms. Differential saving propensities do not depend upon 'an identifiable class of hereditary barons – a class of capitalists "with permanent membership" – distinguished by a high saving propensity and of a "permanent" class of workers distinguished by a low savings propensity'. Instead, Kaldor has 'always regarded the high savings propensity out of profits as something which attaches to the nature of business income, and not to the wealth (or other peculiarities) of the individuals who own property' (Kaldor, 1966, p. 310).

What then explains the differential saving propensities? Kaldor's alternative justification relies entirely on the distinction between retained business profits, which by definition are saved *in toto*, and personal income. This distinction is combined with two additional elements: (i) the empirical observation that the marginal retention rate out of profits is high, and (ii) the hypothesis that the saving propensity out of personal income does

for an analysis of this case. The original responses to Samuelson and Modigliani (1966) are Pasinetti (1966) and Robinson (1966).

not adjust in a way that compensates for variations in the share of retained profits in income.

The validity of the latter hypothesis depends on the desire and ability of personal income receivers to 'declare their own dividends' through counterbalancing portfolio adjustments. If share prices automatically appreciate in line with the level of retained profits then the retention policies of firms will not influence households' budget constraint and thus may have no impact on the level of consumption. But, for any given net supply of shares from firms to the household sector, the equilibrium price of shares will be determined by households' demand for shares. It is therefore not a foregone conclusion that share prices will appreciate in line with retained earnings. And, if they do not, households as 'ultimate wealth-owners' may not be able to fix the aggregate saving ratio independently of firms' retention policies. Kaldor's neo-Pasinetti theorem provides a rigorous formulation of this argument.

Algebraically, the neo-Pasinetti model can be stated as follows:

$$jI = s_w[W + (1 - s_p)P] - (1 - s_g)\left[\frac{\mathrm{d}(qK)}{\mathrm{d}t} - jI\right] \tag{3.8}$$

$$I = S = s_w[W + (1 - s_p)P] - (1 - s_g)\left[\frac{\mathrm{d}(qK)}{\mathrm{d}t} - jI\right] + s_p P \tag{3.9}$$

where s_w, s_g, s_p and j denote households' saving propensities out of distributed incomes and capital gains, the profit retention ratio and the proportion of investment financed by the issue of new securities; q is the financial valuation ratio (Tobin's q); K, I, W and P represent the capital stock, real investment, real wages and real profits respectively.

Equation (3.8) is the equilibrium condition for the securities market and equation (3.9) gives the condition for equilibrium in the product market. Substituting (3.8) into the left-hand side of (3.9) we get

$$S = jI + s_p P \tag{3.10}$$

and since household saving, S_h, is equal to the difference between total saving and retained earnings we have

$$S_h = S - s_p P = jI \tag{3.11}$$

It follows that aggregate net saving of the personal sector is fully determined by the amount of new securities issued by firms.

Unfortunately, the assumptions of the model are very stringent. It is implicitly assumed, first, that the households' portfolio contains only one asset, company-issued securities: a household decision to save represents a decision to buy securities. It follows that, in the aggregate, households can only abstain from spending current income to the extent that firms issue new shares.[16] A one-asset assumption is, however, incompatible with other aspects of the model. For the model to make sense, workers must be paid in money. Otherwise the distribution of income would not be freely variable, and this variability is required to guarantee the existence of equilibrium in the product market: aggregate saving is equal to personal saving plus retained earnings and, for any given amount of new issues, it is changes in the distribution of income which bring about the equilibrium between saving and investment. The distributional mechanism thus implies the existence of money and hence that households have a choice with respect to the composition of their portfolio.

Interpretation of the model is also tricky on the company side. If investment and new-issue decisions are to determine the level of profits and not vice versa, then firms must have access to additional sources of finance apart from current profits and new issues. If they did not, then the need to finance investment expenditures would oblige them to issue securities so as to offset exactly the gap between current retained profits and desired investment.

In conclusion, Kaldor's treatment of financial issues in the neo-Pasinetti model is restrictive and the detailed assumptions of the model are open to criticism. There is thus a need to examine the sensitivity of the main conclusions to changes in the assumptions of the model.

3.7 WOOD

The neo-Pasinetti theorem was an important source of inspiration behind Wood's more detailed analysis (1975) of the financial behaviour of firms. The post-Keynesian distribution theory associated with Kaldor, Robinson and Pasinetti used a differential saving function and the equilibrium condition, $S = I$, to derive a link between growth and profitability. A similar nexus between growth and profits characterises Wood's theory, but it is built on very different foundations.

Firms will, according to Wood, wish to finance a fixed proportion, α, of their investment expenditure through retained earnings. If s_p is the retention ratio then this implies that

$$s_p P = \alpha I \tag{3.12}$$

or

$$\pi = \frac{\alpha}{s_p} \frac{g}{\sigma} \tag{3.13}$$

[16] The adjustment of desired household saving to jI is possible because (i) household consumption is positively related to capital gains and (ii) the financial valuation adjusts endogenously to clear the market for securities.

where π is the share of profits, σ the output–capital ratio, and g the rate of accumulation. The rate of accumulation in turn can be written

$$g = s(\pi)\,\sigma \qquad (3.14)$$

where $s(\pi)$ is the average saving propensity. Equation (3.14), in fact, defines Harrod's warranted growth rate and, like Harrod, Wood takes σ to be an exogenous constant in long-run growth. For any given saving function $s(\pi)$, equations (3.14) and (3.13) yield solutions for g and π in terms of the three parameters α, σ and s_p.

It should be noted that, unlike Kaldor, Wood does not require differential saving propensities: it is the combination of a Harrodian warranted rate with the finance constraint (3.12) which determines profitability. But, if the equations are to be more than mere identities, then the parameters α, σ and s_p must be exogenously given. If faster accumulation is accompanied by an increase in the retention rate or a decrease in the internal financing requirement, then profitability need not bear any relation to the rate of growth. Is it reasonable to posit constant values of α and s_p? Wood suggests that it is. Ultimately, I have failed to be convinced by his argument. In some cases it may be costly – or even impossible – for individual firms to deviate strongly from the prevailing standards of prudent finance, but variations in financial behaviour do exist both across firms and temporally for the same firm. Furthermore, financial standards are not time-invariant, and changes in the standards may be influenced by variations in accumulation rates.

3.8 KALDORIAN CYCLES

So far the main focus has been on long-run growth. One of the most striking stylised facts, however, is the trade cycle: production and employment exhibit marked fluctuations around the trend. Kalecki has argued that cycle and trend should be analysed together, the long-run trend evolving as the sequence of short-run equilibria unfolds, and Kaldor and other post-Keynesians have expressed similar views (see, for example, Kaldor, 1954). In fact, however, most analytical work has proceeded to analyse trend and cycle separately. This also applies to Kaldor's (1940) classic trade-cycle model, which describes cyclical fluctuations around a stationary equilibrium. In spite of its failure to deal with the question of growth, the model has a number of features which have made it the subject of almost continuous attention ever since its publication.[17] One of the

---

[17] Chang and Smyth (1971), Torre (1977), Varian (1979), Dana and Malgrange (1984) and Semmler (1986) are among the recent papers which discuss the original model and attempt to generalise it.

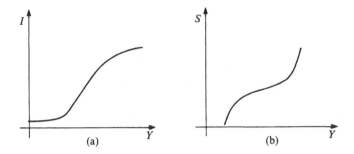

Figure 3.1: (a) Investment and (b) saving in Kaldor's model of the trade cycle.

main attractions of the model is that 'it appears to generate self-sustaining cycles without the need for rigid specification of parameters and the use of time lags and initial shocks' (Chang and Smyth, 1971, p. 37). Instead, the cyclical behaviour of the economy is generated by a combination of (i) non-linearities in the investment and/or saving functions and (ii) endogenous shifts in the two functions caused by the gradual changes in the capital stock.

The working of the model can be described briefly as follows. For any given capital stock, desired investment and saving will be functionally related to income and the functional forms are, Kaldor argued, likely to be non-linear in the manner indicated by figure 3.1. Depending on the position of the two curves, there will be either one or three equilibrium positions (see figure 3.2a–c), and the position of the curves is determined by the size of the capital stock. A large capital stock implies that lower rates of desired investment will be associated with any given rate of output, and, although the saving function may also be affected by changes in the capital stock, it is, Kaldor argued, the shifts in investment which will dominate. The configuration in figure 3.2a therefore corresponds to a 'small' capital stock, 3.2b to a 'normal' stock and 3.2c to a 'large' stock.

Assume now that initially the economy is at the unique equilibrium position, *A*, in figure 3.2a. At this equilibrium, there is a high rate of investment, the capital stock is growing and the curves will be shifting. After some period of time, the configuration will be as in figure 3.2b, the economy still remaining at the high equilibrium point, *A*. Investment, however, is high and causes further shifts in the curves. Eventually, a point is reached where the *A* and *B* equilibria coincide, and, if net investment is still positive, this equilibrium will be followed by the configuration in figure 3.2c with output contracting rapidly until a new equilibrium has been reached at *C*. If the equilibrium at *C* entails negative rates of net investment, then a reverse movement of the curves will now take place until

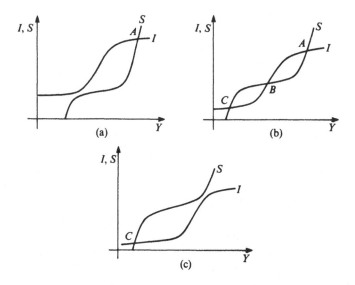

Figure 3.2: Equilibrium positions in Kaldor's model: the positions correspond to (a) a small, (b) an intermediate and (c) a large capital stock.

eventually the 'high' equilibrium at A becomes the only equilibrium as in figure 3.2a.

The model can be formalised in a set of two differential equations,

$$\dot{Y} = \alpha[I(Y, K) - S(Y, K)] \tag{3.15}$$

$$\dot{K} = I(Y, K) - \delta K \tag{3.16}$$

where α is an output adjustment coefficient and where it has been assumed that realised investment is always equal to desired *ex ante* investment. Chang and Smyth (1971) provide a rigorous analysis of the system (3.15)–(3.16) and establish the conditions required for the perpetual fluctuations described above.

The model can be generalised to cover the case of cyclical fluctuations around an exogenous growth trend (see Dana and Malgrange, 1984), but it is not obvious how it could be turned into a model of endogenous cyclical growth. Since the original model yields endogenous fluctuations, this may seem surprising, but problems arise in the specification of the relations between investment and saving on the one hand and the capital stock on the other.

From the point of view of long-run theory, it is reasonable to assume that both the investment and the saving functions are linearly homogeneous in output and the capital stock. This assumption would be in line with most work on saving and investment, and indeed, in line with Kaldor's own later theories (e.g. the 1957 model described above). Homogeneity of degree one in the saving and investment functions will, however, lead to steady growth. With homogeneity, equations (3.15)–(3.16) can be rewritten

$$\hat{Y} = \frac{\alpha}{\sigma}[I(\sigma, 1) - S(\sigma, 1)] \tag{3.17}$$

$$\hat{K} = I(\sigma, 1) - \delta \tag{3.18}$$

where $\sigma = Y/K$. Hence

$$\hat{\sigma} = \frac{\alpha}{\sigma}[I(\sigma, 1) - S(\sigma, 1)] - I(\sigma, 1) + \delta \tag{3.19}$$

From (3.19) it is readily seen that σ will converge monotonically toward some equilibrium value. The equilibrium – corresponding to $\hat{\sigma} = 0$ – may not be unique: the non-linearities in Y for given K may imply the existence of three equilibria, two stable and one unstable. But this complication does not affect the fact that asymptotically the economy will exhibit steady growth; if the saving and investment functions are linearly homogeneous then the model cannot produce endogenous cyclical growth.

Another, and perhaps equally important, criticism of the model concerns the total neglect of the labour market. For situations of significant unemployment, one may choose to ignore the labour market in short-run analysis, but it is difficult to see how such a procedure could be justified if the analysis is to be extended to the medium and long term. At the very least, one should include an upper bound (the natural rate of growth) on the feasible long-run growth rate. Kaldor's model fails to do this. Like the standard Keynesian short-run model, it is built around the product market. In this respect, Kaldor's analysis is in sharp contrast to another classic paper: Goodwin (1967) develops a model of cyclical growth in which the labour market and the bargaining strength of workers take the front seat.

3.9 GOODWIN

The starting point for Goodwin's famous paper is the Marxian conception that the strength of workers depends inversely on the size of the reserve army of labour, and that a strong working class will demand and gain an increasing share of wages in income. The rise in wages, in turn, has adverse effects on the rate of accumulation and hence on the employment rate, and this interaction between the size of the reserve army of labour, the distribution of income and the rate of accumulation produces a cyclical growth path.

Goodwin formalised the process in a system of non-linear differential equations,

$$(1 \overset{\frown}{-} \pi) = -a + be \tag{3.20}$$

$$\hat{e} = c - d(1 - \pi) \tag{3.21}$$

where π is the share of profits in income, e is the employment rate and a, b, c and d are positive constants.

Equation (3.20) says that the rate of growth of labour's share in income is positively related to the level of the employment rate, the rationale being that higher rates of employment strengthen workers in the struggle over distributive shares. Equation (3.21) relates the rate of growth of employment to the share of wages in income. The equation is based on three assumptions: (i) that all profits are invested and all wage income spent on consumption, (ii) that the output–capital ratio is constant, and (iii) that the rate of growth of the labour force is constant. Assumptions (i) and (ii) imply that the rate of growth of the capital stock is equal to the rate of growth of output and proportional to the share of profits in income (the proportionality factor being the constant output–capital ratio), and assumption (iii) transforms the rate of growth of output into a proportional rate of change of the employment rate.

For any given initial values of e and π, the solution to (3.20)–(3.21) yields a closed trajectory in the (e, π)-plane: if left undisturbed, the model will, as shown in figure 3.3, produce conservative cyclical fluctuations in distributive shares and in the employment rate. This, and most other qualitative results, will also hold for the 'general Goodwin model' where the linearity assumptions have been dropped and (3.20)–(3.21) are replaced by[18]

$$(1 \overset{\frown}{-} \pi) = \varphi(e); \quad \varphi' > 0 \tag{3.22}$$

$$\hat{e} = \psi(1 - \pi); \quad \psi' < 0 \tag{3.23}$$

Generalisations of the model which go beyond (3.22)–(3.23) will, however, change the qualitative properties of the model: the trajectories will no longer be closed orbits in the (e, π)-plane if direct feedbacks from π to $(1 \overset{\frown}{-} \pi)$ (or from e to $\hat{e}$) are introduced. In this sense the model is structurally unstable. If, for instance, workers' militancy and thus the change in the share of wages are positively related to the current profit

---

[18] Goodwin mentions this without proof; a proof is given in Groth (1981) as well as in Desai and Pemberton (1981).

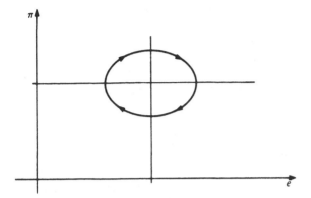

Figure 3.3: Cyclical fluctuations in employment and income distribution in Goodwin's model of a growth cycle.

share as well as to the rate of employment, then the steady-growth equilibrium becomes stable.

Goodwin's paper has attracted much attention and a large literature is devoted to extending and generalising the model.[19] The focus of almost all the contributions has, however, remained exclusively on the labour market. The flow of investment has been treated as an accommodating variable which adapts to the flow of saving. Saving, in turn, is determined by income distribution and, in spite of attempts to introduce money-wage bargaining, the distribution of income is decided in the labour market. Extensions of the model which include money-wage bargaining have in effect merely modified the labour-market relation describing the determination of distributive shares: it has been assumed that changes in money wages depend on expectations concerning price changes (as well as on the employment rate) and that price changes depend on the level of distributive shares. The net effect is that money illusion (or inflation effects on the relative bargaining positions) may produce a direct feedback from the level of distributive shares to changes in distribution.

In Goodwin-type models, class struggle over distribution is thus confined to the labour market. There are no effective-demand problems and investment adapts to clear the product market no matter what prices and wages are set in the wage-bargaining process.[20] Essentially, both output and investment are passive variables in the model and, also from a strictly Marxian point of view, this aspect of the model seems unsatisfactory: the

[19] See, for example, Desai (1973), Groth (1981), Shah and Desai (1981), Goodwin *et al.* (1984), van der Ploeg (1983), Semmler (1986).
[20] Shah and Desai (1981) and Wolfstetter (1982) are possible exceptions.

control over production and investment decisions is, one would think, an important weapon of capital in the class struggle.

In conclusion, the Goodwin model and the associated literature suffer from two interrelated weaknesses: it pays no attention to effective demand (or realisation problems, as Marx would put it), and it treats production and investment as passive and accommodating variables.

3.10 KALECKI

Kalecki does not fit easily into either a post-Keynesian or a neo-Marxian category. Coming from a Marxian tradition and anticipating many aspects of Keynes's analysis, he combines elements from the two traditions, and his work has been extremely influential among both post-Keynesians and neo-Marxists. His famous dictum, for instance, that 'workers spend what they earn and capitalists earn what they spend' is reflected in post-Keynesian distribution theory. Like the post-Keynesian theory, the dictum is based on a semi-classical saving assumption. Kalecki, however, did not use the saving function to determine the share of profits in income.

In his theory, the equilibrium condition for the product market determines the absolute level of profits while the share of profits is determined by firms' pricing decisions: there is imperfect competition and firms act as price-makers and set a mark-up on cost. Kalecki conceded that mark-up decisions might be influenced by the state of demand, but he attached little importance to this possibility. In normal conditions, he argued, there will be both unemployment and spare capital capacity, and changes in demand will affect the level of production (utilisation rates) rather than the price–cost margin. Production levels influence the *rate* of profit but there is no direct influence of demand on distributive shares.

How then do firms fix prices? Profit margins and distributive shares are, Kalecki argued, determined by 'the degree of monopoly'. At times he used the term almost synonymously for the profit margin, and this prompted the accusation that a tautology was involved. The accusation is not warranted: the degree of monopoly is a shorthand expression for a range of factors which influence the pricing decisions of firms. Primary among these factors are the degree of monopolisation in the industry, the elasticity of demand, and the strength and militancy of workers. But, although the theory is not tautological, there are problems with Kalecki's view of pricing and distribution. Some of the problems will be taken up in greater detail in chapter 8 but here I wish to focus on one particular aspect: the direct influence of workers on distribution.

The view that workers can influence the distribution of income directly is at the heart of Goodwin's Marx formalisation, but it is not clear how any such influence can be compatible with money-wage bargaining and the determination of output and production by demand. Kalecki thought it was. He argued that[21]

[T]he existence of powerful trade unions may tend to reduce profit margins for the following reasons. A high ratio of profits to wages strengthens the bargaining position of trade unions in their demands for wage increases since higher wages are then compatible with 'reasonable profits' at existing price levels. If after such increases are granted prices should be raised, this would call forth new demands for wage increases. It follows that a high ratio of profits to wages cannot be maintained without creating a tendency towards rising costs. This adverse effect upon the competitive position of a firm or an industry encourages the adoption of lower profit margins. Thus, the degree of monopoly will be kept down to some extent by the activity of trade unions, and this the more the stronger the trade unions are.

(Kalecki, 1954, quoted from Kalecki, 1971a, p. 51)

This sort of reasoning lies behind the advocacy by some left Keynesians of union militancy and increasing wage demands as a remedy against unemployment.[22] The reasoning, however, is not convincing. Increasing money wages in any one firm will make that firm less competitive and give its workers a rising real wage. It is also likely to cause a decline in the production of the firm, but other firms and industries will be stimulated and the overall effect on employment and output may not be negative. However, just as one needs to consider these expansionary effects on other industries, so one should take into account the fact that increased militancy and higher wages in any one firm will lessen the competitive pressure on rival firms. Consequently, they may raise their profit margins, leaving the overall effect on the profit share indeterminate. The microeconomic argument thus does not generalise to the level of the economy as a whole.

Kalecki (and some later stagnationists) appear to want their cake and eat it too. They suggest that an increase in union militancy and in money wages will (i) raise real wages and the share of wages in income as well as (ii) stimulate demand and thereby lead to an expansion in output and employment. The argument for increases in real wages, however, depends on the assumption that real demand will fall if firms raise prices *pari passu* with money wages. It is the inability of firms to compensate for rising

---

[21] A very similar argument can be found in Kalecki (1971b).
[22] For Pigou and the neoclassical economists, price increases would have real-balance effects causing a decline in demand and rising real wages. They therefore accept the view that rising money wages produce higher real wages, but reverse the stagnationist conclusion concerning output and demand.

wages which explains the power of unions to affect real wages, and it is difficult to see how one can reconcile this argument with the view that rising real wages stimulate aggregate demand and employment. A uniform increase in wages cannot simultaneously increase the competitive pressure on all firms.

Strong and militant unions and/or greedy firms may well cause severe conflict over distributive shares. Unions will push up money wages and firms respond by raising prices and the result may be (accelerating) inflation. Joan Robinson long ago (1962) labelled this the 'inflation barrier', and more recently Rowthorn (1977) has analysed the inflationary process caused by distributional conflict. Inflation in turn may have direct effects on demand, and it may also induce government intervention, e.g. deflationary fiscal and monetary policies and/or a restrictive incomes (wages) policy. Kalecki, however, does not take these factors into account and in any case, it is difficult to see how any such complications could produce clear-cut conclusions in support of his position.

In conclusion, Kalecki's theory of pricing and distribution is not tautological, but he did not manage to combine effective demand with a direct Marxian influence of class struggle on distributive shares in a fully convincing manner. He highlighted the importance of firms' mark-up decisions for the theory of distribution and pointed out some of the factors affecting these decisions. But his arguments that money-wage claims have direct effects on distribution is based on microeconomic reasoning which cannot be extended to the macroeconomic level and which fits badly with the rest of his theory.[23]

3.11 CONCLUDING REMARKS

The development of theories which help us understand the dynamic properties of capitalism is a daunting task, and, although the work reviewed in this chapter has been extremely important, it still leaves many questions unanswered. It is the purpose of the ensuing chapters to address some of those questions.

Harrod argued that a free market capitalism will face two problems: instability of the warranted growth path and inequality of the warranted and natural growth rates. Harrod's framework has been criticised but his

---

[23] The foregoing criticism of the view that money-wage rises will cause an increase in both real wages and employment does not imply that an exogenous decline in the mark-up factor (e.g. caused by a change in the conjectured elasticity of demand) may not have both of these effects. It is the link between money wages and real wages which causes problems. In order to establish this link, one would need a decline in real demand and output rather than an expansion. The effects of changes in the desired profit margin will be analysed in chapter 8.

argument has not been answered convincingly. We need to look seriously at some of the criticisms of Harrod's analysis, but the problems he identified should not be assumed away at the outset, as did both the neoclassical economists and Kaldor (1957). Can Harrod's conclusions survive the introduction of a choice of technique? Will a variable average saving rate alleviate the difficulties pointed out by him? The questions remain open.

A theory which is to enhance our understanding of actual historical processes must explain the stylised facts of advanced capitalism. Prominent among these facts are the persistence of cyclical fluctuations in output and employment and the absence of a long-run trend in the employment rate. The theory should analyse and explain both cycle and trend, and one would like the trend to emerge as the 'slowly changing component of a chain of short-period situations' (Kalecki, 1968) rather than as the result of some exogenous long-run factor. The theory should pay attention to monetary aspects and to the effects of finance on both investment and saving. Last, but not least, one would like to combine both Keynesian and Marxian elements within the same theoretical model. Both Keynesian and Marxian analyses have produced fundamental insights into the working of capitalist economic systems, but it is unsatisfactory if these insights cannot be expressed within a common theoretical framework. Class conflict and effective demand have each been extensively analysed, but attempts to include both in the same model have often been frustrated, either one or the other leading a shadow existence in the combined theory. Why is this? Why do we seem to find so little room for class conflict in models of effective demand and vice versa?

These are some of the questions motivating the analysis in the ensuing chapters.

CHAPTER 4

The model

4.1 INTRODUCTION

I consider three types of agents: firms, banks and households. Firms decide the levels of employment, production and investment. The decisions are based on the maximisation of expected profits, but expectations will not always be fulfilled. Finance for investment is obtained from three different sources: retained earnings, new issues and bank loans.

Banks accept deposits from households and extend loans to firms, and there is no credit rationing: firms can borrow as much as they wish at the prevailing interest rate. The rate of interest, however, may vary over time, an assumption which makes the elastic supply of money (credit) compatible with a range of different monetary regimes.

Households supply labour, consume output and hold financial assets. There may be involuntary unemployment, but households are not quantity-constrained in any other market.

The model differs from standard Keynesian and Kaleckian theory in several respects. One important difference concerns price and output adjustments: production levels are only imperfectly flexible and firms' short-term expectations may not be fulfilled. Consequently, the economy will not necessarily be in short-run equilibrium. Discrepancies between actual and expected demand may arise, and it is assumed that any such discrepancies cause accommodating price changes. In contrast to most Keynesian models, prices are thus flexible (in both directions) even in the very short run.

It is important to be clear about the reasons for this departure from Keynesian orthodoxy and about the structure of the model. The chapter therefore opens with a discussion of price flexibility and disappointed expectations. This discussion is followed by a description of the behavioural assumptions for the three types of agents. The presentation in the main text emphasises the intuition behind the assumptions, more technical material being relegated to an appendix.

4.2 PRICES AND SHORT-TERM EXPECTATIONS

Keynesian models almost invariably follow the *General Theory* in assuming that short-term expectations are fulfilled and that firms are on their supply curves for output. The equivalent assumption is made by Kalecki in the context of imperfect competition. He posits flat cost curves and a constant mark-up factor and assumes that variations in demand are reflected entirely in quantity adjustments. In the *Treatise on Money*, however – as well as in early drafts of the *General Theory*[1] – Keynes took a different approach and allowed expectations to be disappointed; here we shall follow the Keynes of the *Treatise*.

As Joan Robinson and Kalecki have always insisted, a long period is nothing but a sequence of short periods and as such has no independent existence. But why should one use a Keynesian/Marshallian short period with satisfied short-period expectations as the basic unit of analysis? Is it not possible, instead, to analyse movements over time directly as a sequence of ultra-short-run equilibria? In fact, there are good reasons for trying to do so. If animal spirits stay constant and short-term expectations are always fulfilled, then the economy must evolve along a time path which is consistent with the initial long-period expectations; effectively, the economy must be in long-run equilibrium.[2] The reason is simple. With constant animal spirits, firms will only revise their initial long-term expectations if these expectations are proved wrong, and erroneous long-term expectations must involve a divergence between expected and actual outcomes in some short period: if long-period expectations are falsified by events at time *t*, then these events will also confound short-period expectations at time *t*.

Unless one believes that agents have perfect foresight over the infinite future, the notion of short-period equilibrium may thus be of limited use: the possibility of disappointed expectations must be allowed for in an extension of Keynesian theory to cover long-run developments. Indeed, disappointed short-term expectations – with direct effects on production and employment decisions and cumulative effects on long-term expectations and investment – would appear to be among the most important factors driving the economy.[3]

What happens if short-term expectations are disappointed? Firms have made production decisions in anticipation of a certain level of demand,

---

[1] See Keynes (1973), pp. 180–1.

[2] Or equilibrium over an infinite period of time, to use Hicks's terminology (Hicks, 1965, p. 24).

[3] Recent developments in orthodox macroeconomics appear to be based on the opposite view: great effort has gone into investigating the possibility of endogenous cycles in a model with perfect foresight (e.g. Grandmont, 1985).

but, when output appears, demand turns out to be different. The necessary accommodation can be achieved in two ways: through adjustments in either quantities or prices.

The level of production, by assumption, cannot adjust instantaneously, and a quantity adjustment must involve a change in stocks and/or the direct rationing of demand. A particular case of rationing is the lengthening of queues, but, although one can point to industries where queues play an important role (e.g. shipbuilding), instances of quantity-rationing are hardly significant in the general picture of capitalist economies. I therefore have few qualms in leaving out quantity-rationing altogether. Stocks and stock movements, on the other hand, are obviously of importance but, if anything, stock movements tend to amplify fluctuations in other demand components over the trade cycle. Disregarding stocks and stock movements should therefore bias the model toward steady growth rather than toward instability and cyclical fluctuations. With this bias in mind, I shall abstract from stocks too.

Having left out both stocks and quantity rationing, the accommodation will have to come via price adjustments: changes in *prices* must equate the demand for output to (the predetermined level of) production. Can prices perform this function and establish equilibrium in the product market when expectations are disappointed? There will be several mechanisms to consider: real-balance and interest-rate effects may play a part, but there may also be distributional effects. Labour-market contracts are cast in terms of money wages, and there is neither perfect foresight nor *instantaneous* feedbacks from output prices to money-wage rates. The real-wage rate and the share of profits in income therefore respond to unanticipated movements in money prices, and aggregate demand is, as we shall see, inversely related to the share of profits in national income.

The assumption that prices are flexible and that they adjust to clear the product market is at odds with most 'Keynesian' models.[4] There is also a widespread view that empirically prices and profit margins are constant, but the evidence is not clear and some case studies do indicate considerable price flexibility. In either case, the qualitative property of price flexibility need not imply that prices will in fact exhibit large fluctuations. Prices act as signals to changes in output, and the mechanism here is that described already by Marshall: a market clearing price is established in the ultra-short run, but this price will – in general – deviate from the short-run supply price, thus giving firms an incentive to change future levels of

---

[4] Most notably the fix-price literature associated with, among others, Benassy (1975) and Barro and Grossman (1976). From an exegetical point of view this literature fails to represent Keynes's analysis and, more importantly, as a positive contribution it is open to both theoretical and empirical objections; see, for example, Kahn (1977) and Skott (1983).

production. The amplitude of fluctuations in prices and distributive shares will therefore depend, *inter alia*, on the speed with which the level of production reacts to short-run disequilibrium. If firms expand production rapidly as soon as actual prices exceed short-run equilibrium prices, then prices need never deviate very much from the short-run equilibrium level; they may appear to be fixed.

To summarise, in contrast to a traditional Keynesian approach I shall allow actual demand to fall short of – or exceed – the anticipated level. Price and/or quantity accommodation must come into effect when this happens, and I have chosen to rely entirely on price adjustments: unanticipated changes in demand are reflected in price movements, but price movements guide current decisions concerning changes in future output.

There are three reasons for this procedure. Price rigidities are often seen as a major source of problems in market economies. If only prices were perfectly flexible then, it is argued, unemployment would rapidly disappear. The assumption of perfectly flexible prices is one way of challenging the validity of this view: in the present model it will not be possible to blame unemployment on rigid prices. The second reason has already been alluded to: stocks and stock movements are well-known sources of short-term fluctuations in production, and leaving out this source of instability should create a bias toward steady growth. The argument for endogenous cycles is thus strengthened if it can be shown that cycles arise even in models of pure price adjustment. The neglect of stocks and stock changes, finally, is analytically convenient. If unanticipated changes in demand are reflected in stock movements then production decisions will be influenced by both the level of stocks (reflecting past surprises in demand) and the change in stocks (the current surprise). With price signals, one avoids the cumulative effect of past surprises on current decisions. Output adjustments based on price signals are thus easier to model than adjustments based on stock signals.[5]

4.3 PRODUCTION

The view that firms are guided by the profit motive is almost universal in economics. It has been endorsed by Marxians and proponents of the free market alike. There are of course exceptions: Baumol (1959) and his

---

[5] Models which allow for disappointed short-term expectations often assume that the change in output is proportional to the level of excess demand,

$$\dot{Y} = \mu(I - S)$$

This adjustment assumption could be justified by the existence of flexible prices and an ultra-short-run Marshall mechanism. Alternatively, it is compatible with fixed prices and direct quantity-rationing, but, since the change in production depends exclusively on

followers, for instance, have argued that the level and/or growth of sales are the prime objectives of firms. Here, however, I follow the majority view and assume that firms aim to make as much profit as possible. For analytical convenience this proposition will be embodied in the assumption that firms maximise profits (see the discussion in chapter 2).

One of the constraints on profit maximisation is 'technology', but technology should not be seen as a purely technical matter. The productivity of both labour and capital depends on a range of social factors: industrial relations, the strength and militancy of workers, the quality and attitudes of management, to mention just some of the important influences. The interaction of social and more narrow technical factors can be crucial for the analysis of spatial differences in economic performance as well as for the explanation of changes over time in the performance of a single economy.[6] For the time being, however, I shall leave aside these issues and assume that there is a given hybrid socio-technical production function.

I consider two inputs, labour and capital, and in accordance with the empirical evidence it is assumed that excess capital capacity is the normal state of affairs. A theoretical justification for this assumption is given below. With respect to labour, on the other hand, it is assumed that employed workers are fully 'utilised' at all times: there is no labour-hoarding. The appropriateness of this assumption can be questioned. Labour-hoarding is widespread at certain times, and, as a result, movements in output and employment do not always follow each other closely in the short run. To simplify the analysis, I ignore this complication.

To avoid aggregation problems, it is assumed that all firms face the same production function and that it is of the fixed-coefficient type,

$$Y_i = \min\{\lambda L_i, \sigma K_i\} \tag{4.1}$$

where the subscript denotes variables at the firm level. Empirically, the fixed-coefficient production function seems reasonable. Okun's law does not suggest diminishing returns to labour in the short run, and detailed firm-level evidence reported in Fay and Medoff (1985) shows wide variation between firms but is compatible with constant returns to labour for the 'representative' firm.

With respect to short-run analysis, the use of fixed coefficients can also be given some theoretical support: an *ex ante* choice of technique may exist, but, once investment has been carried out and the new plant and machinery has been installed, the firm will face a fixed-coefficient pro-

current excess demand, it is not consistent with fixed prices and inventory accommodation. See Skott (1988b) for an analysis of a fix-price model with rationing.
[6] See Bowles *et al.* (1986), Bowles (1985), Skott (1985a).

duction function. When it comes to long-term questions, however, this argument loses its force. Capital goods may not be malleable, but the analysis of long-term movements should not ignore the *ex ante* choice of technique: steady growth can only be compatible with profit maximisation if firms regard the existing technique as optimal.

I shall return to this issue in chapter 5, but for the time being the fixed-coefficient production function can be interpreted as follows. Capital goods last a long time, and the choice of technique will be governed by expected average long-run cost conditions rather than by short-term fluctuations. If the economy does not diverge too far from a steady-growth path then the steady-growth pattern of relative costs will determine the profit-maximising choice of technique, and the constant parameters λ and σ in equation (4.1) may represent this choice.

In equation (4.1) time subscripts have been left out. Production is not, however, instantaneous. The production process takes time and at any moment the rate of output, Y, is predetermined by past production decisions. Discrete time lags are difficult to handle analytically, but the effects of production lags can be approximated within a continuous time framework by taking the rate of growth of Y at time t, $\hat{Y}_t$, as the decision variable at time t. The approximation is close if the production lag is short and the time path of Y is smooth (differentiable). Smoothness, in turn, may be justified by an appeal to the existence of adjustment costs.

4.4 ADJUSTMENT COSTS

Changes in employment and production are subject to adjustment costs. If the firm wishes to expand production, it may need to raise its expenditure on job advertising, and it is easy to construct simple search models where increases in wage rates and/or improvements in working conditions are also necessary in order to attract more workers. A reduction in the work-force, on the other hand, entails redundancy payments and may lead to a deterioration in industrial relations with negative effects on productivity. Numerically high rates of growth of employment will thus be associated with high adjustment costs, and the standard convexity assumption seems reasonable. The position of the adjustment-cost function will, however, depend on the state of the labour market.

The rate of employment influences the position of the adjustment-cost function through its effects on the social relations of production as well as on the availability of labour with the desired qualifications. A high rate of employment strengthens workers *vis-à-vis* management. It may lead to increased shop-floor militancy, and, as the threat of redundancy loses its edge, more surveillance is needed in order to prevent shirking and to

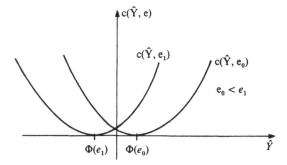

Figure 4.1: The adjustment-cost function for two different values of the rate of employment.

extract the same amount of work effort (Bowles, 1985). Managerial resources will thus be tied up in the day-to-day running of the firm. High rates of employment, furthermore, are likely to lead to an increase in the turnover of the labour force, and the gross recruitment needs associated with any given rate of expansion are thus raised at a time when low unemployment makes it difficult to attract new workers.

All of these effects combine to make it less attractive and more costly to expand production. High employment and a high turnover of the labour force, on the other hand, may allow firms to contract production and employment more rapidly without incurring the costs associated with compulsory redundancies (redundancy payments as well as negative effects on productivity of a deterioration in industrial relations). For positive rates of expansion, the cost of adjustment will therefore be an increasing function of the rate of employment while for negative rates it is decreasing in the rate of employment. The following simple specification of the total adjustment costs of a firm with output Y_i and growth rate $\hat{Y}_i$ satisfies these conditions:

$$c_i = Y_i c(\hat{Y}_i, e); \quad c_1 \gtrless 0 \quad \text{for} \quad \hat{Y}_i \gtrless \Phi(e); \quad c_{11} > 0;$$

$$c_2 \gtrless 0 \quad \text{for} \quad \hat{Y}_i \gtrless \Phi(e); \quad \Phi' < 0 \qquad (4.2)$$

where $c(.,.)$ is the adjustment-cost function and $\Phi(e)$ defines the growth rate of output which minimises these costs given the rate of employment. Note that employment, e, is a macroeconomic variable: the cost of adjustment for an individual firm depends on its own rate of expansion and the state of the labour market in the economy as a whole. Figure 4.1 illustrates the relation between changes in output and the costs of expansion for two different values of the rate of employment.

Firms choose the rate of growth of output so as to balance the costs of changes against the benefits of moving toward the desired position. For any given rate of employment, there will be a positive relation between the rate of expansion of output and the ratio of desired to actual output, $Y*/Y$. The effects of employment on the rate of expansion are also straightforward. An increase in the rate of employment will make expansion more costly and hence depress the growth rate when the firm wishes to expand. An inverse relation between the aggregate employment rate and the rate of expansion also applies when the firm wants to reduce production: in this case a higher rate of employment facilitates the adjustment and thus induces a faster rate of contraction. These considerations are summarised mathematically in equation (4.3):

$$\hat{Y}_i = h\left(\frac{Y*_i}{Y_i}, e\right); \quad h_1 > 0, \ h_2 < 0 \tag{4.3}$$

Note that this equation includes simple adjustment functions as special cases. Let μ_1 and μ_2 be the (asymmetric) speeds of adjustment for expansionary and contractionary movements, respectively, and assume that μ_1 and μ_2 depend on the state of the labour market, $\mu_j = \mu_j(e)$. Then

$$\hat{Y}_i = \begin{cases} \mu_1(e)\dfrac{Y*_i - Y_i}{Y_i} & \text{if} \quad Y*_i > Y_i \\[2ex] \mu_2(e)\dfrac{Y*_i - Y_i}{Y_i} & \text{if} \quad Y*_i < Y_i \end{cases} \tag{4.4}$$

and (4.4) is a special case of (4.3).

4.5 DEMAND

Equation (4.3) describes a relation between desired output, $Y*$, and changes in actual production, but how is $Y*$ determined? Demand clearly plays an important part, but in order to be more precise one needs to consider the market environment. Perfect competition is no serious candidate: it is not – and never has been – a good approximation to the market conditions faced by the majority of firms. Instead, a simple specification of imperfect competition is required.

In the present context, an attempt to capture oligopolistic interdependencies is analytically forbidding. A pure monopoly specification, on the other hand, assumes that demand depends exclusively on the price of the monopolist (ignoring advertising etc.), and this assumption is not really satisfactory. In general, demand will be influenced by the behaviour of rival firms and, furthermore, most firms recognise this to be the case. I

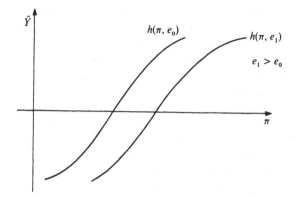

Figure 4.2: The output-expansion function for two different values of the rate of employment.

shall therefore adopt the following specification of the conjectured demand function:

$$p_i = p^\rho B_i Y_i^{-\gamma} \tag{4.5}$$

In equation (4.5), p_i is the price of the firm's own output and p is the average price of output from rival firms: the conjectured demand depends on own price as well as on the prices charged by rival producers, but the firm does not take into account the possible influence of its own pricing and production decisions on the prices charged by rival producers. For simplicity, the price of rival firms is identified with the average price for the economy as a whole, p, and constant elasticities of the demand function (constant values of ρ and γ) also help to simplify the analysis.

4.6 THE OUTPUT-EXPANSION FUNCTION

Assuming that the expected growth rate of demand is independent of the firm's price–output combination (see p. 53) then $Y*_i$ – the current rate of output which the firm would have chosen had its output level been perfectly flexible – is determined myopically by the standard static conditions for profit maximisation. When there is excess capital capacity, we therefore get

$$Y*_i = \left[\frac{\lambda}{w}(1 - \gamma) B_i p^\rho \right]^{1/\gamma} \tag{4.6}$$

$$\pi*_i = \gamma \tag{4.7}$$

where π represents the profit share.

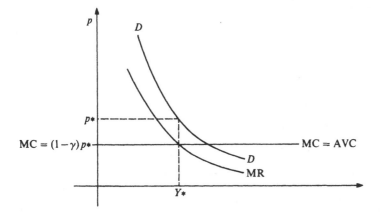

Figure 4.3: Traditional determination of price and output in short-run equilibrium.

Since $Y_i \gtreqless Y*_i$ for $\pi_i \lesseqgtr \pi*_i = \gamma$, equation (4.3) can be rewritten

$$\hat{Y}_i = h(\pi_i, e), \quad h_\pi > 0 \quad \text{and} \quad h_e < 0 \tag{4.8}$$

Equation (4.8) is the *output-expansion function* for the representative firm, and I shall assume that the same functional form applies to the economy as a whole. The aggregate output-expansion function is then given by

$$\hat{Y} = h(\pi, e); \quad h_\pi > 0, \quad h_e < 0 \tag{4.9}$$

The appendix at the end of this chapter provides a more rigorous derivation of equation (4.9).

The output-expansion function is illustrated in figure 4.2, which shows the relation between the share of profits and the growth of production for two values of the rate of employment. This function takes the place of static supply functions in standard theory. The connection between the output-expansion function and the static theory is most easily seen if we disregard the influence of labour-market conditions on the expansion of output. The static supply–demand framework is illustrated in figure 4.3. The combination of excess capital capacity, constant money wages and constant productivity of labour produces a horizontal marginal-cost curve. The short-run equilibrium value of $Y*$ is found at the intersection of this curve with the perceived marginal revenue curve. Figure 4.4 describes the outcome when there are finite adjustment speeds and mistaken expectations: firms have chosen output Y_0 in the expectation of demand DD, but actual demand turns out to be $D'D'$. As a result, the

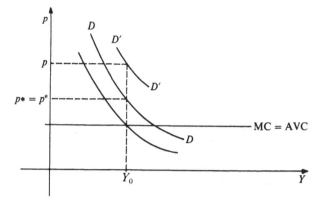

Figure 4.4: Determination of price (and income distribution) in ultra-short-run equilibrium when short-term expectations fail to be fulfilled.

realised price and profit share exceed the expected (short-run equilibrium) levels; $p > p* = w/[\lambda(1 - \gamma)]$, $\pi > \pi* = \gamma$. This price signal now induces an expansion in production, $\hat{Y} > 0$, the speed of adjustment being related to the share of profits in income. Matters become slightly more complicated when we allow the rate of employment to influence the costs of adjustment, but the imperfect flexibility of output and the lack of perfect foresight still distinguish the present approach from standard static theory.

4.7 INVESTMENT

For Kalecki the investment function was the central *pièce de résistance*,[7] and Bliss, in a very different tradition, commented on the great difficulty of writing down the decision problem, never mind solving it.[8] The difficulties stem from the long-term character of the investment decision. In other areas of economic decision-making it may be just about possible to ignore intertemporal issues, but not so with investment. The investment decision is essentially intertemporal, and uncertainty and 'animal spirits' cannot be ignored.

A range of different specifications of the investment function has been proposed to capture the predictable elements in the investment decision, but no consensus exists even within individual schools of thought. Since the investment function is also likely to exhibit instability over time, results which depend heavily on a particular specification of the function

---

[7] Kalecki (1968).   [8] Bliss (1975), p. 323.

must be suspect. I shall therefore postpone the derivation of a complete investment function until chapter 6. At that stage a precise specification will be needed, but for the moment we can do with less.

With respect to short-run issues I follow normal practice and regard the rate of investment as an exogenous variable: this part of the analysis will focus on the influence of changes in parameters and exogenous variables – including investment – on the equilibrium outcome. But, when the period is extended to the medium and long term, it is no longer satisfactory to consider investment exogenous. Long-run investment is primarily induced rather than autonomous, and in steady growth the utilisation ratio of capital must be at the desired level: if it were not, then firms would not maintain a constant rate of accumulation. Large amounts of unwanted excess capacity would depress the rate of accumulation and, conversely, a prolonged period with less than desired capacity would lead to an acceleration in investment plans. But what determines the desired rate of utilisation, $u*$? In particular, can we give a theoretical justification for the assumption used above in the derivation of the output-adjustment function that firms maintain excess capital capacity?

Firms with positive pure profits face a threat of new entry, and although new entry will not affect the current level of demand – entry is not instantaneous – it will reduce future demand: the expected future value of the parameter B in equation (4.5) will be affected, and, if firms recognise this possibility, it will be reflected in their current behaviour. The literature on limit-pricing has suggested an effect on current price and output decisions, but here I shall take a different approach. Following Spence (1977), it is assumed that – instead of deviating from the price and output combination which maximises short-term profits – firms use excess capacity as a strategic deterrence to new entry.

Underlying this alternative approach is the assumption that entry – and hence expected future demand – will depend on the amount of excess capacity. This assumption can be justified by an extension of the limit-price argument: the expected rate of new entry (or the probability of new entry) may be determined, not by the actual price, but by the price which would prevail if all existing capital capacity were fully utilised. Excess capacity can deter entry because it demonstrates commitment to the particular line of business and signals the willingness of the firm to defend its position – should new entry take place – by expanding production and cutting prices.

Strategic deterrence provides a possible theoretical explanation for excess capacity, and I shall assume that the deterrence effect is sufficiently important to ensure the existence of excess capacity at all times. A detailed specification of the connection between excess capacity and expected future demand is postponed until chapter 6 (appendix 6A) where it is needed in order to derive a complete investment function. All we require for present purposes is the general notion that (expected) rates of entry depend on the amount of excess capacity as well as on the amount of pure profits.

The ratio of pure profits to total revenue is constant in steady growth, and I assume that the desired rate of utilisation, $u*$, is a decreasing function of this ratio,

$$u*_i = \kappa \left(1 - \frac{\text{ATC}_i}{p_i} \right) \tag{4.10}$$

where ATC is average total cost and where

$$\kappa(x) = 1 \quad \text{for} \quad x \leqslant 0$$

$$\kappa'(x) < 0 \quad \text{for} \quad x > 0$$

Average total cost depends on the wage rate, w, and the cost of capital (as well as on the parameters of the production function). The cost of capital in turn is determined by the cost of finance, ι, the rate of depreciation, δ, and the price of new capital goods, and I shall assume that the price of capital goods is equal to the general price level p. Using (4.1), average total cost is then given by

$$\text{ATC}_i = \frac{w}{\lambda} + \frac{p(\iota_i + \delta)}{u_i \sigma} \tag{4.11}$$

For the representative firm we have $p_i = p$, $\iota_i = \iota$ and $u_i = u$, and substituting these values into (4.10)–(4.11), we get the following equation,

$$u* = \kappa \left(1 - \frac{w}{p} \frac{1}{\lambda} - \frac{\iota + \delta}{u \sigma} \right) \tag{4.12}$$

The determination of desired utilisation is illustrated in figure 4.5. The share of pure profits is an increasing function of the rate of utilisation (given the other parameters), and, when there are positive pure profits, the desired utilisation rate is in turn decreasing in the share of pure profits. The relation between actual utilisation and desired utilisation defined by (4.12) thus has the shape indicated in the figure, $\bar{u}$ being the value of u yielding zero pure profits, and the equilibrium value of utilisation is found at the intersection with the 45° line.

The utilisation rate will not necessarily satisfy (4.12) in short-run equilibrium. Output adjusts very much faster than the capital stock to unanticipated changes in demand, and utilisation will therefore usually deviate from the desired level. However, equation (4.12) imposes restric-

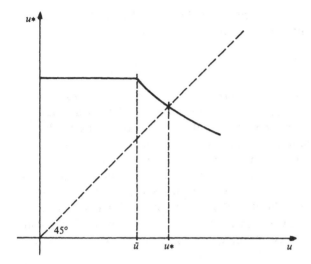

Figure 4.5: Determination of the desired rate of utilisation.

tions on the long-run properties of the investment function: persistent deviations of the utilisation rate from the desired level will lead to changes in the rate of accumulation, and a constant rate of accumulation thus requires that $u = u*$.

4.8 INVESTMENT – FINANCE

Investment needs to be financed, and, in analogy with the budget constraint of households, firms face a financial constraint,

$$pI = s_p P + vN\hat{N} + M(\hat{M} - i) \tag{4.13}$$

where P, I, i, M, N and v represent gross nominal profits, real investment, the interest rate on bank loans, the amount of bank loans, the existing number of securities and the price of securities respectively.

The parameters s_p and $\hat{N}$ reflect the financial decisions of firms. The choice of s_p and $\hat{N}$ may be subject to additional finance constraints (see chapter 7) but the two parameters are not derived from profit maximisation. In a simple Modigliani–Miller world, the valuation of an individual firm is independent of its financial structure, and maximisation therefore gives no guidance to the value of s_p and $\hat{N}$. Outside the Modigliani–Miller world, the valuation of a firm will be affected by financial decisions, but it is difficult to say exactly how, and socio-institutional and historical factors are likely to be important in the determination of financial behaviour.[9]

4.9 BANKS

Most of current macroeconomics takes the money stock as an exogenous variable. It may be subject to random shocks and thus a cause of disappointed expectations and possibly of cyclical fluctuations, but banks and endogenous variations in the money stock rarely figure in the story. The exogeneity assumption may have been appropriate for an earlier period in history, but it is anachronistic in a model of contemporary capitalism.[10] Today, outside money is of little quantitative importance, and recent attempts by central banks to control wider definitions of the money supply have met with limited success. An alternative Wicksellian approach to the analysis of monetary issues therefore seems more relevant.

I shall assume that firms may borrow from banks and that they face no quantity constraints: they can borrow as much as they wish at the ruling rate of interest, but the rate of interest need not remain constant over time. Households deposit their liquid assets with banks, and neither firms nor households hold cash. For simplicity, it is assumed that banks do not hold company-issued securities, that there are no costs involved in banking and that lending and borrowing rates coincide. Banks then have neither costs nor profits: interest payments by firms to banks are exactly equal to interest payments received by households.

In recent years the endogenous-money approach has been associated mainly with post-Keynesian writers like Kaldor and Moore,[11] but an

---

[9] See Wood (1975) for a non-neoclassical account of the determination of the financial parameters.

[10] See Chick (1983, 1986) for a discussion of the evolution of the banking system and the demands which this puts on monetary theory.

[11] E.g. Kaldor (1982) and Moore (1984). The debate between monetarists and post-Keynesians on this issue echoes earlier debates between the currency and banking schools at the beginning of last century, and support for the post-Keynesian position can in fact be found in unlikely quarters. Jean-Baptiste Say argued that 'almost all produce is in the first instance exchanged for money . . . and the commodity, which recurs so repeatedly in use, appears to vulgar apprehensions the most important of commodities, and the end and object of all transactions, whereas it is only the medium. Sales cannot be said to be dull because money is scarce, but because other products are so. There is always money enough to conduct the circulation and mutual interchange of other values, when those values really exist. Should the increase of traffic require more money to facilitate it, the want is easily supplied . . . In such cases, merchants know well enough how to find substitutes for the product serving as medium of exchange or money:* and money itself soon pours in, for this reason, that all produce naturally gravitates to that place where it is most in demand' (Say, 1844, pp. 133–4). The footnote, *, reads: 'By bills at sight, or after date, bank-notes, running-credits, write-offs, & c. as at London and Amsterdam.'

infinitely elastic supply of finance at prevailing interest rates need not exclude all monetarist concerns. The desire of firms to borrow will depend on interest rates and, in principle at least, one can conceive of a system where banks adjust interest rates continuously so as to make firms wish to increase their bank liabilities at a constant rate. In between the polar cases of constant interest rates and constant growth in the money stock is the more realistic case where monetary authorities do change interest rates over time but fail to control the amount of bank lending. I shall return to these issues in chapter 7. Until then, it is assumed that banks pursue a policy of constant real interest rates and that the money supply – the level of bank finance – accommodates.

4.10 HOUSEHOLDS

Households receive wage income as well as a return on their financial wealth. They own no physical capital goods and their (non-human) wealth is held in the form of money (deposits with banks) and securities. Interest is being earned on bank deposits, and the return on securities comprises both dividend payments and capital gains. Household incomes are either spent on consumption or used to augment the financial assets.

The desired stocks of financial assets are related to current income flows, and the saving–consumption decision aims to achieve these desired stock–flow ratios. In reality households differ but I abstract from these differences and consider a single representative household. Algebraically, household behaviour is described as follows:

$$pC + vN(\hat{v} + \hat{N}) + M\hat{M} = W + (1 - s_p)P + vN\hat{v} + iM \tag{4.14}$$

$$\alpha(P - \delta pK - rM) = vN \tag{4.15}$$

$$\beta pY = M \tag{4.16}$$

where C is consumption in real terms, N and M are the number of securities and the money stock (bank deposits) held by households, v is the price of securities, and r is the real rate of interest on bank deposits, $r = i - \hat{p}$. Note that the assumptions on banks in section 4.9 ensure that households are the only holders of securities and that the amount of household deposits with banks is equal to the amount of bank loans to firms.

Equation (4.14) is households' budget constraint, and equations (4.15) and (4.16) describe the behavioural assumptions. It is assumed (equation

Baumol (1977) suggests that this is the foundation for Say's law in its strongest form. This interpretation is dubious, but Say certainly undermines the assumption of an exogenous money supply (Skott, 1985b).

(4.16)) that the demand for money is proportional to national income. Modifications of this simple quantity-theory assumption are discussed in chapter 7.

The demand for financial securities (equation (4.15)) is assumed proportional to the level of profits net of depreciation and (real) interest payments.[12] In other words, it is assumed that the economy-wide price–earnings ratio is constant over time. This specification has the virtue of simplicity, but it may also have a somewhat neoclassical flavour: if the level of profits is given, then share valuation is independent of firms' pay-out decisions. In fact, no important conclusions of the model depend on this precise specification. It would be easy to relate vN to, say, total distributed incomes or total consumption, and this change would not affect the qualitative results of the analysis.[13]

Equations (4.14)–(4.16) can be used to derive saving and consumption functions. Substituting (4.15) and (4.16) into (4.14), we get

$$pC = pY - s_p P - vN\hat{N} - M(\hat{Y} - r)$$

$$= pY\left[1 + \alpha\hat{N}\left(\beta r + \frac{\delta}{u\sigma}\right) - \beta(\hat{Y} - r) - \pi(s_p + \alpha\hat{N})\right] \qquad (4.17)$$

and hence

$$\frac{C}{Y} = (1 - a) - b\pi \qquad (4.18)$$

$$\frac{S}{Y} = a + b\pi \qquad (4.19)$$

where

$$a = -\alpha\hat{N}\left[\beta r + \frac{\delta}{u\sigma} + \beta(\hat{Y} - r)\right]$$

$$b = s_p + \alpha\hat{N}$$

The composite parameters a and b are influenced by $\hat{Y}$ and u as well as by the simple parameters of the system (4.14)–(4.16), and they need not be constant over time. Apart from this modification, the saving–consumption system is similar to the simple Kaldorian specification, and, indeed,

[12] The simplifying assumption that α and β are constant is not entirely satisfactory. The returns on bank deposits and securities are i and $\langle(1 - s_p)/\{\alpha[1 - \delta/(\pi u\sigma)] - r\beta/\pi\}\rangle + \dot{v}$, respectively, and the relative rates of return will not in general be constant over time. I shall return to this problem in chapter 7.

[13] An alternative specification is used in Skott (1981) where the demands for both money and securities are related to nominal consumption expenditure.

equations (4.14)–(4.16) represent a generalised version of Kaldor's neo-Pasinetti theorem.

4.11 WAGE RATES AND EMPLOYMENT

Workers have no direct influence on firms' production and pricing decisions, but they do play a part in the determination of (money) wage rates. Furthermore, the productivity of both capital and labour may depend on work intensity and hence on the attitudes and skills of workers.

It is in the interest of workers to minimise work intensity and maximise real wages, but the strength and militancy with which workers pursue these aims will depend on their position *vis-à-vis* firms. If the rate of employment is high, the threat of redundancy carries little weight, and workers will be in a strong position; low employment rates, conversely, give firms the upper hand. Movements in productivity and wage rates should thus depend on the state of the labour market, the size of the reserve army of labour.

One aspect of the conflictual relation between workers and firms has already been touched upon in the discussion of adjustment costs. A strong and militant working class will make the expansion of production and employment less attractive: it makes for a 'bad business environment' and increases uncertainty and, furthermore, managerial resources, which otherwise could have been used to plan and execute an expansion, become occupied with industrial-relations issues. Apart from the marginal effect on expansion rates, one might have expected an effect on average productivity. The empirical evidence does not, however, suggest that productivity varies inversely with the rate of employment over the cycle, and I shall ignore this possibility. Note, however, that the effect of unemployment on work intensity and hence on productivity would be difficult to distinguish observationally from the effect of a standard neoclassical production function with diminishing returns to labour, and the implications of diminishing returns to labour are examined in chapter 6.

The influence of unemployment on wage settlements is traditionally described in terms of a Phillips curve. A simple version says that wage inflation is determined by the rate of unemployment,

$$\hat{w} = \theta(e); \quad \theta' > 0, \quad \theta'' > 0 \tag{4.20}$$

but the relation is usually extended in various ways. Workers care about real wages, and the rate of wage inflation may therefore depend on expected price changes. If workers have a target real wage, one may also want to include the difference between target and actual real wages,[14] and additional 'wedge effects' arise in models which include taxation.

The inclusion of price expectations and a target real wage may have important implications. There is abundant evidence that workers do not foresee short-run movements in prices,[15] but, if one considers a steady-growth path with a constant rate of price inflation, future price increases will be anticipated. The actual real wage thus cannot deviate from the expected real wage, and if expected real wages fall short of the target, then the rate of wage inflation may accelerate. In other words, if workers have a target real wage,

$$\left(\frac{w}{p}\right)* = \chi(e) \tag{4.21}$$

then steady growth requires that $w/p = (w/p)*$.

A relation like (4.21) has been used by, among others, Rowthorn (1977) and Marglin (1984a), but their reasons for introducing it do not fully convince me: the imposition of a constant target real wage seems peculiar. The value of labour power contains a large historical element, to use Marx's terminology, and one would expect a target real wage to be a moving average of past real wages. If, say, real-wage rates have been high over a prolonged period then it is implausible to assume that the workers' target real wage will remain unchanged. These issues – and the implications of introducing an equation like (4.21) – will be examined in greater detail in chapter 8. Until then I shall ignore the possible effects of target real wages.

A brief comment, finally, on the definition of the employment rate, e. It is assumed that the labour supply is inelastic in the sense that all offers of employment at the ruling wage rate will be accepted by unemployed members of the labour force. The rate of employment is thus unambiguous.

4.12 CONCLUDING COMMENTS

This completes the description of the main assumptions of the model. The implications of changes in some of the assumptions will be examined in chapters 7 and 8, and a detailed specification of the investment function

---

[14] The state of demand in the product market (or the utilisation rate of capital) may also play a part: it could affect the willingness of firms to concede wage increases. However, utilisation and employment move together over the cycle.

[15] It looks as if wage bargains in the sixties were based on the assumption of constant prices: workers appear to have had static expectations concerning the price level. A prolonged period of high inflation changed this, and for the more recent period workers' expectations are better described by the assumption of static expectations concerning the rate of

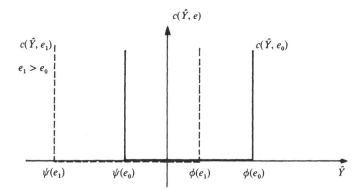

Figure A4.1: The adjustment-cost function for two different values of the rate of employment in the simple-bottleneck specification.

will be needed for the examination of cyclical fluctuations in chapter 6. But the stage has been set for the analysis of ultra-short-run, short-run, and steady-growth equilbria.

APPENDIX 4A

The aggregate output-expansion function can be derived explicitly from microeconomic profit maximisation if a simple specification of the firms' decision problems is adopted.

Assume that

1 all firms face the same fixed-coefficient production function,

$$Y_i = \min\{\lambda L_i, \sigma K_i\} \tag{a4.1}$$

2 the adjustment-cost function takes the form

$$c(\hat{Y}_i, e) = \begin{cases} 0 & \text{for} \quad \varphi(e) \le \hat{Y}_i \le \psi(e), \quad \varphi' \le 0 \text{ and } \psi' \le 0 \\ \infty & \text{elsewhere} \end{cases} \tag{a4.2}$$

Equation (a4.2) describes a simple bottleneck: no adjustment costs are associated with growth rates of production between $\varphi(e)$ and $\psi(e)$ but the cost of adjustment speeds outside this interval is prohibitive. This adjustment-cost function is depicted in figure A4.1.

3 all firms have excess capital capacity

4 expected future demand is independent of the firm's current price–output combination

5 the expected growth rate of demand – of $(p^p B_i)^{1/\gamma}$, see equation (4.5) –

inflation. This assumption on price expectations has been used in econometric work by, for example, Grubb (1986) and Nickell (1987).

lies within the expected future limits on output growth, i.e.
$\varphi(e) < [\rho(\hat{p}/\gamma) + (\hat{B}_i/\gamma)]^e < \psi(e)$.

Assumptions 1, 3 and 4 imply that

$$Y*_i = \left[\frac{\lambda}{w}(1 - \gamma)B_i p^\rho\right]^{1/\gamma} \tag{a4.3}$$

$$\pi*_i = \gamma. \tag{a4.4}$$

where $Y*_i$ and $\pi*_i$ denote the output and profit share the firm would have chosen if production had been perfectly flexible. Assumptions 2 and 5 now imply that the firm will adjust its rate of production towards $Y*_i$ and that the adjustment will be as fast as possible. Since disappointed expectations show up as a deviation of realised profit shares from the short-run equilibrium level, γ, it follows that

$$\hat{Y}_i = \begin{cases} \psi(e) & \text{for} \quad \pi > \gamma \\ \hat{Y}*_i^e & \text{for} \quad \pi = \gamma \\ \varphi(e) & \text{for} \quad \pi < \gamma \end{cases} \tag{a4.5}$$

Equation (a4.5) describes the production decisions of an individual firm. For the aggregate economy we get

$$\hat{Y} = \sum_{j=1}^{3} \sum_{A_j} \frac{Y_i}{Y}\hat{Y}_i \tag{a4.6}$$

where

$$A_1 = \{i \mid \pi_i > \gamma\}$$
$$A_2 = \{i \mid \pi_i = \gamma\} \tag{a4.7}$$
$$A_3 = \{i \mid \pi_i < \gamma\}$$

Assuming that

$$\sum_{A_j} \frac{Y_i}{Y} = l_j(\pi); \quad \frac{dl_1}{d\pi} > 0 \quad \text{and} \quad \frac{dl_3}{d\pi} < 0 \tag{a4.8}$$

it follows that

$$\hat{Y} = h(\pi, e); \quad h_\pi > 0 \quad \text{and} \quad h_e < 0. \tag{a4.9}$$

CHAPTER 5

Ultra-short-run, short-run and steady-growth equilibria

5.1 INTRODUCTION

This chapter explores some properties of the model set out in the previous chapter. The complete time path of the economy, however, cannot be derived on the basis of assumptions in chapter 4. We have described some steady-growth conditions which the investment function must satisfy, but a complete investment function has not been specified, and the model thus remains 'open': a set of initial values does not suffice to determine the future evolution of the economy.

The analysis in this chapter falls in three parts. In analogy with the traditional Marshallian analysis of individual markets I shall examine the *ultra-short* run with exogenously given (predetermined) levels of output and investment, the *short* run with flexible output, exogenous investment and a given predetermined capital stock, and the *long* run of steady growth where the capital stock is flexible and the utilisation ratio is at the desired level.

The examination is initially carried out on the assumption that there is a given technique, but this assumption is subsequently relaxed, and it is shown that an endogenous choice of technique will not have the implications suggested by neoclassical models. The chapter closes with a brief discussion of the effects on the steady-growth path of changes in the strength and militancy of workers, in 'animal spirits', in saving propensities and in the growth of the labour force.

5.2 ULTRA-SHORT-RUN EQUILIBRIUM

Equilibrium in the product market requires that

$$Y = C + I \tag{5.1}$$

Both output and investment are predetermined in the ultra-short run and equation (5.1) together with the consumption function, equation (4.19), determine the share of profits in income,

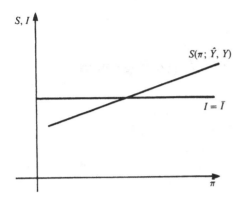

Figure 5.1: Determination of the equilibrium value of the share of profits when both Y and $\hat{Y}$ are given.

$$\pi = \frac{[(I + \alpha\hat{N}\delta K)/Y] - \beta\hat{Y} + \beta r(1 + \alpha\hat{N})}{s_p + \alpha\hat{N}} \tag{5.2}$$

Equation (5.2) gives π as a function of decision variables of the firm sector (I, Y, $\hat{Y}$, $\hat{N}$, s_p, K), household behaviour (α, β), the real rate of interest (r) and the rate of depreciation (δ).

The outcome is illustrated in figure 5.1, and the interpretation of the equation is as follows. Confronted by particular values of the variables under the direct control of firms, the accommodating variable π (or p) adjusts so as to make households wish to consume exactly $Y - I$. Excess demand at the initial profit share leads to price and profit increases which raise the level of retained earnings and depress aggregate demand. The equilibrium value of π depends on the share of investment in output as well as on the retention rate and household saving. Household saving, in turn, is determined by the desired increase in money holdings (which depends on $\hat{Y}$) and by the value of new issues: new and old securities are perfect substitutes, and the price of securities (which depends on profits net of depreciation and interest costs) adjusts endogenously so as to clear the securities market.

Whereas output and investment are predetermined, the growth rate of production, $\hat{Y}$, is flexible. It is not, however, an accommodating variable. The value of $\hat{Y}$ captures firms' supply decisions, and its current value is given by the output-expansion function, equation (4.9), reproduced here as equation (5.3),

$$\hat{Y} = h(\pi, e); \quad h_\pi > 0, \ h_e < 0 \tag{5.3}$$

Substitution of (5.3) into (5.2) would give the ultra-short-run equilibrium value of π in terms of exogenous and predetermined variables.

5.3 THE SHORT TERM – OUTPUT ADJUSTMENT

The level of production is predetermined in the ultra-short run, and an increase in investment must be accompanied by an identical reduction in consumption. Traditional short-run analysis, in contrast, assumes that output has been given time to adjust, and as a result a positive multiplier relation between investment and consumption prevails. But in the present model the appropriate definition of short-run equilibrium is unclear; more precisely, the model highlights some problems which are glossed over in traditional analysis.

It is hardly reasonable to assume that the short-term expectations of all firms are fulfilled in short-run equilibrium and that no individual firm has an incentive to change its level of production and employment. An equilibrium condition of this kind would be far too restrictive. But if this condition fails to be satisfied then how does one define short-run equilibrium? Is the economy in short-run equilibrium when the average profit share equals the static equilibrium value ($\pi = \gamma$) or should one define equilibrium by the condition that the rate of growth of the economy as a whole must be zero [$h(\pi, e) = 0$]? The two definitions are equivalent if (i) the distribution of π-values for individual firms is symmetric around the economy-wide average and (ii) the speed of adjustment of each individual firm is symmetrical in the share of profits (i.e. if $h(\gamma + x_i, e) = -h(\gamma - x_i, e)$ for all values of x_i and e).[1] But, except in this special case, the two definitions will differ.

One resolution of the ambiguity is as follows. In standard short-run analyses one assumes that the total labour force, as well as the capital stock, is constant. It is readily seen that with this assumption the economy will converge to a state where $\hat{Y} = 0$, and the zero growth condition might thus seem the most appealing short-run equilibrium definition. What are the properties of this equilibrium? With a given labour force, the employment rate becomes proportional to the level of output. The equilibrium

---

[1] Let $l(\pi)$ be the density of production yielding a profitability of π. Then the average (economy-wide) rate of growth of production is given by

$$\hat{Y} = \int_{\underline{Y}}^{Y_x} \hat{Y}_s \, ds$$

$$= \int l(\pi) h(\pi, e) \, d\pi$$

Since $h_\pi > 0$, it follows that if $l(\underline{\pi} + x) = l(\underline{\pi} - x)$ and $h(\gamma + x, e) = -h(\gamma - x, e)$ then

$$\hat{Y} = \int l(\underline{\pi} + x) h(\gamma + (\underline{\pi} - \gamma + x), e) \, dx$$

$$\gtreqless \int l(\underline{\pi} + x) h(\gamma + x, e) \, dx = 0 \quad \text{for} \quad \underline{\pi} \lesseqgtr \gamma$$

condition, $\hat{Y} = 0$, and the output-expansion function, equation (5.3), therefore define a locus in the (π, Y) plane,

$$0 = h(\pi, Y) \tag{5.4}$$

This locus describes combinations of profitability and output (employment) which make the average rate of expansion equal to zero; it is effectively the short-run supply curve. The level of demand, Y^d, is a function of both the share of profits, π, and the rate of production, Y and equation (5.2) defines the combinations of (Y, π) which satisfy $Y^d = Y$. Substituting $\hat{Y} = 0$ into (5.2) yields

$$\pi = \frac{[(I + \alpha\hat{N}\delta K)/Y] + \beta r(1 + \alpha\hat{N})}{s_p + \alpha\hat{N}} \tag{5.5}$$

Equations (5.4) and (5.5) determine the short-run equilibrium values of Y and π. In order to derive an explicit solution one would need to specify a functional form for the output-expansion function, and the solution will in general be somewhat messy. In the simple case, however, where the two equilibrium definitions coincide (where $\hat{Y} = 0$ is equivalent to $\pi = \gamma$), we get

$$Y = \frac{I + \alpha\hat{N}\delta K}{\gamma s_p + \alpha\hat{N}(\gamma - \beta r) - \beta r} \tag{5.6}$$

The investment multiplier is $1/[\gamma s_p + \alpha\hat{N}(\gamma - \beta r) - \beta r]$ and it should be noted that the size of the multiplier depends on the financial decisions of firms ($\hat{N}$ and s_p), on the distribution of income (γ) and the real rate of interest (r) as well as on saving and portfolio choices of households (α, β).[2]

A short-run equilibrium with $\hat{Y} = 0$ is illustrated in figure 5.2a–d. The equilibrium condition for the product market (shown in figures 5.2a and 5.2b) determines π as a function of $\hat{Y}$ and Y, and by assumption $\hat{Y} = 0$; hence $\pi = \pi(Y)$, $\pi' < 0$. The rate of growth of production, however, will only be zero if $h(\pi, Y) = 0$, and this imposes a link between π and Y as depicted in figure 5.2c. The outcome is shown in figure 5.2d, which superimposes the supply curve from 5.2c on the equilibrium condition in 5.2b.

Equation (5.6) describes a traditional short-run equilibrium: the rate of investment is exogenous and constant, and output and employment have had sufficient time to adjust fully to their equilibrium levels. In reality, investment is not constant, and neither are the capital stock and the size of

---

[2] The expression $\alpha\hat{N}\delta K$ appears in the numerator of (5.6) because it enters the consumption function as a constant. The valuation of securities is equal to $-\alpha\delta K$ plus an expression which is proportional to the rate of output. This implies that the value of new issues and hence the saving function contain the constant term $-\alpha\hat{N}\delta K$.

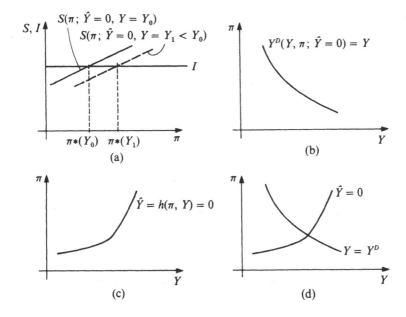

Figure 5.2: Determination of short-run equilibrium. (a) Product-market equilibrium for two different values of Y when $\hat{Y} = 0$. (b) Combinations of (Y, π) which clear the product market when $\hat{Y} = 0$. (c) Locus of (Y, π)-values with $\hat{Y} = 0$. (d) Short-run equilibrium.

the labour force. The short-run equilibrium described by equation (5.6) is thus at best a temporary equilibrium. It is itself shifting over time, and the economy may never attain the equilibrium position. In fact, the focus on stationary equilibria ($\hat{Y} = 0$) is unlikely to be helpful: if the economy experiences long-term growth and/or fluctuations in output, then there must be systematic deviations from stationariness.

The traditional equilibrium is characterised by a static relation between autonomous expenditure and total output, and the present model can be used to generalise this notion: for any given *path* of investment and any given initial rate of employment, equations (5.2) and (5.3) trace out the resulting *path* of output, employment and profitability. A one-dimensional functional relation between I and Y is replaced by a mapping between the time paths of I and Y. The relation between the two time paths is complex, but two special cases may illustrate the principle.

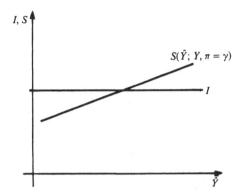

Figure 5.3: Determination of the rate of growth of output which gives product-market equilibrium.

The first case arises when the output-expansion function takes the simple form,

$$\hat{Y} = h(\pi); \quad h(\gamma) = 0, \quad h' \gg 0 \tag{5.7}$$

Equation (5.7) assumes that the rate of expansion of output is independent of the rate of employment. In terms of the short-run supply function, equation (5.4), this corresponds to the case where supply is perfectly elastic at $\pi = \gamma$. It is assumed, furthermore, that production responds very quickly to deviations of π from γ, and, in the limiting case where $h' \to \infty$, the supply response is instantaneous and $\pi = \gamma$ at all times. Substituting this condition ($\pi = \gamma$) into equation (5.2) gives a 'modified short-run equilibrium condition',

$$\hat{Y} = \frac{[(I + \alpha \hat{N} \delta K)/Y] - \gamma s_p - \alpha \hat{N}(\gamma - \beta r)}{\beta} + r \tag{5.8}$$

Equation (5.8) describes the relation between I, Y and $\hat{Y}$ which ensures that the product market clears at the desired supply price, $\pi = \gamma$. The equation says that, if output is perfectly flexible, then the complex relation between the path of investment and the path of output reduces to a simple contemporaneous relation between investment, output and the growth of output.

The most striking difference between (5.8) and traditional short-run equilibria is the appearance of the growth rate of production. The equation suggests that equality between demand and supply in the product market can be maintained entirely through adjustments in the growth rate of output. Neither instantaneous adjustments in Y nor changes in prices and income distribution are needed in response to a shift in I; finite changes in $\hat{Y}$ will suffice. The mechanism is illustrated in figure 5.3: the share of saving in income is positively related to the growth rate of income, and S/Y can adjust to I/Y through variations in $\hat{Y}$.

This result, however, should be interpreted with care. An increase in the rate of growth of output and employment reduces consumption and raises the rate of saving because households wish to maintain a constant ratio of money balances to total money income. In order to achieve this objective, the increase in money stocks (current saving) must be proportional to the change in money income. Now, comparing two different steady-growth paths, we may expect that the rate of growth of households' money deposits equals the rate of growth of money income, but it is not plausible to suggest that a sudden and unanticipated increase in the growth rate of employment and income leads to an immediate decline in consumption. A large fraction of the unexpected rise in incomes may go into saving, but households will not reduce consumption below what it would have been in the absence of an increase in incomes. The present specification of the money-demand equation, however, has left out lags in the adjustment of money demand to changes in income flows. This neglect of lags simplifies the analysis greatly but if adjustments in (the growth of) money balances are not instantaneous then finite changes in $\hat{Y}$ cannot maintain equilibrium in the product market in the face of discrete and unanticipated changes in investment. Equation (5.8) should thus be seen as a modified *short*-run equilibrium, which assumes that both $\hat{Y}$ and Y have been given time to adjust, rather than an *ultra-short*-run equilibrium.

The second example of a simple relation between the time paths of investment and output arises when both investment and the labour force grow exponentially at the same rate, n. In this case the general output-expansion function, equation (5.3), is retained, but a particularly simple time path of investment is imposed. It can be shown – see appendix 5A – that, in this case, the rate of growth of production and employment will also converge to n and that, asymptotically, both the rate of employment and the share of profits in income will be constant. The share of investment in output converges to a constant, too, and asymptotically there is thus a constant multiplier relation between investment and output, the size of the (asymptotic) multiplier being determined by the (constant) ratio between investment and the labour force.

The above examples are but special cases, and there is little point in pursuing the implications of arbitrary restrictions on the time path of investment and/or on the functional forms. Instead, it seems more fruitful to maintain the general framework of equations (5.2) and (5.3) but to introduce additional structure on the determination of investment. Once we move beyond the short run, it is no longer satisfactory to treat investment as an exogenous variable: not all time paths of I are equally plausible.

5.4 THE MEDIUM TERM – UTILISATION AND WARRANTED GROWTH

In the second example above it was assumed that investment grows exponentially at a constant rate. Steady growth, however, is inconceivable unless the rate of capital utilisation is at the desired level, and so far we have failed to take this restriction into account.

The steady-growth condition on utilisation has been derived in chapter 4 and, as in the discussion of short-run equilibrium, a distinction must be made between the individual firm and the economy as a whole. It would be far too restrictive to require that the rate of capital utilisation be at the desired level for each individual firm. But 'on average' the utilisation rate must be as desired: accelerating investment programmes of firms who find themselves short of capacity must be offset by the contracting programmes of firms whose demand expectations have been disappointed.

This definition of the average utilisation rate compatible with steady growth[3] is in principle straightforward, but exact derivation of the utilisation rate is riddled with difficulties. The function determining the desired utilisation rate for an individual firm is non-linear and the investment response to deviations from the desired level is also likely to be highly non-linear (so that the average $u*$ fails to be a simple weighted average of desired utilisation at the firm level).[4] I shall ignore these aggregation problems and assume that equation (4.12), describing the desired utilisation of the representative firm, is directly applicable at the aggregate level. The following condition for steady growth then applies:

$$u* = \kappa \left(1 - \frac{w}{p} \frac{1}{\lambda} - \frac{\iota + \delta}{u* \sigma} \right) = \kappa \left(\pi - \frac{\iota + \delta}{u* \sigma} \right) \tag{5.9}$$

The cost of finance and depreciation, $\iota + \delta$, is determined by the gross

---

[3] Should one call it the non-accelerating accumulation rate of utilisation or – among friends – the NAARU?

[4] Similar aggregation problems – relating for example to sectoral and geographical mismatch – are encountered in the definition of the NAIRU (non-accelerating inflation rate of unemployment) (and play a part in the attempts to explain the persistence of inflation at high rates of unemployment, e.g. Nickell, 1987). See also the discussion on p. 65 of the deviation of π from γ in short-run equilibrium.

profit rate, Tobin's q (q), and the expected rate of growth of demand for the firm's product,[5]

$$\iota + \delta = \frac{\pi u \sigma}{q} + (g_f + \delta)\left(1 - \frac{1}{q}\right) \tag{5.10}$$

where g_f is the expected growth rate of demand for the representative firm. It seems reasonable to suppose that g_f is related to the growth rate of the economy and, for simplicity, it is assumed that $g_f = g_w$ where g_w is the growth rate of the economy as a whole (the warranted rate of growth).

The second term on the right-hand side of (5.10) appears because future increases in demand lead to equiproportionate increases in earnings and in the desired capital stock, and if $q > 1$ then the cost of investment is less than the value of the associated increase in earnings. This anticipated difference between the financial valuation and the cost of future gross investment is reflected in the current valuation of the firm.

Tobin's q is defined by

$$q = \frac{M + vN}{pK} \tag{5.11}$$

and using equations (4.15) and (4.16) to substitute for M and vN, we get

$$q = \left[\beta(1 - \alpha r) + \alpha\left(\pi - \frac{\delta}{\sigma u}\right)\right] u \sigma \tag{5.12}$$

---

[5] Tobin's q gives the ratio of financial valuation to replacement cost. The financial valuation of a firm is the sum of equity valuation and bank loans. Let current dividends be $(1 - s_p)P$ where P represents gross profits, $P = \pi u \sigma p K$, and assume that dividends are expected to grow at the same rate as the market for the firm's product (g_f). Equity valuation, vN, is then given by

$$vN = \int_0^\infty (1 - s_p) \pi u \sigma p K \exp(g_f t) \exp(-(\hat{N} + \bar{r})t)\,dt$$

$$= [(1 - s_p) \pi u \sigma/(\bar{r} + \hat{N} - g_f)]p_0 K_0$$

where $\bar{r}$ is the return on equity and $\hat{N}$ is the rate of growth of the number of shares ($\exp(-\hat{N}t)$ thus represents the share of dividends at time t which accrues to shares which had been issued already at time 0).

If the real rate of interest on bank loans is r, the average real cost of finance will be

$$\frac{\bar{r}vN + rM}{vN + M} = \frac{\pi u \sigma}{q} + \frac{1}{q}\left[qg_f - s_p \pi u \sigma - \hat{N}\frac{vN}{pK} + (r - g_f)\frac{M}{pK}\right]$$

$$= \frac{\pi u \sigma}{q} + g_f - \frac{1}{q}(g_f + \delta)$$

where $q = (vN + M)/pK$ is Tobin's q and where we have used the finance constraint, equation (4.13).

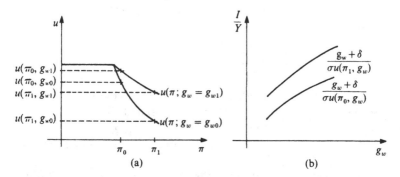

Figure 5.4: The share of investment in output as a function of (a) utilisation and (b) the rate of growth.

Equation (5.9) can therefore be written

$$u* = \kappa \left(\left(\pi - \frac{g_w + \delta}{u* \sigma} \right) \left(1 - \frac{1}{q} \right) \right)$$

$$= \kappa \left(\left(\pi - \frac{g_w + \delta}{u* \sigma} \right) \left\langle 1 - \frac{1}{u* \sigma \{ \beta(1 - \alpha r) + \alpha[\pi - \delta/(\sigma u*)] \}} \right\rangle \right)$$

(5.13)

It is readily seen that if

$$\sigma \left[\beta(1 - \alpha r) + \alpha \left(\pi - \frac{\delta}{\sigma} \right) \right] > 1$$

(5.14)

then equation (5.13) has a unique solution,

$$u* = u(\pi, g_w); \quad u* < 1, \quad u_\pi < 0, \quad u_g > 0$$

(5.15)

The condition (5.14) has a simple economic interpretation. If it is satisfied, then $q > 1$ for $u = 1$ and it follows that 'excess profits' can be made. There is then a need to deter entry and the desired utilisation rate is below unity. Furthermore, the higher the value of q (at $u = 1$), the higher are excess profits and the lower is the desired degree of utilisation. If on the other hand $q < 1$ (for $u = 1$) then profits cannot cover the costs of capital at any rate of utilisation and there is no need to maintain excess capacity to deter entry, hence $u* = 1$. Empirically, one rarely observes full-capacity utilisation, and then only at the peak of the cycle, and I shall disregard the case where $u* = 1$.

Equation (5.15) is effectively an investment function. If u is above $u*$ then investment accelerates and, if it is below, investment decelerates. If the growth rate of the economy is g_w and the output capital ratio is $1/u\sigma$ then steady growth implies that the share of investment in output must be $(g_w + \delta)/u\sigma$ where δ is the rate of depreciation of capital.[6] In specifying u as a function of profitability and growth, equation (5.15) thus determines the share of investment in output as a function of profitability and growth. This is shown in figures 5.4a and 5.4b.

The investment–output ratio must be compatible with equilibrium in the product market and the equilibrium condition is given by equation (5.2). Substituting $\hat{Y} = g_w$ and $I/Y = (g_w + \delta)/\sigma u$ into (5.2) we get[7]

$$\pi* = \frac{[(g_w + \delta)/(u\sigma)] - \beta g_w + \beta r + \alpha\hat{N}[\beta r + \delta/(\sigma u)]}{s_p + \alpha\hat{N}}$$

$$= \pi(u, g_w); \quad \pi_u < 0, \quad \pi_g > 0 \tag{5.16}$$

Equations (5.3), (5.15) and (5.16) are necessary conditions for steady growth. The three equations contain four endogenous variables – e, g_w, u, π – but the extra degree of freedom is illusory. The rate of growth of the labour force, n, is exogenously given, and

$$\hat{e} = g_w - n \tag{5.17}$$

In steady growth we therefore have

$$g_w = n \tag{5.18a}$$

or

$$e \leqslant e_0 \tag{5.18b}$$

where e_0 is defined by the condition that $eh_e = 0$ for $0 \leqslant e \leqslant e_0$.

Notice that if $e_0 = 0$ then steady growth requires that $g_w = n$, and the warranted rate of growth must equal the natural rate (assuming that a warranted growth path exists). Harrod's first problem, the inequality of warranted and natural growth rates, thus finds no place in the present model when $e_0 = 0$. It may be reasonable, however, to suppose that the partial derivative of h with respect to e vanishes for small values of e: beyond a certain point, changes in unemployment may affect neither the strength of workers nor the availability to individual firms of workers with the required skills (whether unemployment is, say, 25 per cent or 30 per cent is hardly significant for firms' production decisions).

---

[6] To see this, write $I/Y = (I/K)(K/Y) = (g_w + \delta)/u\sigma$.

[7] The second inequality, $\pi_g > 0$, implicitly assumes that $1/(\sigma u) - \beta$ is positive. The latter condition is satisfied if $M < pK$.

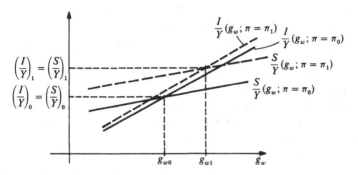

Figure 5.5: Effects on the profit share of changes in the rate of growth.

Consider first the possibility that $e > e_0$. Substituting equation (5.15) in (5.16), we get

$$g_w = g(\pi) \tag{5.19}$$

Equation (5.19) is the equilibrium condition for the product market under steady growth: it specifies combinations of the share of profits and the rate of growth which clear the product market. The sign of the derivative of $g(\pi)$ is ambiguous, but empirically the most likely outcome is a positive value (see appendix 5B). I shall therefore concentrate on this case and assume that

$$g'(\pi) > 0 \tag{5.20}$$

A reversal of this inequality would affect some of the comparative results in section 5.7, but the analysis of the existence and stability of steady-growth paths could be carried out quite analogously if $g' < 0$.

Figure 5.5 shows the effects on the profit share of changes in the growth rate. For given π, both I/Y and S/Y are functions of the growth rate g_w, and the initial steady-growth configuration (g_{w0}, π_0) is determined by the intersection of the investment and saving curves corresponding to $\pi = \pi_0$. An increase in the rate of growth to g_{w1} leads to excess demand at the old profit share, but changes in π shift the two curves and a new steady-growth equilibrium is obtained for $\pi = \pi_1$.

Equations (5.19) and (5.20) can be used to determine the steady-growth solution. By assumption $e > e_0$, and $g_w = n$ is thus a precondition for steady growth. Substituting $g_w = n$ in equation (5.19) gives the equilibrium value of π, $\pi* = \pi(n)$, and from (5.3) we then get

$$n = h(\pi*, e) \tag{5.21}$$

Since $h_e < 0$ for $e > e_0$, it follows that there is at most a single steady-growth path with $e > e_0$. But can we be sure that there are any solutions at all to

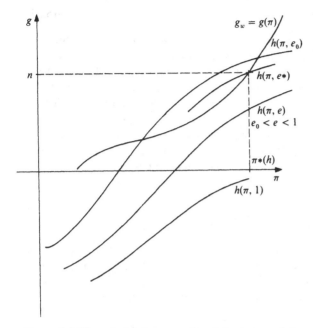

Figure 5.6: The relation between the profit share and the rate of growth (equation (5.19)) and the output-expansion function for different values of the rate of employment.

(5.19)–(5.21)? In order to address this question we consider the family of output-expansion functions,

$$\hat{Y} = h(\pi; e) \tag{5.22}$$

where the rate of employment is now used to parametrise the relation between π and $\hat{Y}$. Figure 5.6 depicts the relation for three values of e: $e = e_0$ ($\simeq e \leq e_0$), $e = 1$ and some intermediate value of e.[8] Since $h_e \leq 0$, an decrease in e shifts the locus in a westerly direction, and for any point ($\hat{Y}$, π) between the loci associated with $e = e_0$ and $e = 1$ there will be a rate of employment, e, such that $\hat{Y} = h(\pi; e)$. A solution with $g_w = n$ thus exists if and only if

---

[8] The analysis here is very similar to Joan Robinson's discussion of a 'relation between the rate of profit *caused* by the rate of accumulation and the rate of accumulation which that rate of profit will *induce*' (Robinson, 1962, p. 48). A key difference is the dependence of the output-expansion function ('the rate of accumulation which that rate of profit will induce') on the rate of employment as well as on the share of profits. There are also, however, important differences with respect to the determination of pricing and of capital utilisation.

$$h(\pi*(n); 1) \leqslant n \leqslant h(\pi*(n); e_0). \tag{5.23}$$

The first inequality is automatically satisfied: as e increases it becomes progressively more difficult to expand employment, and if $e = 1$ then it is logically impossible for the rate of growth of employment to exceed the rate of growth of the labour force. What about the second inequality? Will $\lim_{e \to 0} h(\pi*, e)$ exceed n? I shall argue on pp. 78–9 that this is indeed a reasonable expectation, but the traditional neoclassical argument based on variations in the output–capital ratio is not convincing, and the justification for the second inequality is not nearly as strong as that in favour of the first: a capitalist economy may not be capable of steady growth at the natural rate.

5.5 CHOICE OF TECHNIQUE AND THE NATURAL RATE

In neoclassical theory, variations in the capital–output ratio (the choice of technique) ensure that warranted and natural rates of growth coincide. The equalisation even takes place at full employment, i.e. $h(\pi, 1) = n$ or perhaps more plausibly $h(\pi, e*) = n$ where $e*$ is the 'natural rate of employment'.

The utilisation rate of capital has been treated as a choice variable in the previous section, but so far the technical output–capital ratio has been assumed given and constant. It is time to relax this assumption and allow for an *ex ante* choice of technique. When they make their investment decisions, firms can choose from a range of blueprints. But, once investment has been carried out and the new plant and machinery has been installed, a fixed-coefficient production function applies. The *ex ante* production function is given by

$$Y = F(L, K) \tag{5.24}$$

and it is assumed that there are constant returns to scale.

The question is whether endogenous changes in the output–capital ratio will ensure that $n \leqslant h(\pi(n), e)$ for $e \leqslant e_0$. Assume therefore that the economy is moving along (in the neighbourhood of) the warranted growth path associated with a particular choice of technique and that $e \leqslant e_0$. Assume, furthermore, that the growth rate is below the natural rate. Does this imply that firms have an incentive to change relative input proportions, that in other words, a steady-growth path of this sort cannot be viable as soon as one allows for a choice of technique? In order to investigate this question, it seems reasonable to assume that firms choose the technique which minimises unit costs at the utilisation rate defined by equation (5.15). Alternatively, it could be assumed that firms minimise costs at full-capacity utilisation. This would affect the algebra but not the qualitative results.

Along the steady-growth path, unit labour costs are determined by the mark-up factor and real unit capital costs by the output–capital ratio and the cost of finance. But the cost minimisation is based on microeconomic decisions, and, in assessing the optimality of the choice of technique, the firm takes both money-wage rates and unit capital costs as given; although the firm has some control over its own output price, the unit price of capital goods – purchased from other firms – is by assumption independent of the firm's choice of technique. The choice of technique is thus determined by the following minimisation programme:

$$\min w_0 L + p_0 K \frac{\iota_0 + \delta}{u_0} \tag{5.25}$$

subject to

$$\iota_0 + \delta = u_0 \sigma_0 \frac{\pi_0}{q_0} + (g_{w0} + \delta)\left(1 - \frac{1}{q_0}\right)$$

$$F(L, K) = 1$$

where σ_0, w_0, ι_0, p_0, u_0, π_0 and g_{w0} are the existing technical output–capital ratio and the existing wage, cost of finance, price, utilisation rate, profit share and growth rate respectively. By assumption, there are constant returns to scale and perfectly elastic factor supplies, and unit costs are therefore independent of the scale of production.

The minimisation problem determines a new value of the maximum output–capital ratio σ_1 as a function of the existing ratio σ_0 and the existing steady-growth values of the other parameters. However, this new choice of technique affects the steady-growth solutions for profitability and utilisation (see equations (5.13) and (5.16)), and the stage is therefore set for a second round of minimisation determining σ_2 as a function of σ_1 and the steady-growth parameters associated with σ_1.

A full solution to the choice-of-technique problem is a fix-point for this iterative process. It is a value of the technical output–capital ratio, $\sigma*$, with the property that, if $\sigma*$ describes the existing technique and $w*$, $\iota*$, $p*$, $u*$, $\pi*$ and g_w^* are steady-growth values associated with $\sigma*$, then $\sigma*$ itself solves the minimisation problem (5.25).

The detailed properties of any such solution(s) will depend *inter alia* on the exact specification of the production- and output-expansion functions. For present purposes, however, this does not matter a great deal. The main point here is that the introduction of a choice of technique will not guarantee a warranted rate of growth which is greater than or equal to *n* for $e < e_0$. The choice of technique, the value of $\sigma*$, does influence the warranted growth rate, but neither the rate of growth of the labour force nor the size of the reserve army plays any role in the determination of the choice of technique in (5.25). As a result, the introduction of a neoclassical production function and an *ex ante* choice of techniques makes it no more likely that warranted and natural growth rates will coincide; only by chance would this happen. The 'rational' behaviour of firms may determine the cost-minimising technique, but if the real wage rate does not adjust to clear the labour market then the choice of technique does little to solve the macroeconomic problems of employment and growth.[9]

In view of these results I shall henceforth ignore the choice of technique altogether: even if one sweeps aside the lessons of the capital controversy, the choice of technique may not perform the role attributed to it in neoclassical theory, and it is not clear that the neglect of technical choice imparts any particular bias to the analysis.

5.6 'ACCUMULATE, ACCUMULATE'

If one cannot rely on the choice of technique to raise the warranted growth rate above the natural rate for low rates of employment, are there then no mechanisms to ensure that employment rates do not fall indefinitely?

Marx clearly thought that capitalism was an immensely dynamic system. 'Accumulate, accumulate! That is Moses and the Prophets!' (*Capital*, vol. 1, chapter 24, section 3). Keynes was less confident but still believed that the desire to expand was deeply rooted in human psychology. He argued that

decisions to do something positive, the full consequences of which will be drawn out over many days to come, can only be taken as a result of animal spirits – of a spontaneous urge to action rather than inaction ... [but] if the animal spirits are dimmed and the spontaneous optimism falters, leaving us to depend on nothing but a mathematical expectation, enterprise will fade and die.

(Keynes, 1936, pp. 161–2)

More recently, writers such as Baumol (1959) and Marris (1964) have suggested that firms (or, more specifically, the managers who run them) are interested in growth for its own sake, which if true would be a further argument in favour of capitalist dynamism.

In the context of the present model of profit-maximising firms, the

---

[9] There are close similarities here with the analysis of Wood (1975), pp. 125–7. In both cases the equalisation of warranted and natural growth rates is prevented because prices (real wages) fail to reflect labour-market conditions: real wages are determined by firms' pricing decisions (mark-up decisions) and are independent of variations in employment (for $e \leqslant e_0$).

condition for steady growth at the natural rate is that $h(\pi*(n), e_0) \geq n$.[10] Substitution of reasonable parameter values into the equations suggests that the inequality will in fact be satisfied,[11] but how robust is this result? Is it purely fortuitous that the parameter constellation is such that the inequality holds? Some parameters appear to be completely arbitrary: why, for instance, should firms retain 75 per cent of gross profits and not, say, 20 per cent or 95 per cent? And what would happen if firms changed their retention policies? Will endogenous forces generate other changes which imply that the economy remains sufficiently dynamic and that $h(\pi*, e_0) > n$?

In fact, the result is quite robust. As shown in note 11, profits must exceed depreciation even if the rate of growth is zero, and for all reasonable parameters we have $u\sigma\pi* > g_w + \delta$ (see appendix 5C); i.e. the net rate of profits exceeds the growth rate. With a capital–output ratio of about 2 and a 10 per cent rate of depreciation, the *minimum* gross share of profits associated with 3 per cent growth is thus 26 per cent. A priori, it would be difficult to say whether a profit share of 26 per cent is sufficient to generate a 3 per cent growth in output, but an affirmative answer could perhaps be justified by an upsurge of small-scale business at very low rates of employment. With no hope of employment in established firms, the best option may be to start out on one's own even if the net return on investment is low.[12] In any case, I shall assume that the inequality $h(\pi*(n), e_0) > n$ is satisfied. Logically, it is perfectly possible for the inequality not to hold: reversal of the inequality simply indicates that steady growth at the natural rate would be impossible.

To some this may seem an unsatisfactory conclusion. The gut reaction of most economists is probably that the viability of capitalism does not depend on particular parameter values. If the choice-of-technique

---

[10] The condition $n \leq h(\pi*(n), e_0)$ is necessary and sufficient for steady growth at the natural rate. It is possible, however, that we may have $n > h(\pi*(n), e_0)$ but $n + \Delta < h(\pi*(n + \Delta), e_0)$. In other words, the economy may have a warranted growth path with $g > n$ even if the inequality fails to be satisfied. The set of n-values which satisfy (5.23) need not be connected.

[11] Using the benchmark values in appendix 5C, we get $25\% \leq \pi* \leq 40\%$. For $g_w = 0$ we have

$$\pi* = \frac{(1 + \alpha\hat{N})\delta/(\sigma u)}{s_p + \alpha\hat{N}}$$

and since $s_p \leq 1$, we get

$$\pi\sigma u \geq \delta$$

In other words, even at $g_w = 0$ the rate of profits net of depreciation must be non-negative.

[12] One problem with this justification is that it effectively introduces elements of a dual economy. These elements, although undoubtedly of importance in the real world, do not really fit into a one-sector model. But dual elements may be of central importance for an understanding of spatial differences in growth rates (Skott, 1985a).

mechanism does not always work, then there must be other endogenous forces. But is this belief really justified? At an empirical level there are many examples of capitalist economies which somehow failed to take off or which faded after a while. Without seeing these historical cases as literal illustrations of the model, one may observe that Argentina at the turn of the century had a per capita income more than three times that of Japan and almost twice that of Italy, and its share of agriculture was lower and the share of industry higher than in both those countries;[13] Uruguay prospered in the late nineteenth and early twentieth centuries but subsequently declined relatively and, for a long time, absolutely as well. Clearly, economic systems in general and market economies in particular do not invariably possess mechanisms which stabilise their paths of development.

The fact that capitalism has in fact become dominant in many parts of the world does not imply that the viability of the system is independent of the parameters which characterise the behaviour of agents. If firms – freed from labour constraints and facing a weak working class – had not been strongly dynamic then capitalism would never have emerged as the dominant mode of production. But this dynamic behaviour cannot be deduced a priori. Other behavioural patterns are logically possible and, indeed, if capitalist firms cease to be dynamic then capitalism is doomed as an economic system: it may fade gradually as increasing state intervention becomes necessary to avoid ever-increasing unemployment or it may be shattered abruptly as a result of political struggle.

These questions do not even appear in orthodox economic analysis. Neoclassical theory views the existence of a full-employment steady-growth path as an almost exclusively technical question. Provided the (exogenously given) production function is well behaved and allows sufficient variability in the capital–output ratio then a steady-growth path at full employment will exist for any value of the behavioural parameters. The viability condition for a specific mode of production is thus seen as universal and technical. In contrast, the present theory – like other Keynesian and Marxian models – points to behavioural constraints on the long-term viability of capitalism as a dominant mode of production. One

---

[13] Kuznets (1971), tables 2, 3 and 21, gives the following GDP figures (in 1965 US$) and sectoral shares (%):

	GDP	Agriculture	Industry	Services	
Argentina	443 (1900–4)	33.3	24.8	41.9	(1900–4)
Japan	74 (1874–9)	65.6	34.4		(1879–83)
		38.6	61.4		(1904–13)
Italy	271 (1895–9)	41.7	23.4	34.9	(1891–1900)

of these constraints is the condition that firms must be sufficiently aggressive and dynamic.

5.7 COMPARATIVE DYNAMICS

If the economy follows a steady-growth path (or exhibits fluctuations around a steady-growth path) then equations (5.3), (5.15), (5.16) and (5.18a) can be used to derive comparative dynamic effects of changes in the underlying parameters. This section briefly considers the implications of a couple of possible changes.

Marxian theory has always attributed particular importance to workers' strength as a determinant of income distribution as well as of accumulation. In Goodwin's (1967) formalisation of a Marxian business cycle, the distribution of income is determined directly by wage-bargaining in the labour market while, in the present model, the influence of workers' strength on distribution is indirect: workers' strength affects the production decisions of firms, and production decisions may have delayed effects on the share of investment in income, which in turn affects the distribution of income.

A comparison of steady-growth paths can be used to examine the effects of (semi-)permanent changes in workers' strength and militancy. In the specification of the output-expansion function, however, a single variable – e – captures the effect of workers' strength on output growth, and, if one wants to separate cyclical variations in strength from secular shifts, it is useful to rewrite the expansion function,

$$\hat{Y} = h(\pi, z) \tag{5.26}$$

$$z = z(e; x), \quad z_e > 0, \quad z_x > 0$$

where z is workers' strength and x is an index of secular strength, e capturing the short-run cyclical variations.[14] Using (5.26), (5.15), (5.16) and (5.18a), it is readily seen that an increase in x leads to a decline in the equilibrium rate of employment, and that both the distribution of income and the utilisation rate of capital are unaffected: a change in x affects neither (5.15)–(5.16) nor (5.18a) so $\pi*(n)$ and $u*(\pi*(n))$ are unchanged, and, substituting $\hat{Y} = n$ and the unchanged $\pi*$ into (5.26) and differentiating, we get

$$0 = h_z(z_e de + z_x dx) \tag{5.27}$$

---

[14] The variable x could also be interpreted as an index of structural labour-market conditions embodying, for instance, the degree of regional and occupational mismatch in the labour market.

Hence

$$\frac{de}{dx} = \frac{-z_x}{z_e} < 0 \tag{5.28}$$

The economic interpretation here is that unemployment serves to discipline and contain workers' demands, and more unemployment is needed to perform this task if workers become stronger and/or more militant.

Keynesian theory is the other main inspiration behind the model, and 'animal spirits' has played a key role in Keynesian and post-Keynesian thought. In terms of the present model, there are two possible interpretations of changes in animal spirits. The first interpretation is that of a shift in the output-expansion function. If (5.3) is replaced by

$$\hat{Y} = ah(\pi, e) \tag{5.29}$$

then the buoyancy of animal spirits can be represented by the parameter a. Since a change in a leaves the other equations unchanged, $\pi*$ and $u*$ will not be affected and differentiating (5.29) it follows that

$$0 = n\,da + ah_e\,de \tag{5.30}$$

An increase in a will thus raise the equilibrium level of employment. Notice that a shift of this kind in animal spirits is very similar in its effects to a change in workers' strength. In both cases, it is only the output-expansion function which is affected, and an increase in workers' militancy has exactly the same effect on the steady-growth configuration as a decline in animal spirits.

As an alternative interpretation, an increase in animal spirits could be represented by an upward shift in the steady-growth investment function, i.e. by a downward shift in equation (5.15). If we replace this equation by

$$u* = \frac{u(\pi, n)}{a} \tag{5.31}$$

where, again, the parameter a represents animal spirits, and substitute (5.31) into (5.16) we get

$$\pi* = \pi\left(\frac{u(\pi*, n)}{a}, n\right) \tag{5.32}$$

and

$$d\pi* = \pi_u\left[u_\pi d\pi* \frac{1}{a} - \frac{u(\pi*, n)}{a^2}\,da\right] \tag{5.33}$$

If $g'(\pi) > 0$ in (5.19) then $\pi_u u_\pi / a < 1$ (see appendix 5B) and (5.33) implies that $d\pi*/da > 0$. From (5.3) it follows that $e*$ will then also increase. The steady-growth value of u on the other hand will fall: the term in the square brackets on the right-hand side of (5.33) is $du*$ and $\pi_u < 0$. An upward shift in the investment function thus raises the rate of employment and the profit share but reduces the utilisation of capital.[15]

Turning now to changes in saving behaviour, the results are less clear-cut and, in some cases, surprising: a rise in the corporate retention rate, s_p, produces a standard Keynesian 'paradox of thrift' – it leads to a decline in the share of profits and in the rate of employment – but a rise in α (one of the parameters describing the saving and portfolio choices of households) may cause both profitability and employment to go up.

A change in the retention rate, s_p, affects equation (5.16) but leaves the other equations intact. Substituting (5.15) in (5.16) and writing the equation explicitly as a function of s_p, we get

$$\pi* = \pi(u(\pi*, g_w), g_w, s_p); \quad \pi_u < 0, \quad \pi_g > 0, \quad \pi_s < 0 \tag{5.34}$$

Differentiating (5.34) (and setting $g_w = n$) yields

$$d\pi* = \pi_u u_\pi d\pi* + \pi_s ds_p \tag{5.35}$$

and hence $d\pi*/ds_p < 0$ (still assuming that $\pi_u u_\pi < 1$; see (5.20) and appendix 5B). A fall in $\pi*$ is in turn translated into a fall in employment (via the output-expansion function, equation (5.3)).

The effects of an increase in α are best seen for the simple (and empirically not unrealistic) case where $\hat{N} = 0$. Equations (5.3), (5.16) and (5.18a) are then unaffected, and equation (5.15) is shifted downwards. Including the parameter explicitly in (5.15), substituting in (5.16) and differentiating, we get

$$d\pi* = \pi_u(u_\pi d\pi* + u_\alpha d\alpha) \tag{5.36}$$

and for $\pi_u u_\pi < 1$ it follows that $d\pi*/d\alpha > 0$ (both π_u and u_α are negative). A rise in $\pi*$ is in turn associated with higher employment.

An increase in the saving parameter α may thus raise employment along the steady-growth path, but what is the reason for this paradoxical non-paradox of thrift in a Keynesian model? Although α describes the saving and portfolio preferences of households, it may have no effects at all on the saving propensity of the economy: households in aggregate can only save current income in the form of securities if firms issue new securities, i.e. if $\hat{N} > 0$. When $\hat{N} = 0$, the greater desire of households to hold financial securities will simply lead to a rise in the price of existing securities. This rise produces capital gains (which tend to stimulate consumption), and the process comes to a halt when the price of securities has risen in proportion to the change in α, at which point households have

---

[15] Note that shifts in the investment function could be caused by changes in the threat of new entry as well as by changes in animal spirits.

reached the new desired portfolio composition without having saved as much as a penny out of current income. The increase in α has not affected the saving propensity, but it has changed the value of financial assets and thus the financial valuation of firms. The rise in valuation – in Tobin's q – reduces the cost of finance to firms, and it is this valuation effect which may stimulate the economy. Outside the simple case where $\hat{N} = 0$, changes in α will affect the saving propensity, but the total effect on employment remains positive as long as the valuation effect dominates this saving effect.

So far we have considered changes in workers' strength, in 'animal spirits' and in the saving parameters. None of these changes have direct effects on the long-run rate of growth. The model contains homeostatic forces which keep the actual rate of growth in line with the growth of the labour supply in efficiency units (i.e. adjusting for changes in labour productivity). Changes in workers' strength, in 'animal spirits' or in the saving function therefore only affect the long-run rate of growth in so far as they influence the rate of technical progress or the rate of growth of the labour supply. One might expect, for instance, that higher animal spirits would go hand in hand with greater technical dynamism and faster technical progress. The preceding analysis has not taken any such effects into account, but it may be of interest to consider the influence of changes in the natural rate of growth on the endogenous variables.

The profit share varies directly and utilisation inversely with changes in the rate of growth when $g'(\pi) > 0$. The outcome for employment, however, is ambiguous (even when $g'(\pi) > 0$): if $h_\pi(d\pi*/dn) > 1$ (< 1) then the rate of employment in steady growth will rise (fall). To see this, differentiate equation (5.3) to give

$$dn = h_\pi \frac{d\pi*}{dn} dn + h_e de \qquad (5.37)$$

and hence

$$\frac{de}{dn} = \frac{1 - h_\pi d\pi*/dn}{h_e} \qquad (5.38)$$

Equations (5.37) and (5.38) say that a marginal increase in n will cause an increase (decrease) in the employment rate if the output-expansion function is sensitive (insensitive) to variations in the profit share.

5.8 CONCLUDING COMMENTS

The analysis of ultra-short-run, short-run and steady-growth equilibria has a couple of noteworthy features which have not yet been commented upon.

The first point concerns the rate of inflation. Chapter 4 has discussed various hypotheses about the influence of the rate of unemployment on wage inflation, and this Phillips-curve relation is usually a main building-block of macroeconomic theories. In fact, recent debates in macroeconomic theory have focused strongly on the correct specification of this particular relation, and it may be surprising that the analysis in this chapter has made no reference at all to the specification of the Phillips curve: I have analysed the different equilibria without any reference to absolute prices and wages or to the rate of inflation.

This neglect of monetary aspects has been possible because the equilibrium values of all real variables (employment, investment, production, distributive shares) depend upon neither absolute prices nor inflation. If one wants to know the rate of inflation then reference must be made to the Phillips curve, but the model is recursive, and the shape of the Phillips curve does not matter for the determination of the real side of the economy.

The model thus has 'neutrality' properties which superficially resemble those of many monetarist models: real outcomes are homogeneous of degree zero with respect to proportional variations in wages, prices and the stock of money. Unlike monetarist theories, however, the present model assumes that the stock of money is an endogenous variable, and this difference is crucial. A monetarist might argue that 'if the money supply is doubled then prices and wages will also double and the new equilibrium will leave real quantities unchanged'. In this model, on the other hand, the corresponding argument would be that 'if money wages double then the prices of output and securities will also double leaving real quantities unchanged'.

Several post-Keynesians have argued strongly in favour of this reversal of the causal chain, and I shall discuss some of the issues in greater detail in chapter 7. However, one important implication of the reversal should be noted in the present context. The neutrality of the real economy with respect to changes in money-wage rates implies that unemployed workers may be *involuntarily* unemployed in Keynes's sense. The problem of involuntary unemployment arises exactly because '[t]here may exist no expedient by which labour as a whole can reduce its *real* wage to a given figure by making revised *money* bargains with the entrepreneurs' (Keynes, 1936, p. 13). There may be unemployment, workers may be willing to accept a cut in real wages, firms may want to expand production and employment if real wages were to fall and profitability to increase, but there is no mechanism to ensure that the fall in real wages and the rise in employment will take place.

APPENDIX 5A

Equations (5.2) and (5.3) imply that

$$\pi = \frac{(I/Y) - \beta[h(\pi, e) - r] + \alpha\hat{N}[\beta r + \delta/(u\sigma)]}{s_p + \alpha\hat{N}} \tag{a5.1}$$

Since $\hat{I} = \hat{L}$ we know that $I/\underline{L} = a$ will be constant and hence

$$u = \frac{Y}{\sigma K} = \frac{Y}{L}\frac{L}{\underline{L}}\frac{\underline{L}}{\sigma K} = \lambda e \frac{\underline{L}}{\sigma K}$$

$$\frac{I}{Y} = \frac{I}{\underline{L}}\frac{\underline{L}}{L}\frac{L}{Y} = \frac{a}{\lambda}\frac{1}{e} \tag{a5.2}$$

Using (a5.1) and (a5.2) we get

$$\pi = \frac{(a/\lambda)(1/e) - \beta h(\pi, e) + \beta r + \alpha\hat{N}\{\beta r + [\delta/(\sigma\lambda e\underline{L}/K)]\}}{s_p + \alpha\hat{N}} \tag{a5.3}$$

The left-hand side of (a5.3) is increasing and the right-hand side (RHS) decreasing in π. It follows that (a5.3) defines π as a function of e. The function need not be monotonic (the sign of $\partial\mathrm{RHS}/\partial e$ is ambiguous), but an increase in e must lead to a decline in $h(\pi, e)$. To see this, we assume the contrary, i.e. assume that both e and $h(\pi, e)$ increase. This implies that the expression for π on the RHS of (a5.3) will fall, but a fall in π is inconsistent with the assumed rise in $h(\pi, e)$. We conclude that $dh/de = (\partial h/\partial\pi)$ $(d\pi/de) + \partial h/\partial e$ must be negative, and since

$$\hat{e} = h(\pi, e) - n \tag{a5.4}$$

it follows that the rate of employment converges monotonically to some constant $e*$ (non-linearity of $h(\pi, e)$ will ensure that $0 \leqslant e* \leqslant 1$). If $e \to e*$ then we must have $\hat{Y} = \hat{L} = n$ asymptotically and, since $\hat{Y} = h(\pi, e)$, $\pi \to \pi*$.

APPENDIX 5B

The slope of $g(\pi)$ depends on both (5.15) and (5.16). Substituting (5.15) into (5.16) we get

$$\pi = \pi(u(\pi, g_w), g_w) \tag{b5.1}$$

and hence

$$(1 - \pi_u u_\pi)d\pi = (\pi_g + \pi_u u_g)dg_w \tag{b5.2}$$

From (5.13) and (5.16) it follows that

$$u_\pi = \kappa' \left[\left(1 - \frac{1}{q} \right) + \left(\pi - \frac{g_w + \delta}{u\sigma} \right) \frac{\sigma u \alpha}{q^2} \right] < 0$$

$$u_g = \kappa' \frac{-1}{u\sigma} \left(1 - \frac{1}{q} \right) > 0$$

$$\pi_u = - \frac{g_w + \delta + \alpha\delta\hat{N}}{\sigma u^2(s_p + \alpha\hat{N})} < 0$$

$$\pi_g = \frac{(1/u\sigma) - \beta}{s_p + \alpha\hat{N}} > 0$$

It seems unlikely that a one percentage point rise in the share of pure profits should cause the desired utilisation rate to fall by more than one percentage point. One would therefore expect the derivative κ' to satisfy $0 \geqslant \kappa' \geqslant -1$. Substituting plausible values for the remaining parameters (a list of benchmark values is given in appendix 5C) it is readily seen that $\pi_u u_\pi < 1$ and $\pi_g u_g + \pi_g > 0$ and, furthermore, that the first of the two inequalities appears to be the more stringent.

APPENDIX 5C

The following parameter values would seem in accordance with generally accepted stylised facts:

$$\sigma u = \frac{Y}{K} \approx \tfrac{1}{2}$$

$$\beta = \frac{M}{pY} \approx \tfrac{1}{2}$$

$$\alpha = \frac{vN}{P - \delta pK - rM} \approx 20$$

$$\delta \approx \tfrac{1}{10}$$

and

$$0 \leqslant r \leqslant \tfrac{4}{100}$$

$$0 \leqslant \alpha\hat{N} \leqslant \tfrac{1}{2}$$

$$0 \leqslant g \leqslant \tfrac{1}{10}$$

$$\tfrac{1}{2} \leqslant s_p \leqslant 1$$

The steady-growth profit share is given (equation (5.15))

$$\pi* = \frac{[(g_w + \delta)/(\sigma u)] - \beta(g_w - r) + \alpha\hat{N}[\beta r + \delta/(\sigma u)]}{s_p + \alpha\hat{N}(1 + \beta r)}$$

The profit share is increasing in r and since we are mainly concerned to establish a minimum value of π we let $r = 0$. The equation for π then simplifies to

$$\pi* = \frac{g_w[1/(\sigma u) - \beta] + (1 + \alpha\hat{N})\delta/(\sigma u)}{s_p + \alpha\hat{N}}$$

which is increasing in g_w and decreasing in s_p and $\alpha\hat{N}$.

Setting $g_w = 0$, $s_p = 1$ and $\alpha\hat{N} = \frac{1}{2}$, we get $\pi* = \delta/\sigma u = 20\%$. If instead $g_w = 5\%$ then $\pi* = 25\%$, and $\pi* = 30\%$ for $g_w = 10\%$. If $s_p = 1$, $\alpha\hat{N} = 0$ and $g_w = 5\%$ then $\pi* = 27.5\%$.

At the other extreme, let $s_p = \frac{1}{2}$, $\alpha\hat{N} = 0$ and $g_w = 10\%$. Then $\pi* = 70\%$. If, more reasonably, the very low retention rate is accompanied by a high rate of new issues, $\alpha\hat{N} = \frac{1}{2}$, and if $g_w = 5\%$, then $\pi* = 37.5\%$.

With intermediate values of $s_p = \frac{3}{4}$ and $g_w = 5\%$ we get $\pi* = 30\%$ for $\alpha\hat{N} = \frac{1}{2}$ and $\pi* \approx 36.7\%$ for $\alpha\hat{N} = 0$.

If $r = 0$, the share of gross profits thus lies between 25% and 40% (and the rate of net profits between $2\frac{1}{2}\%$ and 10%) for the most plausible range of parameter values. A positive real interest rate would shift the profitability figures upwards.

CHAPTER 6

Investment, instability and cycles

6.1 INTRODUCTION

The preceding chapter has examined the properties of ultra-short-run, short-run and steady-growth equilibria, but has not looked at stability issues in any detail. Will a sequence of ultra-short-run equilibria converge to a state of short-run equilibrium and will the economy approach steady growth asymptotically?

Following Harrod, many Keynesians have argued that the steady-growth path (the warranted path) is unstable. The empirical evidence, however, suggests that although both employment and production fluctuate significantly in advanced capitalist countries there is no monotonic divergence from some unstable steady-growth path. Furthermore, average growth rates appear to be broadly in line with the growth in the labour force.

The influence of the rate of employment on firms' production decisions can, as shown in the previous chapter, explain the consistency of warranted and natural growth rates, and as we shall see these class-struggle effects may also explain why Harrodian instability leads to fluctuations in production and employment rather than to monotonic divergence from steady growth.

The homeostatic effects of movements in the reverse army were emphasised by Marx in 1867 in his 'general law of accumulation' (see Marx, 1976, chapter 23) and formalised by Goodwin (1967), but neither Marx's original argument nor Goodwin's formalisation took any account of Keynesian effective-demand problems (realisation problems). The Marxian mechanism can, however, be adapted and introduced into Keynesian models, and it is the purpose of this chapter to do just that. Most of the building-blocks are already in place: the only piece missing is a full specification of the investment function. In previous chapters I have assumed either that investment was an exogenous constant (in ultra-short- and short-run equilibrium) or that the capital stock (the utilisation rate) was at the desired level (in long-run steady growth). Neither of these assumptions is appropriate if one wants to analyse the evolution over time of the sequence of ultra-short equilibria.

6.2 THE INVESTMENT FUNCTION

I have argued in section 4.7 that the rate of accumulation would accelerate if utilisation were to remain above the desired level for prolonged periods, and one may therefore need to distinguish between the short-run and long-run investment function. At any given moment, each individual firm has some view of the trend rate of growth of demand, a view which is reflected in its investment response to unanticipated changes in demand. If, say, the firm expects the trend in demand to be flat, then an investment programme which over one year adds 5 per cent to existing capital capacity may be the appropriate response to a 5 per cent shortfall in capacity below desired levels. If, on the other hand, the trend growth in demand is 10 per cent, this investment programme cannot even prevent utilisation rates from increasing further; an investment programme is needed which in one year adds 15 per cent to existing capital capacity. The short-run investment function, which describes the investment response to deviations of actual from desired utilisation rates, may thus be shifting over time.

The potential instability of the short-run investment function could not be ignored if the purpose had been to specify a universal investment function. I shall, however, confine myself to a more limited task: I shall examine the behaviour of the economy in the neighbourhood of a steady-growth path, and, in the absence of exogenous shifts in animal spirits, the short-run investment function will be stable over time as long as the trend rate of growth is constant. As we shall see, the economy will in fact – given the specification of the investment function – fluctuate around a steady-growth path, and it is thus possible to tell a consistent story of persistent but bounded fluctuations. But, since the model includes an investment function which itself depends on the assumption of near steady growth, this story does not prove global stability of the economy: there is no presumption that eventually all paths of the economy must produce fluctuations within some neighbourhood of the steady-growth path.

What does the short-run investment function look like (conditional on near steady growth)? Let $(g, \pi, u, e) = (n, \pi*, u*, e*)$ be a solution to the steady-growth equations (5.3), (5.15), (5.16) and (5.18a). I then adopt the following specification of the investment function

$$\frac{I}{K} = \sigma u f(u, \pi) \tag{6.1}$$

where $f_u > 0$, $f_\pi \geq 0$ and $\sigma u * f(u*, \pi*) = n$.

The specification (6.1) includes the standard stock-adjustment (flexible-accelerator) function as a special case. To see this, simply recall that the desired utilisation rate of capital is a decreasing function of profitability, $u* = u(\pi, n)$ (see equation (5.15)). The stock-adjustment principle suggests that investment is proportional to the difference between desired and actual capital stock,

$$I = \mu(K* - K) \tag{6.2}$$

and hence (using $u* = u(\pi, n)$ and $K*/Y = 1/u* \sigma$)

$$\frac{I}{Y} = \mu\left(\frac{K*}{Y} - \frac{K}{Y}\right) = \mu\left(\frac{1}{\sigma u*(\pi)} - \frac{1}{\sigma u}\right) = f(u, \pi) \tag{6.3}$$

where both partial derivatives are positive.

The flexible accelerator is often justified with reference to the existence of convex adjustment cost (Eisner and Strotz, 1963; Lucas, 1967; Gould, 1968), but this line of argument is not entirely convincing. Convexity of adjustment costs is a convenient assumption, but, as pointed out by Nickell (1978), 'there seems to be no very good reason why such costs should be increasing at the margin' (p. 37).[1] The rate of investment associated with a given investment programme is determined by the amount of new capacity which will be generated and by the speed with which the programme is carried out. While it may be reasonable to assume that costs are strictly convex in the speed of implementation (at least for rapid speeds of implementation), it is not reasonable to suppose that costs are convex as a function of the size of the programme. On the contrary, one would expect important indivisibilities and increasing returns: (i) the unit cost of new capacity may be smaller for a completely new and purpose-built factory than for marginal additions and modifications to existing plant; (ii) there may be fixed costs associated with the installation of new machinery (e.g. stopping the plant); (iii) information and learning

---

[1] Nickell (1978) goes on to argue that 'In fact it seems very much more plausible that reorganization and training processes are subject to large indivisibilities and consequently give rise to diminishing costs over a considerable range. Furthermore, these processes use information as an input and this is a well-known cause of decreasing costs. Thus, once one has determined how to reorganize one production line, one has determined how to reorganize any number of similar ones. Lastly, there may well be fixed costs associated with the installation of new capital equipment such as the costs of stopping the plant while it is installed. A more general line of argument purporting to give good reason for the strict convexity of $C(.)$ has been that it is more expensive to do things quickly than slowly. This *may* be true for the installation of very large units of machinery over very short periods of time. For example, it is probably cheaper to install a new production line in a month than in a day. But it is not clear that it is more expensive in terms of adjustment costs to install a new production line in a month than to install it in fifty years' (p. 37).

by doing make the costs of installing two machines (or building two plants) less than double the costs of installing only one.

Although one may justifiably feel unhappy about simply postulating (6.1), it is thus doubtful whether much is gained by a rigorous derivation which is based on convex adjustment costs, an assumption which itself lacks plausibility.[2] There is no doubt that the capital stock is less than perfectly flexible, but inflexibility is not the same as convex adjustment costs. A lack of flexibility stems from three sources: the irreversibility of investment (lack of second-hand markets for most investment goods), the existence of a time lag between investment decision and the appearance of new capacity, and the existence of indivisibilities and increasing returns which make it costly or impossible to adjust the capital stock continuously in response to changes in output and demand. It is not obvious that the hybrid assumption of convex adjustment costs gives an adequate representation of (the effects of) these inflexibilities.

Both Marxian and post-Keynesian theory have often been accused of being without 'choice-theoretic foundations'. For the reasons discussed in chapter 2, I have never found this argument very interesting or powerful. It is, however, a widespread view that such foundations are needed and that Keynesians and Marxians have failed to provide them: an explicit microeconomic derivation of the investment function may thus be desirable. The derivation is – not surprisingly – quite technical, and it is relegated to appendix 6A. It should be noted, however, that the derivation does not depend on convex adjustment costs. Instead, it is assumed that the constraints on firms' profit maximisation include an investment lag as well as indivisibilities of the sort described above.

6.3 THE EQUATIONS

With the specification of the investment function now complete, we have all we need. Before embarking on the detailed analysis of the implications of the model, however, it is useful to bring together the relevant equations.[3] The behaviour of the economy can be described algebraically by six equations:

$$S = Y[s(u, \pi) + \zeta h(\pi, e)]; \quad s_u \geq 0, \; s_\pi > 0, \; \zeta \geq 0 \tag{6.4}$$

$$\hat{K} = \frac{I}{K} - \delta; \quad \delta > 0 \tag{6.5}$$

$$\hat{e} = \hat{Y} - n \tag{6.6}$$

[2] In fact I have already implicitly rejected the assumption that investment is subject to convex adjustment costs: it is incompatible with the derivation of u^* in chapter 5, which implies that u^* is independent of the rate of growth.

[3] A simplified version of the model has been analysed in Skott (1989a), and the presentation in this chapter draws heavily on this paper.

$$\hat{Y} = h(\pi, e); \quad h_\pi > 0, \ h_e < 0 \tag{6.7}$$

$$I = Y f(u, \pi); \quad f_u > s_u \geqslant 0, \ s_\pi > f_\pi \geqslant 0 \tag{6.8}$$

$$I = S \tag{6.9}$$

The saving function, which generalises equation (4.17), is the only equation that needs special comment. The saving rate will depend on $\hat{Y}$ as well as on u and π if the parameter β in equation (4.17) is positive. But, as argued in section 5.3, one should not read too much into the direct effect of $\hat{Y}$ on saving: in long-run analysis it may be important to take the effect into account, but it is not an instantaneous effect, and it should not be used to determine ultra-short-run equilibrium positions. Our concern here is with the properties of (a sequence of) ultra-short-run equilibria which stay in the neighbourhood of steady growth, and it is therefore debatable whether the influence of $\hat{Y}$ on saving should be left out. In terms of equation (6.4), however, the absence of a link between output growth and saving corresponds to the special case where $\zeta = 0$ and $S/Y = s(u, \pi)$. The general specification (6.4) thus captures both possibilities.

Both the saving and the investment functions depend on u and π, but it is assumed that saving is more sensitive than investment to changes in π and that relative sensitivities are reversed for changes in u (equation (6.8)). Are these assumptions necessary and are they reasonable? The relative sensitivity of saving to changes in the profit share is essential. If a rise in prices and profits were to raise investment more than saving then the effect would be to increase aggregate demand, and the ultra-short-run equilibrium – the basic equilibrium concept in the model – would fail to be stable.

Fortunately, the evidence in favour of this stability condition is strong. According to equation (4.17), s_π is equal to $s_p + \alpha \hat{N}$, and empirically the order of magnitude of s_p is 75 per cent. The (short-run) effect of profitability on investment, f_π, on the other hand, is small. A formal argument is set out in appendix 6A (p. 110), but intuitively the reason is that firms do not expect a proportional increase in the prices of their own and all rival products to cause a large decline in the volume of demand. More precisely, equation (4.5) implies that the elasticity of (conjectured) demand with respect to proportional changes in both p_i and p is $(1 - \rho)/\gamma$, and ρ is likely to be close to unity. For the representative firm both p_i and p move together, and the relative insensitivity of demand with respect to changes in these prices implies that investment will be relatively insensitive to changes in profitability (in prices): investment decisions are governed by expected future demand which in turn is determined by the underlying level of current demand rather than by temporary deviations of prices from their normal levels.

The second inequality, $s_u \leqslant f_u$, is not central to the model in the same way, but the details of the algebra will depend on the relative sensitivity of saving and investment to changes in utilisation. The justification for the inequality is that the rate of utilisation only affects the average propensity to save indirectly: it influences the share of depreciation in total income, the share of depreciation in turn affects net profits and hence the price of financial assets, and the price of securities, finally, affects saving because of its influence on the valuation of new issues. Using (4.17), the derivative of S/Y with respect to u is $\alpha \hat{N} \delta / \sigma u^2$ and new issues form a very small proportion of the stock of securities,[4] $\hat{N} \approx 0$. It follows that the effect of utilisation on saving is weak, and in the simple case where $\hat{N} = 0$ it vanishes completely.

The remaining equations can be dealt with very briefly. Equation (6.5) relates the change in capital to gross investment and depreciation. Equation (6.6) is based on the production function (4.1) and the absence of labour-hoarding, and it links changes in the employment rate to the growth rate of output. Equations (6.7) and (6.8) restate the output-expansion function, (4.9), and the investment function, (6.1). Equation (6.9), finally, is the ultra-short-run equilibrium condition, (5.1), which has been discussed extensively in section 4.2.

6.4 ANALYSIS

The overall working of the model is as follows. At any given moment, t, the rate of output, Y_t, the employment rate, e_t, and the capital stock, K_t, are all predetermined. The desired ratio of saving to capital, S_t/K_t, and the desired rate of accumulation, I_t/K_t, are both positively related to the share of profits in income, but the restrictions on the saving and investment functions ensure that a unique share of profits will clear the product market and that the product-market equilibrium is stable. The equilibrium condition for the product market thus serves to determine the distribution of income, π_t. With the distribution of income fixed, equations (6.7) and (6.8) determine the rates of growth of output and capital, and (6.6) links the rate of growth of the employment rate to output growth. The complete time paths of Y, K and e are thus determined by the current values of the same three variables.

---

[4] In the UK there were effectively no net issues during the 1970s, and although there has recently been increased activity in this area, new issues still remain small in relation to total market valuation.

6.4.1 Uniqueness of balanced-growth equilibrium

In order to determine the properties of the paths we first reduce equations (6.4)–(6.9) to a two-dimensional system of differential equations. From (6.4), (6.8) and (6.9) one gets

$$\pi = \xi(u, e); \quad \xi_u > 0, \ \xi_e > 0 \tag{6.10}$$

Inserting (6.10) in (6.7) and (6.8) we find an expression for $\hat{u}$,

$$\hat{u} = \hat{u} + \hat{\sigma} = \hat{Y} - \hat{K} = h(\xi(u, e), e) - u\sigma f(u, \xi(u, e)) + \delta \tag{6.11}$$

and combining (6.6), (6.7) and (6.10) we get

$$\hat{e} = h(\xi(u, e), e) - n \tag{6.12}$$

By construction, the model possesses a steady-growth equilibrium at $(g, \pi, u, e) = (n, \pi*, u*, e*)$, but is the steady-growth equilibrium unique? The investment function has been calibrated to this particular steady-growth path so the question is almost illegitimate: steady growth at a different configuration of (g, π, u, e) would be inconsistent with the specified investment function. But in fact, it is readily seen that equations (6.4)–(6.9) cannot have more than a single (non-trivial) steady-growth solution. Setting $\hat{e} = \hat{u} = 0$ and substituting (6.12) in (6.11) we get

$$\sigma u f(u, \xi(u, e)) - \delta = n \tag{6.13}$$

Equation (6.10) implies that (6.13) has a unique solution, $u = u(e)$ with $u_e < 0$, and substituting this solution into the right-hand side of (6.12) gives the equilibrium condition,

$$h(\xi(u(e), e), e) = n \tag{6.14}$$

The function $h(\xi(u(e), e), e)$ is monotonically decreasing in e.[5] It follows that (6.14) has a unique solution, $e = e*$, and substituting this into (6.13) gives the unique solution for $u = u*$.

6.4.2 Local instability of the steady-growth path

The local stability properties of the equilibrium are determined by the Jacobian of the system (6.11)–(6.12). At the equilibrium the Jacobian is given by

[5] We have $dh/de = [h_\pi \xi_e + h_e] + h_\pi \xi_u u'$. The term $h_\pi \xi_u u'$ is unambiguously negative. The term in square brackets includes the positive element $h_\pi \xi_e$. It follows, however, from the definition of ξ that the bracketed sum must be negative. $\pi = \xi(u, e)$ is defined by the equilibrium condition that $s(u, \pi) + \zeta h(\pi, e) = f(u, \pi)$, and the assumptions that $s_u \leq f_u$ and $s_\pi > f_\pi$ imply that the rise in π following an increase in e will be insufficient to offset the depressing effect of the change in e on output growth. To see this, note that $f(u, \pi) - s(u, \pi)$ is decreasing in π (for given u), that π is determined (given u and e) by the condition that $f - s = \zeta h$, and that (from equation (6.10)) a rise in e will raise the equilibrium value of π.

$$J(u, e) = \left\{ \begin{matrix} u[h_\pi\xi_u - \sigma f - u\sigma(f_u + f_\pi\xi_u)] & u(h_\pi\xi_e + h_e - u\sigma f_\pi\xi_e) \\ eh_\pi\xi_u & e(h_\pi\xi_e + h_e) \end{matrix} \right\} \qquad (6.15)$$

and[6]

$$\text{Det} = ue\{(h_\pi\xi_e + h_e)[- \sigma f - u\sigma(f_u + f_\pi\xi_u)] + h_\pi\xi_u u\sigma f_\pi\xi_e\} > 0 \qquad (6.16)$$

$$\text{Tr} = u[h_\pi\xi_u - \sigma f - u\sigma(f_u + f_\pi\xi_u)] + e(h_\pi\xi_e + h_e)$$

$$= u\left(\frac{\partial\hat{Y}}{\partial u} - \frac{\partial\hat{K}}{\partial u}\right) + e\left(\frac{\partial\hat{Y}}{\partial e}\right) \qquad (6.17)$$

The equilibrium will be locally asymptotically stable (unstable) when Tr is negative (positive). The sign of Tr is apparently ambiguous, but in fact Tr will almost certainly be positive and the equilibrium unstable.

Essentially, the positive sign of Tr is ensured if an implicit assumption underlying standard short-run macroeconomics is satisfied. Short-run macroeconomics examines variations in output which are rapid relative to any movements in the capital stock: the *level* of output is related to the level of investment and hence to the *growth* of the capital stock. This assumption in static short-run theory has a dynamic equivalent. Assume that there is a rise, $\Delta\hat{K}$, in the rate of accumulation. Since output (and employment) are initially unchanged, the impact effect of the rise in $\hat{K}$ is to reduce the ratio of output to investment below the short-run equilibrium level, $Y/I = \mu$ where μ represents the multiplier. Adjustments in output, however, *rapidly* restore the multiplier relation and during this adjustment process, $\hat{Y}$ must exceed $\hat{K}$. In fact, $\hat{Y}$ must be many times greater than $\hat{K}$ in order to justify the standard approach which assumes that short-run equilibrium is established so quickly that the capital stock can be taken as fixed in short-run analysis.[7] Algebraically we therefore have,

---

[6] The sum $h_\pi\xi_e + h_e$ is negative (see footnote 5).

[7] The positive sign of $\partial(\hat{Y} - \hat{K})/\partial u$ is closely related to the condition for instability in the Chang and Smyth (1971) model. Chang and Smyth show that instability requires that

$$\alpha(I_Y - S_Y) + I_K > 0 \qquad \text{(i)}$$

Since $\dot{Y} = \alpha(I - S)$, equation (i) can be rewritten

$$\frac{\partial\dot{Y}}{\partial Y} + \frac{\partial I}{\partial K} > 0 \qquad \text{(ii)}$$

and of both I and S are linearly homogeneous in Y and K then (ii) can be transformed to

$$\frac{Y}{K}\frac{d\hat{Y}}{d(Y/K)} - \frac{Y}{K}\frac{d\hat{K}}{d(Y/K)} = u\left(\frac{d\hat{Y}}{du} - \frac{d\hat{K}}{du}\right) \qquad \text{(iii)}$$

Kaldor's reply to Chang and Smyth correctly stated that (i) is 'implicit in *all* Keynesian "short period equilibrium" models' (Kaldor, 1971, p. 45). He did not, however, develop the argument in any detail.

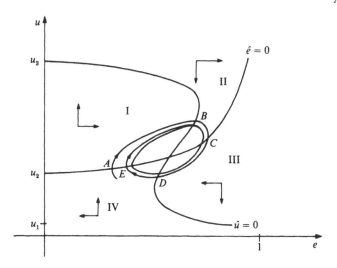

Figure 6.1: Phase diagram for the model described by equations (6.11) and (6.12).

$$d\hat{Y} = \eta d\hat{K} \quad \text{where } \eta \gg 1 \tag{6.18}$$

Since $T_F = u[\partial(\hat{Y} - \hat{K})/\partial u] + e(\partial\hat{Y}/\partial e) = u(\eta - 1)(\partial\hat{K}/\partial u) + e(\partial\hat{Y}/\partial e)$, it follows that the equilibrium is unstable unless the sensitivity of desired output growth to changes in employment is much greater than the sensitivity of the accumulation rate to changes in the output–capital ratio (in capacity utilisation). Appendix 6B gives a precise derivation of the connection between $\partial(\hat{Y} - \hat{K})/\partial u$ and standard multiplier analysis. It is shown that with plausible numerical values the equilibrium is unstable unless $e\,\partial\hat{Y}/\partial e < -9$.

In conclusion: stability cannot be ruled out but instability is the more likely outcome. The main factor which makes for instability is a fast adjustment speed of output outside short-run equilibrium. The destabilising influence of fast output adjustment could be offset if (i) the response of accumulation to changes in utilisation and profitability were sufficiently slow, or (ii) the rate of growth of output were highly sensitive to marginal changes in the employment rate around the balanced-equilibrium point.

6.4.3 Global behaviour – the existence of a limit cycle

In order to establish the existence of a limit cycle one needs to show that (6.11) and (6.12) have a compact positively invariant set in the positive orthant, i.e. that there exists a closed and bounded subset of the positive orthant with the property that, if the initial value of (e, u) belongs to this

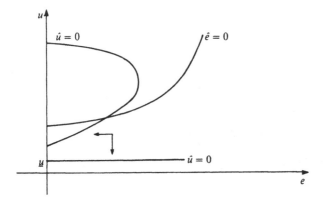

Figure 6.2: Possibility of convergence to a state $(\underline{e}, \underline{u})$ with $\underline{e} = 0$ when assumption (iii) fails to be satisfied.

subset, then the path subsequently traced out by (6.11) and (6.12) will be wholly contained within the subset. If this condition is satisfied then, by the Poincaré–Bendixson theorem, a trajectory starting anywhere within the invariant set (except in the equilibrium point itself) will converge to (or be identical with) a closed orbit (see, for example, Hale, 1969).

In order to prove the existence of a positively invariant compact set we consider the two loci, $\hat{e} = 0$ and $\hat{u} = 0$. The $\hat{e} = 0$ locus is an upward sloping curve, as indicated in figure 6.1. For low rates of employment the curve will be flat but as e approaches unity the curve rises sharply.[8]

The $\hat{u} = 0$ locus is given by the set of solutions to

$$h(\xi(u, e), e) = u\sigma f(u, \xi(u, e)) - \delta \tag{6.19}$$

Since $h_\pi \xi_e + h_e < 0$[9] there is at most one value of e in the interval $[0, 1]$ which solves (6.19) for given u. Furthermore, uniqueness and instability imply that there is exactly one intersection between the two loci and that the slope of the $\hat{u} = 0$ locus is positive and exceeds the slope of the $\hat{e} = 0$ locus at the intersection. Figure 6.1 has been drawn on the additional assumptions that (i) $\hat{K} \leqslant \hat{Y}$ for very small values of u, (ii) $\hat{K} \geqslant \hat{Y}$ for very high values of u and (iii) for low values of e, $\hat{u} = 0$ implies that $e > 0$.

Assumption (i) is plausible but could be dispensed with completely, and violation of the second assumption is inconsistent with the fixed-coefficient production function which implies that there is an upper limit on the output–capital ratio, $Y/K = u\sigma \leqslant \sigma$, and hence that $\hat{u} = \hat{Y} - \hat{K} \leqslant 0$ for

---

[8] This is the most plausible shape of the curve; only the positive slope is important to the argument.

[9] See footnote 5 on p. 95.

$u \geq u_0$ where $u_0 \leq 1$. The third assumption, however, is important. It ensures that there is a floor under the cyclical downturn: with the assumption, perpetual fluctuations around the balanced-equilibrium path are inevitable. If, on the other hand, the assumption fails to be satisfied, the economy will either exhibit perpetual fluctuations around the balanced equilibrium, or it will converge asymptotically to an equilibrium $(\underline{e}, \underline{u})$ where $\underline{e} = 0$. The latter possibility is illustrated in figure 6.2.[10]

When assumptions (i)–(iii) are satisfied, it is intuitively clear that a compact and positively invariant subset of the positive orthant can be constructed. The only problem is (see figure 6.1) whether (e, u) can get stuck in region IV; i.e. is it possible that (e, u) may converge toward a point $(\underline{e}, \underline{u})$ where $\underline{e} = 0$, $\underline{u} \leq u_2$? This possibility is ruled out by the fact that $\dot{u}$ will be bounded above some positive constant when (e, u) is in region IV and e is sufficiently small. A rigorous proof of this proposition is given in appendix 6C.

6.4.4 Description of the cycles

The limit cycle need not be unique, and the precise asymptotic behaviour of the economy may therefore depend on initial conditions. The same qualitative properties of the cyclical fluctuations are, however, shared by all limit cycles, and figure 6.1 can be used to describe the qualitative movement of the economy.

Assume that the economy is at point A in figure 6.1. The utilisation rate as well as the share of profits are relatively low at A, but high rates of unemployment imply that even this modest share of profits is sufficient to generate a rate of growth of production and employment which matches the rate of increase in the labour supply. The high degree of excess capacity, however, depresses the rate of accumulation of capital below the rate of growth of production. The utilisation rate is therefore rising at A. As u increases, the economy moves into the area marked I, the rise in u stimulates investment, and product-market equilibrium is maintained through an increase in π. The rise in profitability in turn causes the rate of growth of output to accelerate. Both the utilisation rate and the rate of employment are thus increasing.

After a while the gradual increase in employment – the cyclical rise in working-class power – starts to exert downward pressure on the growth

---

[10] One possible justification for assumption (iii) could be that exceedingly low rates of employment cause an upsurge in small-scale business (see section 5.6). A modification of the saving function to allow the employment rate to affect the share of saving in income via its effect on the rate of wage inflation could provide an alternative justification. Inflation effects of this kind will be discussed in chapter 7.

rate of production. The rate of accumulation, on the other hand, is rising and at point B accumulation has caught up with output growth: the utilisation rate and the profit share attain their cyclical maxima. Employment is still expanding at B, but class-struggle effects imply that the rate of growth of production is declining and the utilisation rate begins to fall. The decline in u discourages investment, and profitability suffers as prices adjust to maintain product-market equilibrium, the falling profit shares speeding up the decline in the growth rate of output.

At C the rate of growth of employment has become equal to the growth rate of labour supply, and the employment rate has reached its cyclical peak. The share of profits and the utilisation rate are still fairly high, but a tight labour market depresses output growth. The movement which took the economy from A to C is now repeated in reverse: the decline in u is brought to a halt at D, and the gradual recovery of utilisation rates and profit shares from their nadir is started by the stimulus to output growth arising from further falls in employment. After this first stimulus, accelerator effects of u on I/Y lead to rising profitability, and profitability effects (multiplier effects) of π on $\hat{Y}$ accelerate the upward movement back toward the $\hat{e} = 0$ locus at E.

6.5 COMPARISON WITH THE KALDOR AND GOODWIN MODELS

It may be instructive to compare the present model with those of Kaldor (1940) and Goodwin (1967). In contrast to the Chang and Smyth (1971) formalisation of Kaldor's model, I have assumed that both the saving and investment functions are linearly homogeneous in Y and K. Secondly, I have introduced flexible prices and profit margins and related the growth of output to profitability rather than to the excess of desired investment over desired saving. Finally, and most importantly, I have argued that the rate of growth of employment and production will depend on labour-market conditions as well as on the state of demand. Compared with the Goodwin model, the main difference is the explicit modelling of the production and investment decisions. As a result of this difference, the equilibrium condition for the product market becomes the proximate determinant of income distribution, labour-market conditions having no direct impact on distributive shares.

Kaldor's model ceases to produce cycles when saving and investment are linearly homogeneous in output and the capital stock (see section 3.8). We can, however, compare the cyclical path in figure 6.1 with that of the Goodwin model. The Goodwin model produces cycles in employment and profitability, and in the present model π is an increasing function of u and e. The cycles of the two models can therefore be depicted in the same

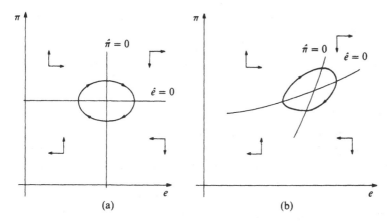

Figure 6.3: Phase diagrams for (a) the Goodwin model and (b) the model described by equations (6.11) and (6.12).

(e, π)-plane. Comparing figures 6.3a and 6.3b, the similarity is striking. Both models imply that employment is increasing when profitability is high and that profitability suffers in periods of high employment. The $\hat{\pi} = 0$ and $\hat{e} = 0$ loci are both rotated slightly in the present model (and as a result the model is not afflicted by the structural instability of the Goodwin model), but the important differences are elsewhere.

In the Goodwin model, the output–capital ratio is constant. The present model, in contrast, predicts that profitability will vary over the cycle and that movements in utilisation and profitability will be positively correlated, a prediction which is strongly supported by the stylised facts (see, for example, Hahnel and Sherman, 1982). Secondly, the mechanism behind the fluctuations differs significantly. In the Goodwin model, the rate of employment has a direct influence on (changes in) distributive shares whereas the present model uses the equilibrium condition that saving equals investment to determine (changes in) distribution. The simple inverse relation between employment and (the change in) profitability thus hides a chain of causal relations: employment affects the rate of output growth, output growth leads to changes in utilisation rates, utilisation influences investment, and investment finally affects profitability through the equilibrium condition for the product market. The Goodwin model short-circuits this chain. It assumes full utilisation of capital and the growth rate of output is therefore equal to the rate of accumulation, and because investment and saving are identically equal (there is no independent investment function) the changes in income distribution can be determined in the labour market without any consideration of effective demand.

In spite of the similarity between figures 6.3a and 6.3b, there are thus radical differences between the two models and the cycles they generate.

6.6 EFFECTS OF SHORT-RUN DIMINISHING RETURNS

It has been argued in chapter 4 that a fixed-coefficient production function may be a reasonable assumption for the short run: a choice of technique and thus the variability of the technical output–capital ratio should be considered in the analysis of long-term growth, but changes in technique may be of limited importance for short-term issues in general and the trade cycle in particular. Nevertheless, fixed coefficients do sometimes give rise to stability problems, and one may wonder whether the model can still produce cycles if a standard neoclassical production function is introduced. Accordingly, let

$$Y = F(L, K); \quad F_1 > 0, \ F_2 > 0, \ F_{11} < 0, \ F_{22} < 0 \qquad (6.20)$$

and hence

$$\hat{Y} = v\hat{L} + (1 - v)\hat{K} \qquad (6.21)$$

where $v = v(u\sigma)$ is the elasticity of output with respect to changes in labour input. Equation (6.21) replaces (6.6), and, since adjustment costs attach to changes in employment, the output-expansion function (6.7) needs to be replaced by an employment-expansion function: the growth rate of employment rather than of output should depend on the deviation of actual levels from short-run equilibrium levels. The short-run equilibrium value of π ($\pi*$), however, may no longer be constant (invariant with respect to changes in the level of demand) even if the conjectured elasticity of demand is constant. If $1/\gamma$ is the elasticity of demand then the first-order condition for profit maximisation implies that

$$\pi* = 1 - (1 - \gamma)v(u\sigma) \qquad (6.22)$$

The deviation from short-run equilibrium levels will thus be a function of both π and $u\sigma$, and (6.7) should be replaced by

$$\hat{L} = \tilde{h}(u\sigma, \pi, e) \qquad (6.23)$$

Turning to the investment function, we retain the assumptions that the rate of accumulation depends on deviations of K from the conjectured optimal level, $K*$, and that $K*$ is proportional to the level of demand, the proportionality factor depending on relative factor prices at the steady-growth path. With these assumptions, $\hat{K}$ is determined by $(u\sigma, \pi)$,[11] and the reduced system replacing (6.11) and (6.12) can be written

$$\hat{u} + \hat{\sigma} = [\tilde{h}(u\sigma, \pi, e) - u\sigma f(u\sigma, \pi)]v(u\sigma) \tag{6.24}$$

$$\hat{e} = \tilde{h}(u\sigma, \pi, e) - n \tag{6.25}$$

The trace of the Jacobian at the balanced-growth equilibrium becomes

$$\mathrm{Tr} = v(u\sigma)u\sigma\left[\frac{\partial \hat{L}}{\partial(u\sigma)} - \frac{\partial \hat{K}}{\partial(u\sigma)}\right] + e\frac{\partial \hat{L}}{\partial e}$$

$$= u\sigma\left[\frac{\partial \hat{Y}}{\partial(u\sigma)} - \frac{\partial \hat{K}}{\partial(u\sigma)}\right] + e\frac{\partial \hat{L}}{\partial e} \tag{6.26}$$

and, using the same argument which led to (6.18), we find that the stability condition is unchanged if it is adjustment costs associated with changes in employment which lie behind the slow adjustment of output. Again, the equilibrium will be locally asymptotically unstable unless the sensitivity of output growth to changes in employment is much higher than that of accumulation to changes in the output–capital ratio, and the introduction of a neoclassical production function thus has not improved the prospects for stability. The reasons for instability are essentially Harrodian, and the Harrodian argument as presented here does not depend on any particular production function.

6.7 CONCLUSIONS

This chapter has analysed the behaviour of the economy as a sequence of ultra-short-run equilibria, but, in order to achieve this, an investment function had to be specified. The chosen specification includes a number of standard specifications as special cases, and in appendix 6A it is shown how the specification can be derived from the profit-maximising behaviour of individual firms. Such derivations are often, following Eisner and Strotz (1963) and Lucas (1967), based on the introduction of adjustment costs, but the hybrid assumption of convex assumption costs seems unsatisfactory: it does not capture the underlying sources of

[11] The perceived level of demand, $B^{1/\gamma}$, can be derived from the demand function

$$p_i = p^\rho R Y^{-\gamma}$$

For the representative firm we get

$$B^{1/\gamma} = p^{(1-\rho)/\gamma} Y$$

Hence, if $K^* = \mu B^{1/\gamma}$,

$$\frac{I}{Y} = v\frac{K^* - K}{Y} = v\frac{\mu B^{1/\gamma} - K}{Y} = v\frac{\mu p^{(1-\rho)/\gamma} - 1}{u\sigma} = f(u\sigma, \pi)$$

inflexibility. The analysis in appendix 6A therefore models inflexibility directly in the form of (i) irreversibility of investment, (ii) the existence of an investment lag between the decision to invest and the appearance of new capacity, and (iii) indivisibilities and increasing returns which make the unit costs of capacity higher for marginal additions to existing plant than for completely new and purpose-built plants.

The main point of the chapter, however, is not the derivation of an investment function. The investment function is merely a necessary element in the subsequent analysis of the time path of the economy. This analysis shows that the steady-growth path is unstable for reasonable parameter values and that, indeed, instability is closely related to implicit assumptions underlying all standard short-run theory. The traditional Harrodian instability argument is thus vindicated, but instability of the steady-growth path need not imply cumulative divergence from steady growth: the model produces a limit cycle, and the economy exhibits perpetual fluctuations around the steady-growth path. Essentially, the influence of unemployment (the reserve army of labour) on the desired rate of expansion of production generates the turning-points and transforms the divergent movement into cyclical fluctuations. In this respect the model shows similarities with Goodwin's formalisation of Marx's theory of accumulation and crises, but the similarities hide radical differences in the causal structure of the model: unlike Goodwin's model the present analysis integrates Keynesian demand analysis with the traditional Marxian emphasis on the importance of the reserve army of labour.

APPENDIX 6A

The production and investment behaviour – equations (6.7) and (6.8) – can be derived from principles of constrained profit maximisation. Most of the constraints have already been described in chapters 4 and 5 and the main text of this chapter, and the presentation can therefore be brief. The constraints are as follows:

A. Production constraints

All firms face the same production function of the fixed-coefficient type (chapter 4, equation (4.1)),

$$Y_i = \min\{\lambda L_i, \sigma K\} \tag{a6.1}$$

It is assumed that changes in production and employment are associated with adjustment costs, and the adjustment-cost function takes the following simple form (chapter 4, equation (a4.2))

$$c(\hat{Y}_i, e) = \begin{cases} 0 & \text{for} \quad \varphi(e) \leqslant \hat{Y}_i \leqslant \psi(e), \quad \varphi' \leqslant 0 \text{ and } \psi' \leqslant 0 \\ \infty & \text{elsewhere} \end{cases} \tag{a6.2}$$

B. *Constraints on investment*

In place of the standard but unsatisfactory assumption of convex adjustment costs I assume that:

(a) Gross investment is non-negative.

(b) There is a time lag between the investment decision and the appearance of new capacity, and the specificity and non-malleability of capital goods imply that the specific capital goods which are optimal for one investment programme may not be suitable for an alternative investment programme designed to give, say, a larger increase in capacity. When a firm decides to increase its capacity by ΔK, it is therefore committing itself to a complete investment programme,

$$I_{t+h}, \quad 0 \leqslant h \leqslant T$$
$$\Delta K = \int I_{t+h} \mathrm{d}h \tag{a6.3}$$

where T is the lag between the decision to invest and the appearance of new capacity. I assume that the investment lag T is a 'gestation lag' and that all investment is concentrated at time t when the investment decision is made; i.e.

$$I_{t+h} = \Delta K D(h) \tag{a6.4}$$

where $D(.)$ is the Dirac delta function. Letting K_t denote capacity at time $t + T$, I_t still represents the change in K_t.

(c) Indivisibilities and increasing returns imply that the unit cost of new capacity may be a declining function of the amount of new capacity created, and there may also be an inverse relation between the amount of new capacity and the variable unit costs of output produced using that capacity (a new plant of optimal size will have a higher labour productivity that can be obtained on marginal additions to existing plants). For simplicity it is assumed that the unit cost of new capacity, as well as the productivity of workers operating the new capacity, is constant for all investment programmes exceeding a certain minimum size, $\underline{I}$, that cost and productivity conditions are such that firms will never undertake positive investment on a scale below this minimum, and that the minimum investment level moves in line with the average firm size so that the indivisibility constraint is neither relaxed nor tightened over time. Finally, I assume that an individual firm will never be engaged in two different investment programmes at the same time.

C. *Demand expectations*

It is assumed (chapter 4, equation (4.5)) that firms' perceived demand
curve takes the form

$$p_i = p^\rho B_i Y_i^{-\gamma} \tag{a6.5}$$

and to simplify the notation both p_i and p will be measured in terms of unit
wage costs. The perceived current value of the multiplicative constant, B_i,
is determined from the current (observed) values of p_i, p and Y_i,

$$B_{it} = p_i^{-\rho} p_{it} Y_{it}^{\gamma} \tag{a6.6}$$

Firms view (B_{it+h}) as a stochastic process, but I assume that the relevant
characteristics can be adequately represented by certainty-equivalent
point expectations, B_{it+h}, where

$$B_{it+h} = B_{it} \exp\left(\int_t^{t+h} \varsigma_\tau d\tau\right) \tag{a6.7}$$

$$\varsigma_\tau = \varsigma\left(\frac{K_{\tau-T}}{(p_\tau^\rho B_\tau)^{1/\gamma}}\right); \quad \varsigma' > 0, \ \varsigma'' < 0 \tag{a6.8}$$

The expression $p^\rho B$ is a measure of the level of demand facing the firm,
and the use of excess capital as a strategic deterrent explains the appearance of the ratio of capital to demand as a determinant of the expected
growth rate of output. The rate of new entry (or the probability of new
entry) is related to the price which would prevail if all existing capital
capacity were fully utilised rather than to the actual price (section 4.7).
Concavity of the ς-function is a standard assumption, and it is assumed
that the deterrence effect of excess capacity is sufficiently strong to ensure
that available capital capacity never becomes a binding constraint on
output.

As for p, I assume that the firm expects rival firms to return to a
normal price level, $p*$ (recall that in this appendix p_i and p are measured
in terms of unit wage costs). This assumption is reasonable: all firms are
in the same position with respect to both unit costs and demand
elasticity, and in the absence of adjustment costs $m = 1/(1 - \gamma)$ is thus
the optimal mark-up for all firms. Deviations of the mark-up from its
optimal level will induce rival firms to change their rate of production
and, as a result, the average mark-up will in fact fluctuate around a
normal level (see also the steady-growth analysis in chapter 5). In order
to simplify the derivation of the investment function it is assumed that
rival firms are expected to return to 'normal' prices in less than T
periods, T being the length of the investment lag.

D. Cost expectations

There are three aspects of cost expectations: variable cost (unit labour cost), output-adjustment cost, and the cost of capital services. With regard to nominal unit labour costs, w, the firm expects the money price of rival firms to be linearly homogeneous in w, and, if p is homogeneous of degree zero in w, then the expected demand price (deflated by unit labour costs), p_i, is invariant with respect to changes in w (see also the discussion of money-wage neutrality in section 5.8).

The position of the adjustment-cost function depends on the rate of employment, but it is assumed that firms expect e to remain within a range which (i) will allow output to change in line with expected changes in demand (i.e. it is assumed that the expected growth rate of $(p^p B)^{1/\gamma}$ will lie within the expected future limits on the growth of output), and (ii) will allow the actual rate of production T periods hence to reach $Y*_{t+T}$, where $Y*_{t+T}$ is the level of output which the firm currently expects would be optimal at time $t + T$ if production were perfectly flexible. Firms thus do not expect short-run inflexibilities in production to be binding constraints on medium-term growth.

The model, finally, does not distinguish between investment and consumption goods so the price of investment goods is equal to the general price level, and it is assumed that the rate of discount is equal to the real rate of interest on bank loans. This identification of the real rate of interest with the rate of discount may seem questionable: the appropriate discount factor is, arguably, related to the value of Tobin's q, as well as to both profitability and the rate of utilisation (chapter 5, equations (5.10) and (5.12)). It may therefore fluctuate even though the real rate of interest remains constant, but in order to simplify the analysis I assume that firms ignore any such short-run variations in the cost of finance.

E. The decision problem

We are now in a position to set up the firm's decision problem formally. If i and r denote the nominal and real rates of interest, $i = r + \hat{p}$, then the firm must solve the following mathematical problem:

$$\max \int e^{-\int i_\tau d\tau} \frac{w_t}{\lambda} (p_{it} Y_{it} - Y_{it} - p_t I_{it}) dt$$

$$= \max \int e^{-rt} \frac{w_0}{\lambda} \left[(p_{it} - 1) \frac{p_0}{p_t} Y_{it} - p_0 I_{it} \right] dt \qquad (a6.9)$$

subject to

$$\varphi(e) \leqslant \hat{Y}_i \leqslant \psi(e) \tag{a6.9a}$$

$$I_i = 0 \quad \text{or} \quad I_i \geqslant \underline{I} \tag{a6.9b}$$

$$\hat{K}_i = I_i - \delta K_i \tag{a6.9c}$$

$$p_i = p^\rho B_i Y_i^{-\gamma} \tag{a6.9d}$$

where B_i is determined by (a6.7) and (a6.8).

F. Optimal solution

Let $Y*_t$ denote the current rate of output which the firm would have chosen if its output level had been perfectly flexible, and let $Y*_{t+h}$ be the rate of output which the firm expects will be optimal at time $t + h$ (still assuming that output levels were perfectly flexible). The expected growth rate of demand is independent of the firm's price–output combination, and $Y*_t$ is determined myopically,

$$Y*_i = [(1 - \gamma) B_i p^\rho]^{1/\gamma} \tag{a6.10}$$

$$\pi*_i = \gamma \tag{a6.11}$$

By assumption the expected rate of growth of $Y*$ (= the growth rate of demand) is within the limits on the growth of actual output and it follows that

$$\hat{Y}_i = \begin{cases} \psi(e) & \text{for} \quad \pi > \gamma \\ \hat{Y}*_i & \text{for} \quad \pi = \gamma \\ \varphi(e) & \text{for} \quad \pi < \gamma \end{cases} \tag{a6.12}$$

(a6.12) is the output-expansion function for an individual firm and upon aggregation we get (appendix 4A),

$$\hat{Y} = h(\pi, e), \quad h_\pi > 0 \quad \text{and} \quad h_e < 0 \tag{a6.13}$$

In order to derive the investment equation implied by (a6.9) we first consider the simple programme which arises when (i) the 'awkward' constraints, (a6.9a) and (a6.9b), are deleted and both the capital stock and the output level are perfectly flexible, and (ii) rival firms charge 'normal' prices, $p*$. It is readily seen that the solution to this standard programme yields a constant output–capital ratio.

Indivisible investment programmes imply that the firm will be unable to maintain the constant optimal output–capital ratio. Output will change smoothly over time whereas the time path of capital will exhibit discontinuous jumps: (positive) investment will be triggered when the capital-output ratio has dropped to a certain critical value. When the investment lag, T, is introduced, it is the ratio of capital capacity to expected optimal output at time $t + T$ which matters. Recalling that K_t is the capacity at $t + T$, we let K_t^- denote the capacity which will be available if no investment takes place at t. We then have

$$I_{it} = \begin{cases} \underline{I} & \text{if } \quad K_{it}^- \leqslant \varLambda Y*_{it+T} = \varLambda B_{it+T}^{1/\gamma} p*^{\rho/\gamma} p*_i^{-1/\gamma} \\ 0 & \text{otherwise} \end{cases} \tag{a6.14}$$

Equation (a6.14) remains valid when the simplifying assumption (ii) is removed: firms expect p_{t+T} to be equal to $p*$ and it is p_{t+T} which affects $Y*_{it+T}$.

If no new investment projects mature over the period $[t, t + T)$, it follows from (a6.7) and (a6.8) that the ratio of expected demand at time $t + T$ to K_t^- is determined by current profitability and the ratio of current demand to K_t^-. Algebraically,

$$\frac{B_{it+T}^{1/\gamma}}{K_{it}^-} = G\left(\frac{B_{it}^{1/\gamma}}{K_{it}^-}, \pi\right); \quad G_1 > 0, \ G_2 < 0 \tag{a6.15}$$

Since

$$B_{it}^{1/\gamma} = (1 - \pi_i)^{-1/\gamma}(1 - \pi)^{\rho/\gamma} Y_{it} \tag{a6.16}$$

we therefore get

$$I_t = \begin{cases} \underline{I} & \text{if } \quad 1 \leqslant MG\left(\frac{Y_{it}}{K_{it}}(1 - \pi_{it})^{-1/\gamma}(1 - \pi_t)^{\rho/\gamma}, \pi_t\right); \\ & \quad\quad G_1 > 0, \ G_2 < 0 \\ 0 & \text{otherwise} \end{cases} \tag{a6.17}$$

where $M = \varLambda p*^{\rho/\gamma} p*_i^{-1/\gamma}$.

Equation (a6.17) has been derived under the simplifying assumption that Y_i is perfectly flexible. The investment lag, however, implies that the limited flexibility of Y_i over the first T periods is irrelevant for the investment decision: it is sufficient that firms have enough flexibility to enable production at time $t + T$ to match the expected perfect flexibility output, $Y*_{it+T}$. By assumption this is the case, and (a6.17) thus becomes the investment equation associated with (a6.9).

(a6.17) describes the investment behaviour of an individual firm. The equation says that a new investment programme is triggered when a functional expression in u_i, π_i and π reaches unity. It follows that the aggregate level of investment is determined by the density of firms for whom the expression equals one. Assuming that this density, o, is positively related to the functional expression evaluated at the average economy-wide values of u and π (the average values of π_i and π coincide), we have

$$o = H(MG(u(1 - \pi)^{-(1-\rho)/\gamma}, \pi)) = F(u, \pi); \quad F_1 > 0, F_2 \gtrless 0 \qquad (a6.18)$$

By assumption, I is proportional to the average size of firms, and combining (a6.17) and (a6.18) we therefore get the following expression for aggregate investment,

$$I = \int I_s ds = o \epsilon Y = \epsilon Y F(u, \pi) = Yf(u, \pi) \qquad (a6.19)$$

where ϵ is a positive constant.

Will the investment function satisfy the requirement that $f_\pi < g_\pi$? From (a6.18) it is readily seen that provided $(1 - \rho)$ is 'small' then the condition will be satisfied. The parameter ρ is the conjectured elasticity of the demand price of a firm with respect to the prices charged by other firms, and it is reasonable to suppose that ρ is close to unity and the condition satisfied. (G_2 is negative so it is possible that $f_\pi < 0$, but since G_2 will be numerically very small it was assumed in the main text that $f_\pi \geqslant 0$. No qualitative property of the model depends on f_π being positive; the only important condition is $f_\pi < g_\pi$.)

APPENDIX 6B

The connection between $d\hat{Y}$, $d\hat{K}$, the multiplier and the speed of adjustment can be formalised. Assume that the economy is initially at the balanced growth path, and consider the implications of a disturbance in u. From the investment function it follows that

$$\frac{d(I/Y)}{du} = f_u + f_\pi \xi_u \qquad (b6.1)$$

If μ is the investment multiplier, then the effect of the disturbance on the ratio of the short-run equilibrium level of output to actual output is

$$\frac{\partial(Y*/Y)}{\partial u} = \mu(f_u + f_\pi \xi_u) \qquad (b6.2)$$

Assuming that t units of time are needed for the multiplier to work itself out, this implies

$$\frac{\partial\hat{Y}}{\partial u} \simeq \frac{\mu(f_u + f_\pi \xi_u)}{t} \qquad (b6.3)$$

Since

$$\frac{d\hat{K}}{du} = \sigma f + u\sigma(f_u + f_\pi \xi_u) \tag{b6.4}$$

and since the investment multiplier is equal to the reciprocal of the share of investment in income, $\mu = 1/f$, we get

$$d\hat{Y} = \frac{\mu}{t} d\frac{I}{Y} = \frac{\mu}{t}\left[\frac{\sigma f + u\sigma(f_u + f_\pi \xi_u)}{u\sigma} - \frac{f}{u}\right] du$$

$$= \frac{\mu}{t}\left(\frac{d\hat{K}}{u\sigma} - \frac{f}{u} du\right) = \frac{\mu}{t}\left(\frac{1}{u\sigma} - \frac{f/u}{d\hat{K}/du}\right) d\hat{K}$$

$$= \frac{1}{t}\left(\frac{\mu}{u\sigma} - \frac{1}{u\,d\hat{K}/du}\right) d\hat{K} \tag{b6.5}$$

Standard assumptions concerning the size of the investment multiplier, the output–capital ratio and the speed of adjustment of output can be used to derive numerical estimates of the critical values of $u\,d\hat{K}/du$ and $e\,\partial\hat{Y}/\partial e$. If, for instance, the multiplier is equal to 3, the capital–output ratio is 2, and it takes $1/2$ period (year) for the multiplier to work itself out, then Tr can be written

$$\text{Tr} = 11\frac{u\,d\hat{K}}{du} - 2 + \frac{e\,\partial\hat{Y}}{\partial e} \tag{b6.6}$$

It seems unlikely that $u\,d\hat{K}/du$ should fall below 1: one would expect a 1 per cent increase in the output–capital ratio (a 1 per cent increase in the utilisation rate of capital) combined with an increase in the share of profits to induce an increase in the accumulation rate of at least one percentage point (the initial situation being one of normal utilisation and normal profitability at the balanced-growth path). Stability of the balanced-growth path would thus require that

$$\frac{e\,\partial\hat{Y}}{\partial e} < -9 \tag{b6.7}$$

Stability in other words requires that a 1 per cent increase in employment reduces the growth rates of output by at least nine percentage points.

APPENDIX 6C

Consider the transformed variables, $x = \log(u)$ and $y = \log(e)$, and the equivalent system

$$\dot{x} = h(\xi(\exp(x), \exp(y)), \exp(y)) - \sigma\exp(x) f(\exp(x), \xi(\exp(x), \exp(y))) + \delta$$
$$\text{(c6.1)}$$

$$\dot{y} = h(\xi(\exp(x), \exp(y)), \exp(y)) - n \tag{c6.2}$$

For small values of x, we have $\sigma\exp(x)f(\exp(x), \xi(\exp(x), \exp(y))) < \delta$ (the rate of net accumulation becomes negative when utilisation and profitability are sufficiently low), and it follows that

$$\dot{x} \geq h(\xi(\exp(x), \exp(y)), \exp(y)) > h(\xi(\exp(x), \exp(y)), \exp(y)) - n = \dot{y}$$
$$\text{(c6.3)}$$

for, say, $x \leq x_1$.

Let (see figure C6.1)

x_2 = the limit as $y \to -\infty$ of the value of x which solves $\dot{x} = 0$ (c6.4)

y_1 = the value of y at the intersection between the $x = x_2$ line and the $\dot{y} = 0$ locus   (c6.5)

and define the sets A, B, C and D and the variable x_3 by

$$A = \{(y, x) \,|\, y \leq y_1, \dot{x} \leq 0, \dot{y} \leq 0, (x - x_1) \geq (y - y_1)\} \tag{c6.6}$$

x_3 = the value of x at the intersection between the $\dot{x} = 0$ locus and the straight line given by $(x - x_1) = (y - y_1)$ (c6.7)

$$B = \{(y, x) \,|\, y \leq 0, x \geq x_3, \dot{x} \geq 0, \dot{y} \leq 0\} \tag{c6.8}$$

$$C = B \cap \{(y, x) \,|\, \dot{x} = 0\} \tag{c6.9}$$

C is compact so we can define $\underline{y}$,

$$\underline{y} = \min\{y \,|\, (y, x) \in C\} > -\infty \tag{c6.10}$$

Now let

$$D = B \cap \{(y, x) \,|\, y \leq \underline{y} - \delta\} \tag{c6.11}$$

$$E = B \cap \{(y, x) \,|\, \underline{y} = \underline{y} - \delta\} \tag{c6.12}$$

where $\delta > 0$. We want to establish a lower bound for the value of $\dot{x}$ in D. D, however, may not be compact, and we therefore consider first the compact set E and define

$$\epsilon = \min\{\dot{x}(y, x) \,|\, (y, x) \in E\} \tag{c6.13}$$

Since $\partial\dot{x}/\partial y < 0$ (and since $\underline{y} - \delta, x_0) \in E$ implies that there is a $y \geq \underline{y}$ such that $\dot{x}(y, x_0) = 0$) we have $\epsilon > 0$. Using again $\partial\dot{x}/\partial y < 0$ as well as the fact that $(\underline{y} - \delta, x_0) \in E$ for all (y, x_0) in D, we have $\dot{x} \geq \epsilon$ for all (y, x) in D.

Turning now to $\dot{y}$ and using $\partial\dot{y}/\partial y < 0$ and $\partial\dot{y}/\partial x > 0$ we get

$$\dot{y} \geq \dot{y}(\underline{y} - \delta, x_3) = \omega > -\infty \quad \text{for all } (y, x) \text{ in } D \tag{c6.14}$$

Finally, let

$$F = \{(y, x) \mid \epsilon(y - \underline{y} + \delta) - \omega(x - x_3) \geq 0\}$$
$$\cap \{(y, x) \mid y \leq y_1, x_3 \leq x \leq x_2, (x - x_1) \geq (y - y_1)\} \tag{c6.15}$$

It is readily seen that F is a compact and positively invariant set for the system; simply consider the velocity vector of the system along the boundary of F (as illustrated in figure C6.1).

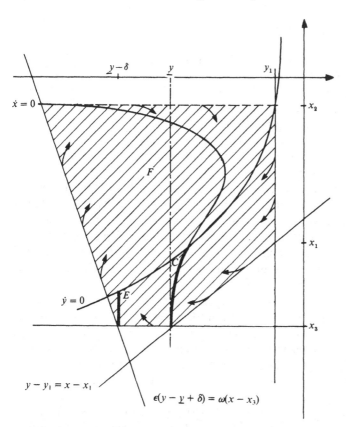

Figure C6.1: Phase diagram for the transformed system.

CHAPTER 7

Finance and money-wage neutrality

7.1 INTRODUCTION

Keynesian theory has always regarded investment as a key variable. Firms decide the level of investment, and income and saving then adapt to bring about the *ex post* identity between saving and investment. But *can* investment plans be independent of saving? Firms need finance in order to execute their investment plans, and the availability of finance – or loanable funds – has been linked to saving by many economists.

Unlike in most Keynesian models I have specified the financial side of the economy in some detail, and the need to finance investment has been introduced explicitly. Short-term finance, however, has not been an active constraint: by assumption firms could borrow as much as they wanted at the prevailing rate of interest. Alternatively, they could use the new-issue market to raise finance: new and old securities are perfect substitutes, and new issues remain a possible source of additional funds even if financial markets take a dim view of the investment project which needs to be financed.

But is the specification of the financial environment and of the financial behaviour of firms satisfactory? In pre-Keynesian economics saving was seen as a constraint on investment – investment in fact was not always distinguished as a separate category – and similar views are common today: the widespread belief, for instance, that government spending must 'crowd out' private investment is based on the assumption that somehow the amount of saving (and finance) is given.

Recently the independence of saving from investment has come under attack from within the Keynesian camp. Asimakopulos (1983) has argued that the independence of investment from saving is not as robust as Keynes stated and that 'the investment market *can* become "congested through shortage of saving" even in a closed economy' (p. 230). He concludes that 'there may be limits, related in some way to the propensity to save, to the extent to which firms are in a position to increase their rate of investment even if short-term credit is available to finance such an increase' (p. 232). This conclusion is clearly at odds with received Keynesian and Kaleckian wisdom, and Asimakopulos's paper has provoked a number of comments.[1]

The need for finance has also played a prominent part in the theories of other post-Keynesians. Wood (1975), Eichner (1976) and Harcourt and Kenyon (1976) have argued that firms need to finance part of their investment expenditure through retained earnings and that investment and pricing decisions are therefore closely related: the financing of high levels of investment (associated with high rates of expansion of output) requires a high mark-up factor, but high mark-up factors (high prices) on the other hand depress demand (and output) and the desired rate of investment. Finance constraints and demand conditions thus give rise to two separate relations linking the mark-up and the rate of investment, and the equilibrium values of both variables can be determined.

In this chapter the specification of the model is re-examined in the light of these different pre- and post-Keynesian views on the role of saving and finance.

7.2 PRE-KEYNESIAN IDEAS

The Keynesian view of investment as an independent variable has always been restricted to the short run. In long-run analysis investment ceases to be an exogenous determinant of output and/or of the distribution of income. Instead, investment is primarily induced: past changes in demand (as well as expected future changes in demand) cause changes in the desired stock of capital and hence in the rate of investment. This induced character of investment is at the centre of Harrod's argument for the instability of the warranted growth path. And induced investment implies that changes in the saving propensity will affect investment decisions. Investment thus is not independent of saving decisions in the long run.

In Keynesian/Harrodian analysis a rise in the saving propensity entails a fall in the level of demand (in the multiplier), and falling demand leads to negative accelerator effects on investment and hence to a (subsequent) decline in the actual level of saving. In contrast to this scenario, pre-Keynesian economics suggests that saving is the dominant variable which not only influences but fully determines the level of investment. Furthermore, in this view the rate of saving is determined solely by the preferences of households: firms may retain some fraction of total profits, but households will take any such retentions into account in their own saving

---

[1] See, for example, Kregel (1984–5, 1986), Richardson (1986), Davidson (1986).

decisions, and the overall rate of saving is independent of the amount of retained earnings.

With respect to short-term analysis, both the causal priority of saving and the determination of aggregate saving through household preferences would be challenged by most economists today. But, when it comes to long-run analysis, the pre-Keynesian view remains dominant. Bliss (1975) has expressed this view succinctly in his critique of the 'Cambridge model'. He argues that

in the semi-stationary state, it is households that 'call the tune' when it comes to saving, not because only households can save, but because when firms save (retain earnings for investment) the ownership rights in those firms appreciate in value along with the new investment and so increase the net worth of the households that share in the ownership of firms, and hence increase their ability to consume if they so wish.   (Bliss, 1975, p. 135)

Bliss's argument finds no support in the present model. It is not households who call the tune in steady growth, nor is the share of saving (investment) in income independent of the parameters describing firms' investment behaviour (see the comparative analysis of changes in s_p and in animal spirits in section 5.7). Why is there this difference between our results and Bliss's analysis?

In a corporate economy the wealth which appears in households' budget constraint is the market value of financial assets, and the portfolio choice is a choice between financial assets. This distinction between financial and real assets is the basic idea underlying both Kaldor's neo-Pasinetti theorem and the generalised neo-Pasinetti formulation in chapter 4, and it is because of this distinction that changes in the distribution of income or in the retention and new-issue policies of firms influence the average rate of saving. But the significance of the form of the saving function can only be assessed in the context of the full model: one also needs to look at the determination of output and investment.

The dependence of the average saving rate on distribution implies that exogenous variations in the rate of investment can be accommodated in the ultra-short run, but the outcome will then feed back and influence future output and investment decisions. Saving may be an accommodating variable in the ultra-short and short run, but this does not exclude the possibility that investment may be determined by household preferences in the long run: saving may 'call the tune' in steady growth. This is the crux of Bliss's argument, and it should be noted that the argument concerns the investment function rather than the saving function: implicitly Bliss imposes assumptions on firms' investment behaviour.

There are major differences between Bliss's general-equilibrium analysis and the theory developed here. Three points, especially, deserve comment:

the role of money and bank credit, the degree of competition in product markets, and the determination of the real-wage rate.

7.2.1 Money and demand

Consider first the question of money and credit. General-equilibrium models have little need – or room – for money, and it is therefore interesting to examine the implications of leaving out bank credit from the present theory and setting households' demand for bank deposits equal to zero. Firms' finance constraint, equation (4.13), then needs to be modified,

$$pI = s_p P + \hat{N}vN \qquad (7.1)$$

and this change is more fundamental than it may seem at first glance. In the original formulation – with an elastic supply of credit – firms could choose the values of I, s_p and $\hat{N}$ independently and let the amount of bank credit accommodate. In contrast, (7.1) implies that investment needs to be financed in full out of retained earnings and new issues, and this precludes a Kaldorian determination of prices and profits via the equilibrium condition for the product market. If firms wish to spend the amount pI on investment they must first ensure the finance of this expenditure, and the *existing* level of profits (in conjunction with the retention rate and the amount of new issues) thus becomes a constraint on investment.

The exclusion of credit from the model also affects the equilibrium condition for the product market: the finance constraint implies that *ex ante* saving and investment will always be equal at the existing distribution of income. To see this, simply observe that when $\beta = 0$, the saving function (4.17) can be written

$$pS = s_p P + \hat{N}vN \qquad (7.2)$$

The values of I, s_p and $\hat{N}$ are chosen such that (7.1) holds, and it follows that $S = I$ at the existing levels of P and vN. Firms deciding to raise the level of investment will adopt financial policies which simultaneously force an identical increase in saving at the existing level of output and the existing distribution of income. Changes in investment thus have no impact on distribution and no multiplier effects on output: the finance constraint and the equilibrium condition for the securities market ensure equilibrium in the product market.[2]

---

[2] When there is a flexible supply of bank credit, firms' finance constraint and the equilibrium condition for the securities market imply that

$$pI = s_p P + vN\hat{N} + M(\hat{M} - i)$$

$$pS = s_p P + vN\hat{N} + M(\hat{Y} - r)$$

Product-market equilibrium thus requires that $\hat{M} - i = \hat{Y} - r$ and substituting this condition into the finance constraint it is readily seen that if I, s_p, $\hat{N}$, $\hat{Y}$ and r are independently given then this equation determines the equilibrium level of profits. Firms control I, s_p and

This specification of the pre-Keynesian S–I nexus differs from standard neoclassical formulations. In this specification, firms are free to choose any rate of investment, and in their provisions to finance the chosen investment rate – new issues and retained earnings – they automatically force households into adopting saving plans with $S = I$.[3] The saving rate is flexible and thus does not define a single warranted growth rate. In contrast, most simple neoclassical models assume that the saving rate is exogenously given and that investment adjusts to saving. The adjustment mechanism, however, is seldom specified, and even in the absence of money and bank credit it is not clear how households could be in a position to prevent firms from issuing new securities and/or retaining profits to finance the rate of investment which they wish to carry out.

7.2.2 Real wages and employment

Once the Keynesian equilibrium condition for the product market has dropped out, effective-demand problems cannot block the way to full employment. But before considering the determination of employment we may note that capital will be fully utilised in the pre-Keynesian system: if there is perfect competition and prices are parametrically given then no firm will wish to produce at utilisation rates u with $0 < u < 1$. Furthermore, the replacement value of physical capital assets will be equal to the market valuation of firms: the rate of discount used by firms in calculating the present value of future profits is determined by the terms on which they can raise finance, and the market valuation reflects the terms on which households are willing to provide funds for investment. A market valuation in excess of replacement cost is a sign of positive pure profits, and individual firms could gain even higher profits by equiproportionate increases in inputs and outputs. Both the utilisation rate and Tobin's q must thus be equal to unity in steady growth, $u* = q* = 1$.

Setting $\beta = 0$ (since by assumption there is no bank credit in this economy) and substituting $q = u = 1$ into (5.12) yields the equilibrium value of π

$\dot{N}$, households decide $\dot{M}$, and prices and profitability accommodate. Firms may have planned to finance a large proportion of investment through bank credit, but they cannot force households to increase bank balances in the same way that they can force households to buy newly issued securities: households always have the option to spend money on consumption (in an attempt to raise real consumption), thereby raising prices and profits and reducing the need for bank credit.

[3] In this respect, the pre-Keynesian system resembles the monetarist system, which assumes that the money supply is exogenous (see section 7.6).

$$\pi* = \frac{1 + \alpha\delta}{\alpha\sigma} \tag{7.3}$$

Note in particular that $\pi*$ is independent of firms' decision variables: it is determined entirely by households (α) and technology (δ, σ). Equation (7.3), which replaces (5.15), represents the long-run investment (cum saving) function for this pre-Keynesian system: if $\pi > \pi*$ then $q > 1$ and accumulation accelerates as firms exploit the possibilities for pure profit.

But how is π determined in the short run? Pre-Keynesian theory assumes that real wages adjust to clear the labour market, and, with sufficient substitutability between labour and capital, full employment may be possible even if the labour supply is inelastic. Here, by assumption, the production function has fixed coefficients, and an elastic labour supply is needed to ensure equilibrium in the labour market. The important point, however, is simple and does not even require instantaneous labour-market clearing: the pre-Keynesian system assumes that low rates of employment are associated with low real-wage rates, and the profit share is thus inversely related to the rate of employment,

$$\pi = \pi(e); \quad \pi' < 0 \tag{7.4}$$

Equations (7.3) and (7.4) determine the steady-growth value of the rate of employment, and it is readily seen that the equilibrium is stable: employment is proportional to the capital stock ($u = 1$), and, if accumulation responds to deviations of π from $\pi*$, we get a simple first-order differential equation:

$$\hat{e} = \frac{I}{K} - \delta - n = \tilde{f}(\pi - \pi*) = f(e* - e); \quad \tilde{f}' > 0, \ f' > 0 \tag{7.5}$$

Household preferences and technology determine the real-wage rate and the distribution of income in the short run (equation (7.4)), and, indirectly, households thus control the growth of output. The rate of growth in conjunction with the production function (and the full utilisation of capital) in turn determine the share of saving in income, and, ultimately, saving and investment as well as the distribution of income are fully determined by household preferences and technology.

This conclusion is independent of whether the technical output–capital ratio is exogenously given or determined as a result of the choice of technique described in (5.25). In the latter case, it is readily seen that $\sigma*$ is independent of firms' financial decisions: the cost of capital, $\iota + \delta$ in (5.25), becomes simply $\pi_0 \sigma_0$, and neither the real-wage rate nor the cost of capital is influenced by the manner in which firms finance their investment expenditure. In this pre-Keynesian system, $\sigma* u*$ is thus independent of financial variables even if σ is a choice variable.

7.2.3 Introducing credit money

Problems arise, however, if bank credit or imperfect competition are introduced into the pre-Keynesian system. In either case the determination of real wages in the labour market may be blocked and the direct link between household preferences and investment is then severed. Consider first the implications of introducing credit into an otherwise unchanged pre-Keynesian system with atomistic competition and instantaneous and costless variations in output and employment.

The steady-growth equilibrium in this system must still satisfy $u* = q* = 1$, and the steady-growth value of π is determined by (7.3), but the short-term determination of w/p and π can no longer take place in the labour market. In a system without bank credit, firms' finance constraint ensures the equality between saving and investment quite independently of distribution, and changes in money-wage rates therefore do not necessarily cause changes in prices – there is no connection between aggregate demand and income distribution. With credit finance and independently determined values of I, s_p and $\hat{N}$, the product market is no longer in neutral equilibrium: the equilibrium condition for the product market determines a unique value of π, and, if equilibrium is to be maintained in the product market, then changes in money-wage rates require price changes which leave real wages unchanged.

The money supply is by assumption accommodating: banks set the rate of interest and then supply the credit demanded by the non-banking sector, and the money market can be in equilibrium at any rate of interest. But the existence of bank crtedit implies that equation (5.2) must be reintroduced as the equilibrium condition for the product market (the equation can be simplified in the present context if we retain the assumption that $\beta = 0$). Firms' finance constraint no longer ensures that this condition is satisfied for any given value of π. Furthermore, in steady growth the equilibrium condition can be rewritten as in (5.16), and this equation (with $\beta = 0$ and $u = 1$) together with (7.4) determine a unique warranted rate, Bank credit and the associated introduction of an independent saving function thus imply that Harrod's first problem reappears: the warranted and natural growth rates need not coincide (and the magnitude of the warranted rate depends on firms' financial decisions).

7.2.4 Imperfect competition

Imperfect competition transforms the condition that average q equals one into the condition that marginal q equals one, but otherwise this change does not have dramatic qualitative implications if there is already bank credit in the system. With atomistic competition the steady-growth path was characterised by $u* = q* = 1$. In contrast, the demand function (4.5) implies that $\pi* = \gamma$ and that $g_w = g(\gamma)$, $u* = u(\gamma, g_w)$ and $q* = q(\gamma, u*)$ (from (5.19), (5.15) and (5.12)). Once again we get a unique warranted growth rate, g_w, which depends on the financial parameters and where $g_w \gtrless n$.

Imperfect competition on its own, however, may be incompatible with the pre-Keynesian adjustment mechanism even if there is no money in the system: equation (7.4) clearly cannot operate if there is a constant conjectured elasticity of demand and firms apply a constant mark-up such that $\pi = \gamma$.

7.2.5 Class conflict and slow adjustment

The theory presented in earlier chapters predicts that under certain conditions the warranted growth rate adapts to the natural rate, and the warranted rate thus cannot depend on the financial parameters. The properties of the steady-growth path, however, are still influenced by firms' financial decisions (as well as by the saving and portfolio choices of households): as shown in section 5.7 an increase in s_p will reduce profitability and employment but raise the rate of utilisation in steady growth.[4] This conclusion, furthermore, does not depend on a non-neoclassical specification of household behaviour. The demand for money follows the simple quantity theory, and the valuation of securities is determined by the net real rate of profit. The specification of the demand for financial assets has deliberately – but perhaps unrealistically – left out any direct influence of firms' retention and new-issue policy on the financial valuation. In spite of these assumptions, the financial behaviour of firms is important in the short term as well as in long-term steady growth.

Equation (5.16), the equilibrium condition for the product market, shows why there must be this influence. The equation says that

$$\frac{S}{Y} = - \alpha \hat{N} \left(\beta r + \frac{\delta}{\sigma u} \right) + \beta(g_w - r) + (s_p + \alpha \hat{N}) \pi$$

$$= \frac{g_w + \delta}{\sigma u} = \frac{I}{Y} \tag{7.6}$$

Assume that changes in s_p have no effect on the steady-growth path, i.e. that $(u*, \pi*, \sigma*, q*, g_w)$ are invariant with respect to changes in s_p. From (7.6) it follows that a rise in s_p must then cause a rise in the real rate of

---

[4] A rise in $\hat{N}$ has the same qualitative effects.

interest, r. The rate of interest, however, influences the value of $q*$ and thus indirectly also ($u*$, $\pi*$, $\sigma*$, g_w). The assumption that changes in s_p have no effects on the steady-growth path has led to a contradiction. As soon as money and bank credit are included in the model, firms' financial decisions will play a role in the determination of the steady-growth solution.

In the pre-Keynesian system, profit maximisation ensured that Tobin's q would be equal to one. How is it possible for the steady-growth value of Tobin's q to vary freely in response to changes in financial parameters in the present model? Have we not overlooked restrictions on q? The answer is no: adjustment costs and the output-expansion function imply that the steady-growth values of π and q are not pinned down by the degree of competition in the product market. In fact, it is this flexibility in the share of profits and the financial valuation which allows long-run growth at the natural rate. The output-expansion function provides the system with an extra degree of freedom: the steady-growth share of profits in income is no longer uniquely determined by the perceived elasticity of demand. The share of profits in steady growth may deviate from the level predicted by standard short-run theory because changes in employment and production are associated with adjustment costs. These adjustment costs depend on the social relations of production, and the sign and magnitude of the deviation therefore depend upon the rate of employment.

The steady-growth condition $g_w = n$ implies that financial decisions cannot influence the warranted growth rate (as in the case with costless adjustment), but firms' financial behaviour plays a part in the determination of $\pi*$, and $\pi*$ in turn is linked with $q*$, $u*$ and $e*$, and – if there is a choice of technique – with $\sigma*$. The steady-growth path thus depends on the financial policy adopted by firms.

7.3 THE ASIMAKOPULOS CRITIQUE

The present theory is firmly Keynesian in its specification of independent investment and saving functions. It also pays careful attention to financial aspects and thus appears to provide a suitable framework for an examination of Asimakopulos's (1983) critique of the treatment of finance in traditional Keynesian models. Asimakopulos has argued that in some circumstances increased saving may provide a stimulus to investment and growth. From a Keynesian perspective this hypothesis looks suspect, but properly understood it is in fact correct: the present theory shows how a rise in (some) saving parameters may stimulate investment and increase the rate of employment.

The key to understanding this result lies in the distinction between saving and valuation effects. The theory shares with all Keynesian models the basic principle that a rise in the average propensity to save will *reduce* the short-run equilibrium level of production (see equation (5.6)). The difference arises in the determination of the average propensity to save, s. In simple flow models, s itself is typically taken as a parameter or s is defined as a weighted average of the propensities to save out of profits and wage income. In the present theory on the other hand, s is determined by the interaction of different parameters describing the behaviour of both households and firms,[5] and some of the parameters which influence the saving propensity will also affect the financial valuation of firms (Tobin's q). Changes in these parameters will thus have both a saving and a valuation effect. The saving effect is deflationary, but the valuation effect will stimulate investment and if the valuation effect dominates then an increase in the saving-cum-valuation parameter will induce higher levels of investment. The interesting point is the direction of the combined effect. In traditional Keynesian/Harrodian theory, the lagged effect of increased saving propensities is to reduce investment, as effective-demand problems lead to excess capacity. The influence of valuation effects poses the possibility that the direction of the lagged effect may be reversed.

Tobin's q is not (directly) affected by changes in firms' financial parameters, s_p and $\hat{N}$. Increases in either of these parameters are therefore unambiguously deflationary. The ultra-short-run effect is to reduce profitability, π, and hence the growth rate of output and employment (equations (5.2) and (5.3)),[6] and, as shown in section 5.7, the long-term effect of a rise in s_p is to reduce the rate of employment in steady growth.

The parameters α and β which describe household behaviour are different: these parameters affect the financial valuation of firms directly. Tobin's q is positively related to both α and β and a change in either of these parameters therefore gives rise to valuation effects (equation (5.12)). The simplest case arises when $\hat{N} = 0$. In this case, a change in α has *only* valuation effects; household saving will not be affected. To see this, simply set $\hat{N} = 0$ in (4.19) and note that the average propensity to save is then completely independent of α. Although a rise in α represents an increase in

---

[5] This implies that the multiplier becomes an endogenous variable. If, for instance, firms were to fix the rate of new issues so as to secure the immediate funding of all investment over and above some normal level (as in the pre-Keynesian system), then the multiplier would vanish: saving would accommodate to investment without any changes in output or distribution. New issues (and, in an obvious extension of the model, bond issues by the public sector) thus have a 'crowding-out' effect: they raise the saving propensity and, because of this, crowd out consumption and income.

[6] The partial derivative $\partial \pi / \partial \hat{N}$ is negative if $\pi - \beta r - \delta/(\sigma u) > 0$. The latter expression represents the share of profits net of depreciation and real-interest payments and is proportional to the valuation of securities. As long as the price of securities is positive, this condition will thus be satisfied.

the desire to hold securities, it cannot affect net saving out of current income unless firms issue new securities. In the absence of new issues, the price of securities will rise, and capital gains increase households' financial wealth without any saving out of current income. The rise in the price of securities comes to an end when the value of the existing volume of securities has reached the new desired level relative to current income flows.

An increase in valuation has no immediate effects on short-run production. From (5.2) it is readily seen that a rise in α leaves the share of profits unchanged when $\hat{N} = 0$, and the growth rate of production therefore remains unaffected. But the increase in the valuation of firms reduces the cost of capital, and this reduction stimulates investment. The positive effects of an increase in α show up when we move beyond the short term and allow the level of investment to vary endogenously. These positive long-term effects have already been analysed: in section 5.7 it has been shown that a rise in α will improve profitability and increase the rate of employment along the steady-growth path when $\hat{N} = 0$.

Outside the simple case of changes in α when $\hat{N} = 0$, changes in α and β will have both saving and valuation effects. Changes in valuation have no immediate impact on the profit share and on the rate of growth of employment and production, and the impact effect of a rise in α or β is thus non-positive. But, if the valuation effect is strong, the medium- and long-term stimulus to investment may be sufficient to offset the negative saving effect, and the steady-growth value of the rate of employment may increase.

These results may be summarised as follows. An increase in the average saving propensity does not stimulate investment and output. On the contrary, the orthodox Keynesian view is vindicated: increased saving propensities depress output and thus future investment. But, in a model with stocks of financial assets, a change in 'saving parameters' will affect both the saving propensity and the valuation of existing assets. The valuation effect may in some cases dominate, and increased 'saving parameters' may thus stimulate investment and growth. In a model with financial stocks, the desire to save will indeed influence the cost of finance as claimed by Asimakopulos but, if one wants to stimulate the economy by raising the desire to save, it is important to choose the right target parameters. The best candidate is households' demand for securities, α; an increase in the retention rate, on the other hand, is unambiguously deflationary. One should also make sure that conditions are such that the valuation effect is likely to dominate the saving effect, i.e. one should examine whether the rate of new issues, $\hat{N}$, is small enough for the valuation effect to dominate the saving effect. Finally, one should not expect the expansionary effects to show up immediately: the impact effect will be negative if $\hat{N} > 0$ even in cases where the long-term effect is expansionary. As a general policy prescription, the suggestion that greater incentives to save may be used to stimulate the economy thus looks more than a little dubious.

7.4 ALTERNATIVE FINANCIAL BEHAVIOUR – A MODIFIED EICHNER–WOOD HYPOTHESIS

We have seen how firms' financial policy may become an important determinant of real outcomes in both the short and the long run. But so far the financial behaviour of firms has been cast in terms of exogenous parameters s_p and $\hat{N}$, and this may not be a reasonable approach: it has been argued by Wood (1975)[7] that firms fix target values for the proportions of finance which are to be obtained from the three different sources. This alternative assumption implies that an increase in investment becomes directly associated with an increase in retained profits as well as in the amount of new issues: firms planning to raise investment will simultaneously plan to increase the amounts of new issues and retained profits.

Wood views the profit retention rate (s_p) as an exogenous parameter and uses the financial condition to establish a link between profitability and capital accumulation (see section 3.7). This pricing mechanism differs radically from the one adopted here, and, in order to make Wood's mechanism compatible with the present framework, one would need to introduce fundamental changes in the assumptions of the model: Wood, for instance, assumes that the growth rate of demand, rather than the level of demand, is dependent upon the price of output. It is possible, however, to examine the implications of a quasi-Wood regime without major changes in the model.

There appears to be no reason to believe that retention rates cannot change over time. Institutional rigidities and established conventions of financial prudence may cause significant inertia, but conventions do change. In an analysis of long-run steady growth it therefore seems unduly restrictive to assume that the retention rate is exogenously given, and, if the retention rate is allowed to vary, then one may retain the pricing and distribution mechanism analysed in the previous chapters and incorporate – at the same time – Wood's requirement that finance be raised in fixed proportions.

Let ν_1 and ν_2 be the desired proportions of finance coming from retained earnings and new issues respectively, i.e. let

[7] See also Eichner (1976) and Harcourt and Kenyon (1976).

$$\nu_1 = s_p \frac{P}{pI}$$

$$\nu_2 = \frac{\nu N \hat{N}}{pI} \tag{7.7}$$

and hence

$$1 - \nu_1 - \nu_2 = \frac{M(\hat{M} - i)}{pI} \tag{7.8}$$

Under this alternative assumption, firms wish to maintain constant values of ν_1 and ν_2, but the parameters s_p and $\hat{N}$ remain the proximate decision variables. There is a feedback from realised values of ν_1 and ν_2 to s_p and $\hat{N}$, but the feedback will not be instantaneous and the parameter s_p, in particular, is likely to be somewhat sticky. For short-run problems, it will thus be reasonable to take s_p and $\hat{N}$ as given. In steady growth, however, s_p, $\hat{N}$ and $\hat{M}$ must satisfy equations (7.7) and (7.8).

Substituting (7.7) and (7.8) into (5.16) we get

$$(1 - \nu_1 - \nu_2) \frac{g_w + \delta}{\sigma u} = \beta(g_w - r) \tag{7.9}$$

In steady growth we have $g_w = n$, and equation (7.9) determines $u*$ as a function of parameters which by assumption are exogenously given. There are two points to note. First, since $u*$ must be positive, we require that sign $(1 - \nu_1 - \nu_2) = \text{sign}(g_w - r)$. The reason for this consistency condition is straightforward. If, say, $(1 - \nu_1 - \nu_2)$ is positive then firms wish to finance part of their investment expenditure through new bank loans (i.e. they want to expand their total bank debt at a rate which exceeds the rate of interest), but the stock of bank loans to firms is equal to the stock of households' bank deposits, and firms, therefore, can only succeed in this policy if households are prepared to accept money balances which grow faster than the rate of interest. If this condition fails to be satisfied, firms may still take out loans from banks, but, since households do not want to increase their money holdings sufficiently fast, they will spend the money on goods and securities. Increased demand for goods and securities raises profitability (hence the amount of retained earnings) and the price of securities (hence the value of new issues), and the money thus returns to firms: their bank balances are improved and the intention that bank loans should finance a given proportion of the expenditure has been frustrated.

The second point concerns the causal interpretation of equation (7.9). The equation corresponds to (5.16) in the original system and (5.16) was derived from the equilibrium condition for the product market, $I = S$. In chapter 5 this condition has been used to determine the distribution of income as a function of the rate of utilisation. In (7.9), however, the distribution of income does not even appear. The change in the mathematical structure of the steady-growth equations should, however, be distinguished from the causal structure of the model, which has not changed: at any moment – in any ultra-short-run period – the distribution of income is determined by a set of predetermined and exogenous variables and parameters. The change compared with the original system is that the parameters s_p and $\hat{N}$ are no longer exogenously given and time-invariant. Instead, they are merely predetermined: like the rate of output and investment they change over time, and it is because of these endogenous changes that the profit share drops out of the steady-growth condition for equilibrium in the product market.

One might ask, however, whether adjustments of s_p and $\hat{N}$ are likely to establish the desired proportionalities between retained earnings and the value of new issues on the one hand and total investment expenditure on the other. In the present model the answer is no. If, say, retained earnings and new issues fail to provide the desired amount of finance then one would expect firms to raise the retention rate and expand the new-issue programme. The effect of this response is to reduce the share of profit (section 5.7). According to equation (7.9), however, an increase in $(\nu_1 + \nu_2)$ requires a decline in $u*$, and a decline in $u*$ is associated with a rise in $\pi*$ (equation (5.15)). The increase in s_p and $\hat{N}$ will thus aggravate the initial imbalance. This instability result is sensitive to the precise specification of the model. It would not arise, for instance, if it had been assumed that households' demand for money were proportional to total *wage* income, $(1 - \pi)pY$, rather than to aggregate income, pY.[8] The instability result does suggest, however, that one needs to be careful when the behaviour of an agent (in this case the firm) is specified in terms of parameters which are not fully controlled by the agent.[9]

7.5 MONEY-WAGE NEUTRALITY RECONSIDERED

In the conclusion to chapter 5 it was pointed out that the model has neutrality properties which superficially resemble those of monetarist models: real outcomes are invariant with respect to proportional changes in prices, wages and the money stock. The causal structure of the present system, however, differs from that of monetarist theories and the model

---

[8] See Skott (1988a).

[9] Disregarding these problems, the comparative results for the quasi-Wood system are qualitatively similar to those for the original system whenever the adjustment process is stable. To see this, simply note that increases in s_p and $\hat{N}$ are associated with increases in ν_1 and ν_2 respectively, when the adjustment process is stable.

exhibits 'money-wage neutrality' rather than 'neutrality of money'. Strict neutrality simplifies the system, but it does depend on restrictive assumptions, and it is time now to examine these assumptions.

Keynes dealt with the implications of changes in money-wage rates in chapter 19 of the *General Theory*. Having described in the previous eighteen chapters how the principle of effective demand determines the equilibrium level of output and employment when money wages (but not prices) are given, he had, finally, to consider whether changes in money wages could shift the aggregate demand and supply schedules so as to ensure full employment. If changes in money wages fail to achieve such a shift then the economic system would possess no endogenous forces to eliminate involuntary unemployment: the labour market is the only market with excess supply, and the money-wage rate is the only 'price' which is under any pressure to change.

Keynes points to a number of different effects of changes in money wages, and Leijonhufvud has subsequently expanded the list and provided a catalogue of the sundry effects which have been identified in the literature (Leijonhufvud, 1968, pp. 319–33).[10] Some of the effects only apply to open economies, and many of the closed-economy effects, by general consent, either are insignificant or have a direction which cannot be unambiguously determined. A fall in money wages may, for instance, 'produce an optimistic tone in the minds of entrepreneurs' but 'if workers make the same mistake as their employers about the effects of a general reduction, labour troubles may offset this favourable factor' and against the expansionary influence one must also count the danger that 'the reduction in wages disturbs political confidence by causing popular discontent' (Keynes, 1936, p. 264).

Disregarding the confusing array of possible effects, the most important economic arguments against money-wage neutrality (in a closed economy) focus on the Keynes effect and the Pigou effect.[11] The Keynes effect is the effect of falling interest rates on aggregate demand, where the fall in interest rates is itself caused by falling money wages. The Pigou effect describes the effect on real consumption of an increase in real balances where, again, the rise in real balances is brought about by a fall in money wages.

Neither Keynes nor Pigou effects have appeared in the present model. The Pigou effect is absent because there are no outside assets whose value

[10] Famous among these effects are the Keynes effect, the Pigou effect and the real-balance effect. Less well known, perhaps, are the Tobin effect and the Lerner effect.
[11] The argument that unanticipated changes in prices cause a redistribution of wealth between creditors and debtors (which could cause bankruptcies) is also powerful. It reinforces the Keynesian argument against money-wage changes as a means for securing full employment.

is fixed in nominal terms: the value of securities is tied to nominal income, and it has been assumed that the real rate of interest on bank deposits (money) is constant. The latter assumption implies that changes in nominal prices are completely neutralised in their effect on the real value of total bank deposits, and constant real rates of interest also cut out the Keynes effect.

The obvious way to remove money-wage neutrality is to abandon the assumption of fixed interest rates, and a change in this direction is all the more appealing since the ability of the banking system to control real rates of interest has been questioned. Indeed, the alleged impossibility of controlling real interest rates has been a monetarist argument in favour of replacing interest-rate targets with targets for the money supply (e.g. Friedman, 1968).

What then happens if the real rate of interest is no longer constant? The answer clearly depends on what alternative assumptions one introduces, but two simple cases deserve consideration. The first is the monetarist case where the rate of growth of the money stock is kept constant, and the second arises if nominal interest rates are constant and exogenous. The distinction between the different cases is of limited importance if one is concerned only with steady growth. In steady growth both the growth rate of the money stock and the real and nominal interest rates will be constant no matter which variable is fixed exogenously. The short-run dynamics of the system – and hence the stability properties of the steady-growth path – may, however, be different in the three cases.

7.6 EXOGENOUS MONEY

Monetarists view the stock of money as exogenous (or directly under the control of the central bank). As a literal description of monetary institutions this view is clearly anachronistic. The days when the supply of money was directly determined by the amount of gold in the economy are long gone, and the evolution of the financial system makes the simple exogeneity assumption less appropriate every day. The endogenous character of the money supply – an infinitely elastic supply of bank loans at the prevailing rate of interest – does not, however, *per se* rule out the possibility of controlling the growth of total bank loans (and total bank deposits).

So far it has been assumed that the supply of money (of bank loans to firms) is perfectly elastic at a given time-invariant real rate of interest. This assumption is now reversed and, instead, it is assumed that banks vary the interest rate on loans to whatever extent is required in order to induce firms to expand their total bank loans at some given growth rate, m.

Individual firms still have unused overdraft facilities with banks, but the interest rate on these overdrafts is adjusted so as to make firms want to increase the balance on these accounts at the given rate. Since firms hold no money themselves, this implies that the money stock of the household sector must grow at the rate m.

The implications of this change are far more dramatic than those associated with the change in the financial behaviour of firms analysed in section 7.5. Using the demand for money, equation (4.16), we have

$$m = \hat{Y} + \hat{p} = h(\pi, e) + \frac{\pi}{1 - \pi} \hat{\pi} + \hat{w} \tag{7.10}$$

Since m, $h(\pi, e)$ and $\hat{w}$ are all finite, equation (7.10) implies that $\hat{\pi}$ is also finite. Consequently, there can be no discrete jumps in the distribution of income: at any moment the share of profits in income is predetermined. Since the level of demand is reflected in the distribution of income, it follows that changes in the rate of investment – if such changes occur – can have no effects on aggregate demand in the monetarist system.

The dynamics of the monetarist system are quite simple. If wage inflation is determined by a simple Phillips curve, $\hat{w} = \theta(e)$, then equation (7.10) can be rewritten as

$$\hat{\pi} = (1 - \pi)[m - h(\pi, e) - \theta(e)] \tag{7.11}$$

and the rate of change of employment is given by

$$\dot{e} = e[h(\pi, e) - n]; \quad h_\pi > 0, \ h_e < 0 \tag{7.12}$$

The steady-growth solution is determined by substituting $h(\pi, e) = n$ into (7.11) and solving for $e*$. Given $e*$, (7.12) can then be solved for $\pi*$. Note that, in contrast to chapter 5, the steady-growth path now depends on the Phillips curve: with an exogenous growth rate of the nominal stock of money, the system has, not surprisingly, lost its money-wage neutrality. The real rate of growth is given by the growth rate of the labour force, and the long-run rate of inflation is also independent of the shape and position of the Phillips curve: it is equal to the difference between the growth in the money supply and the real rate of growth. A shift in the Phillips curve will, however, affect the rate of employment as well as the share of profits along the steady-growth path.[12]

[12] If a target real wage is introduced into the Phillips curve then the rate of wage inflation will be accelerating when actual real wages deviate from the target level. Actual wages must therefore be equal to target wages in steady growth:

$$\left(\frac{w}{p}\right)^{\cdot} = \chi(e), \quad \chi' > 0$$

where the target wage depends on the rate of employment as a proxy for the strength of workers. Since w/p is inversely related to the share of profits in income, equation (*) and the output-expansion function will determine the equilibrium values of $\pi*$ and $e*$

The militancy of workers now influences the outcome directly via money-wage-bargaining as well as through the output-expansion function. The reserve army of labour is a restraint on militancy and an upward shift in the Phillips curve gives rise to increased unemployment in steady growth: the reserve army needs to be expanded in order to maintain the given rate of wage inflation. The change in employment in turn affects profitability along the steady-growth path: if the position and shape of the output-expansion function is unchanged then the reduction in employment leads to a decline in the profit share. Assuming more realistically that the increase in militancy affects both the Phillips curve and the output-expansion function, the effect on employment of an increase in militancy remains unambiguous, but the net effect on profitability becomes indeterminate.

In order to examine the dynamics we derive the Jacobian for the system,

$$J(\pi, e) = \left\{ \begin{array}{ll} -(m - h - \theta) - (1 - \pi)h_\pi & -(1 - \pi)(h_e + \theta') \\ eh_\pi & h(\pi, e) - n + eh_e \end{array} \right\} \tag{7.13}$$

and hence

$$\text{Det} = (h + \theta - m)(h - n + eh_e) - (1 - \pi)h_\pi(h - n) + (1 - \pi)eh_\pi\theta'$$

$$\text{Tr} = -(1 - \pi)h_\pi + eh_e - (m + n) + 2h(\pi, e) + \theta(e)$$

At the steady-growth equilibrium we have $(h + \theta - m) = (h - n) = 0$ and hence $\text{Det} = (1 - \pi)eh_\pi\theta' > 0$ and $\text{Tr} = -(1 - \pi)h_\pi + eh_e < 0$. The steady-growth path is thus locally asymptotically stable. In fact, the system is globally stable. If $x = \log(1 - \pi)$ and $y = \log(e)$ then (7.11) and (7.12) can be written

$$\dot{x} = h(1 - \exp(x), \exp(y)) + \theta(\exp(y)) - m \tag{7.14}$$

$$\dot{y} = h(1 - \exp(x), \exp(y)) - n \tag{7.15}$$

The Jacobian for (7.14) and (7.15) is given by

$$J(x, y) = \left\{ \begin{array}{ll} -\exp(x)h_\pi & \exp(y)(h_e + \theta') \\ -\exp(x)h_\pi & \exp(y)h_e \end{array} \right\} \tag{7.16}$$

and

$$\text{Det} = \exp(x)\exp(y)h_\pi\theta' > 0$$

$$\text{Tr} = -\exp(x)h_\pi + \exp(y)h_e < 0$$

Since the product of the diagonal elements $(-\exp(x)h_\pi\exp(y)h_e)$ is strictly positive, the conditions of Olech's theorem (Olech, 1963) are satisfied and the system is globally asymptotically stable.

Before jumping to monetarist conclusions, it should be noted that, even if the banking system follows an active interventionist policy aimed at stabilising the growth of nominal income, the success of this policy in generating stable growth depends on strong assumptions. If one introduces a simple modification and lets the parameter β vary with the rate of interest, then fluctuations in the rate of interest will entail fluctuations in the growth of nominal income when m is constant. Furthermore, it is well known that, if $\beta = \beta(i)$, instability may result unless some generalised form of the Cagan condition is satisfied (Cagan, 1956; Peel and Metcalfe, 1979; Groth, 1988). 'Goodhart's law' also complicates matters. Outside simple models, there is a range of moneys and near-moneys, and the possibilities of substitution between existing assets and of financial innovation combine to make monetary control very tricky: the particular money stock which is being controlled may cease to bear any relation to nominal output as agents switch to assets outside the chosen definition of 'money'. The simple quantity-theory specification may thus be particularly misleading in the case where banks actively aim to control the growth of the money stock.

Finally, it was assumed that banks could and would adjust interest rates to whatever extent needed in order to induce firms to increase their loans at the given rate. Traditionally, high interest rates have been recommended to curb excessive growth of the money stock and, conversely, if the growth rate of the money stock threatens to fall below the chosen rate then low interest rates are used to stimulate the demand for money. Recent experience in a number of countries, however, suggests that extremely volatile interest rates may be required in order to generate stable growth in the money stock, and a high degree of volatility in interest rates may endanger the stability of the financial system (see Kaldor, 1982, and other exponents of the 'endogenous money view'). Let us therefore look more closely at the mechanism whereby variations in interest rates bring about the control of the money stock.

A rise in interest rates has direct effects on both saving and investment. The effect on saving works through two channels: a rise in the real rate of interest (i) reduces the price of securities and hence the value of new issues, and (ii) raises households' interest income and reduces saving out of non-interest income. Both of these saving effects work in the same direction: they imply a direct relation between consumption and the rate of interest. Note that the second of the two effects is a real-balance effect: the rise in interest rates implies that real balances will expand unless there is an increase in consumption and a fall in saving out of current non-interest income (see Arestis and Hadjimatheou, 1982, for empirical work which includes this kind of real-balance effect).[13]

---

[13] An increase in the rate of interest (given the rate of inflation) is equivalent in its effects on saving and consumption to a decline in the rate of inflation (given the nominal rate of interest). If households do not earn interest on their money holdings (or if the rate of

Investment may be affected by changes in interest rates because of the effect on the cost of finance: a rise in the rate of interest on bank loans leads to a decline in Tobin's *q*. This effect is closely related to the Keynes effect. The only difference is that in this case the change in the rate of interest is directly under the control of the monetary authorities and not the indirect result of a change in the level of money wages. The direction of the effect is unambiguous – a rise in interest rates depresses investment – but the strength of the effect and the speed with which it comes into operation have been the subject of considerable debate (see Desai and Weber, 1987). The saving and investment effects are contradictory in their influence on aggregate demand – a rise in interest rates stimulates consumption and depresses investment – and, by assumption, the money stock is proportional to aggregate income. It is therefore not surprising that large fluctuations in interest rates may be needed in order to control the growth in the stock of money and it should be noted, furthermore, that successful control of the growth in the money stock depends on the relative strength of the saving and investment effects. If the Keynes effect dominates the real-balance effects then interest rates should be raised in order to reduce the growth in the money stock (and nominal incomes), but if the real-balance effect is dominant then reductions in interest rates are required. Monetarist policies have prescribed a rise in interest rates in order to lower the growth rate of the money stock and have thus been based on the implicit assumption that the Keynes effect on investment exceeds the real-balance effect on saving: since the direct effects on saving are adverse, the policy only works if it succeeds in controlling the rate of investment.

This conclusion needs to be modified if one allows for induced changes in financial behaviour. It is not, however, obvious that all such changes facilitate monetarist control. The financial behaviour of households is described by the parameters α and β representing the ratio of the stock of securities to profit income and the ratio of the money stock to total current income. An increase in interest rates raises households' return on money holdings and causes a capital loss on securities. One might therefore expect rising interest rates to be associated with a tendency for α to fall and β to rise. The net effect on household saving of these changes is uncertain: a rising value of β will raise the saving propensities whereas a fall in α reduces saving as long as $\hat{N} > 0$.

Changes in interest rates may also affect firms' financial decisions. A rising interest rate makes bank loans more expensive, but it also reduces

interest on money holdings is invariant with respect to changes in the loan rate) then variations in the loan rate have no real-balance effects, and if the rate of new issues is zero (negative) then the overall effect on household saving vanishes (is reversed).

the stock-market valuation of firms. The latter effect is hardly conducive to higher levels of new issues, and it also militates against a higher retention rate and reductions in dividends. The net effect of a rise in interest rates on the retention rate and the amount of new issues, s_p and $\hat{N}$, is therefore unclear.

Leaving aside these doubts, induced changes in the financial parameters can potentially obviate the need to control the rate of investment: induced financial changes may reconcile variations in investment with a constant level of aggregate demand. Consider, for instance, the case where firms' financial behaviour is affected by changes in interest rates. Substituting $\hat{M} = m$ into firms' financial constraint, (4.13), we get

$$pI = s_p \pi p Y + eN\hat{N} + M(m - i) \tag{7.17}$$

or, using (4.15) and (4.16),

$$I + \beta i(Y + \alpha \hat{N}) = Y[s_p \pi + \alpha \hat{N}(\pi - \delta u \sigma + \beta \hat{p}) + \beta m] \tag{7.18}$$

The interpretation of (7.18) is as follows. If the rate of investment is increased then banks raise interest rates in order to prevent an expansion of nominal incomes. The left-hand side of (7.18) is thus increased, and the equality is maintained through changes in financial parameters: current production is predetermined but banks set i at a level which induces firms to choose values of s_p and $\hat{N}$ which satisfy (7.18) at the given share of profits in income (see equation (7.10)). In other words, I, s_p and $\hat{N}$ are no longer chosen independently, and we get a model which closely resembles the pre-Keynesian system described above. While in the fixed-interest case (chapters 4–6) firms choose I, s_p and $\hat{N}$ and let dM adjust, they are now, by assumption, induced to choose a financial policy which – at the given level of profitability – makes the amount of bank loans expand at the rate d$M = mM$, and either s_p or $\hat{N}$ must therefore play the accommodating role in (7.18). It is important to note that in (7.18) Y and π are the existing, predetermined levels of output and profitability: the equation describes a financial constraint and not a relation between some future expected variables.

Comparing (7.18) and the ultra-short-run equilibrium condition, (5.2), it is readily seen that the product market will in fact clear at the given profit share. The product market can – as in the pre-Keynesian system – be in equilibrium at any value of π. Induced changes in firms' policies towards retained profits and new issues affect the saving function and hence the size of the multiplier: a rise in the rate of investment is accompanied by increases in the retention rate and/or the rate of new issues, and the resulting fall in the multiplier offsets the stimulating effects of increased investment. With induced changes in financial behaviour,

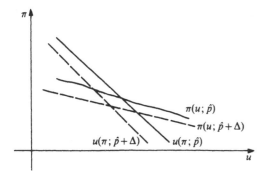

Figure 7.1: Effects of a rise in the rate of inflation on the share of profits.

equilibrium in the product market *may* thus be compatible with constant (exogenous) growth rates of nominal income and variable (autonomous) investment decisions.

7.7 CONSTANT NOMINAL INTEREST RATES

Consider, finally, the case where the nominal rate of interest is held constant. In chapter 5 the steady-growth path has been described by four equations – (5.3), (5.15), (5.16), (5.18a) – but these four equations no longer suffice to define the steady-growth path. Substituting $r = i - \hat{p}$, the equations can be written

$$n = h(\pi, e) \tag{7.19}$$

$$u = u(\pi, n; \hat{p}), \quad u_\pi < 0, \quad u_{\hat{p}} < 0 \tag{7.20}$$

$$\pi = \pi(u, n; \hat{p}), \quad \pi_u < 0, \quad \pi_{\hat{p}} < 0 \tag{7.21}$$

A rise in the rate of inflation thus shifts both the desired utilisation curve (7.20) and the market equilibrium curve (7.21) in a southwesterly direction as shown in figure 7.1.[14] The shift in the utilisation curve is related to the Keynes effect: changes in Tobin's q following a change in the real interest rate affect the desired utilisation rate and hence the steady-growth share of investment in total output. The market-equilibrium curve shifts because of the saving effects associated with changes in the real rate of interest.

The net effect on $\pi*$ of these shifts depends on the relative size of the shifts in the two curves. Unless, however, the shift in the market equilibrium curve is much smaller than the shift in the utilisation curve, $\pi*$ will be a decreasing function of the rate of inflation (see figures 7.1 and

[14] Both curves are negatively sloped in the u–π plane but, as argued in appendix 5B, $\pi_u u_\pi$ is less than unity and the utilisation curve is steeper than the market-equilibrium curve.

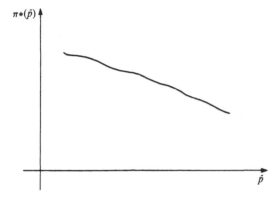

Figure 7.2: The share of profits in steady growth as a function of the rate of inflation.

7.2). In steady growth we have $\hat{w} = \hat{p}$ and if the Phillips curve takes the simple form

$$\hat{w} = \theta(e), \quad \theta' > 0 \tag{7.22}$$

then equations (7.20)–(7.22) yield an inverse relation between $\pi*$ and $e*$. Equation (7.19) on the other hand describes a positive relation between $\pi*$ and $e*$ and the equations (7.19)–(7.21) thus define a unique steady-growth equilibrium. Note that, just as in the monetarist case, the shape and position of the Phillips curve has become an important determinant of the long-term solution. The assumption of fixed real interest rates has been abandoned, and as a result the system has lost its money-wage neutrality.

With respect to the dynamics of the system, one would expect strong saving effects to stabilise the steady-growth path and the Keynes effect on investment to be destabilising. This expectation is readily confirmed for a simplified version of the model. As shown in appendix 7A we have the following result. If

(i) $\hat{N} = 0$,

(ii) households' demand for money is proportional to total wage income (rather than to total nominal incomes), and

(iii) the real rate of interest which influences investment is $\tilde{r} = i - \hat{w}$ rather than $r = i - \hat{p}$,

then the movement of the economy can be described in terms of two differential equations. Furthermore, the trace of the Jacobian exceeds (falls short of) the trace for the fixed real-interest system in chapter 6 if and only if the deflationary investment effects dominate the expansionary saving effects of a rise in real interest rates.

In terms of stability conditions, the constant *real* interest thus represents an intermediate case. If investment effects dominate saving effects then a necessary condition for monetarist stabilisation is satisfied, but the stability condition for a regime of fixed nominal interest rates will be more stringent than those for the constant real-interest regime. If, on the other hand, the saving effects are dominant, then the growth in the money stock is inversely related to the rate of interest and the standard policy prescriptions for monetary control will be unsuccessful and destabilising. Furthermore, constant nominal interest rates will have a better chance of stabilising the economy than a fixed real rate of interest.

7.8 CONCLUDING COMMENTS

The pre-Keynesian belief that in the long run households determine the level of saving (and investment) finds no support in the present theory. On the contrary, firms' financial decisions influence the outcome both in the short run and in steady growth. In this chapter I have discussed the reasons for this difference and the assumptions underlying the pre-Keynesian story.

Two differences between the pre-Keynesian system and the Keynesian theories are particularly important. The pre-Keynesian system, first, excludes the existence of bank credit, and the Keynesian multiplier vanishes if firms are forced to finance all investment through new issues and/or retained earnings. The exclusion of bank credit (and other forms of endogenous money creation) from the pre-Keynesian system implies that effective-demand problems cannot arise: the equilibrium condition for the securities market and the finance constraint ensure equilibrium in the product market, and equality between saving and investment can be established through variations in the market value of securities (the rate of interest). There are therefore no effective-demand problems in the pre-Keynesian system, and equilibrium in the product market does not require any particular real-wage rate. It follows that variations in money wages need not cause proportionate variations in nominal prices and this opens up the possibility that the real-wage rate may be determined exclusively by the equilibrium condition for the labour market.

The second difference concerns the specification of competition in the product market. Imperfect competition may cause firms to adopt a fixed mark-up, thereby preventing the real-wage adjustment required by the pre-Keynesian system. It is not, however, imperfect competition which causes effective-demand problems; these may arise also under perfect competition if there is an endogenous supply of bank credit. The pre-

Keynesian system thus requires perfect competition as well as the absence of credit money.

Having looked at the differences *vis-à-vis* the pre-Keynesian system, I examined the effect of changes in households' saving and portfolio decisions on the long-run outcome, and some novel results emerged. The influence of household saving has always been acknowledged in Keynesian theory, but it has been argued that a rise in saving propensities is unambiguously deflationary. I have shown that this need not be the case: an increase in the parameters describing household saving *may* in some cases stimulate the economy. The valuation effects on investment of an increase in Tobin's *q* may dominate the deflationary effects of a rise in saving propensities. Empirically, however, this result is likely to be of little importance.

In contrast, the financial behaviour of firms and the overall monetary and financial environment can be of crucial importance for the properties of the economy. A respecification of firms' financial behaviour along the lines suggested by Eichner and Wood produced no dramatic changes in the behaviour of the system, but a change in the monetary regime may alter the qualitative properties of the economy: *if* banks succeed in adjusting interest rates so as to induce firms to expand their bank liabilities by a constant rate, then the steady-growth path becomes stable. This result is not surprising given the simple quantity-theory specification of the demand for money, a specification which may be acceptable as a first approximation as long as banks do not attempt to control the growth of the money supply. Stability of the steady-growth path, however, depends critically on the precise specification of the demand function as well as on the successful manipulation of interest rates to attain the constant growth in the money stock.

As a third possibility, finally, I looked at a regime with fixed nominal interest rates. The results for this case are less clear-cut although there is a presumption that the steady-growth path will be unstable.

The three assumptions – constant real interest rates, constant nominal interest rates and constant money-supply growth – represent the simplest specifications of the monetary regime. In terms of stability the constant real-interest regime is an intermediate case. This regime is also the one which best fits the stylised facts: nominal interest rates as well as the growth rate of (the different measures of) the money supply have historically fluctuated more than real interest rates. Analysis of the two alternative specifications does, however, indicate the potential importance of changes in the overall monetary and financial structure, and this should be borne in mind in the interpretation of the results in chapters 4–6. It should be noted in particular that the system loses its money-wage neutrality when one leaves the regime with fixed real interest rates. Inflation and the determination of money wages will then be important, and further consideration of the Phillips curve becomes desirable. The determination of money wages therefore is one of the issues addressed in the next chapter.

APPENDIX 7A

It is assumed that
  (i) $\hat{N} = 0$
  (ii) $M = \beta w L$
  (iii) the rate of interest which influences investment is $\tilde{r} = i - \hat{w}$
  (iv) $\hat{w} = \theta(e)$
If $\tilde{r}*$ is the steady-growth value of $\tilde{r}$ then the saving function – (4.19) – can be written

$$\frac{S}{Y} = \beta(\hat{Y} - \tilde{r}*) + s_p \pi - \beta(\tilde{r} - \tilde{r}*) \tag{a7.1}$$

The investment function is given by

$$\frac{I}{Y} = f(u, \pi, \tilde{r} - \tilde{r}*); \quad f_{\tilde{r}} < 0 \tag{a7.2}$$

and

$$\pi = \pi(u, e, \tilde{r}) \tag{a7.3}$$

where

$$\pi_{\tilde{r}} \gtrless 0 \quad \text{for} \quad \frac{d(I/Y)}{d\tilde{r}} \gtrless \frac{d(S/Y)}{d\tilde{r}} \tag{a7.4}$$

Both saving and investment vary inversely with changes in the rate of interest and $\pi_{\tilde{r}}$ is thus positive (negative) if the saving (investment) effect is dominant.

Using $\tilde{r} = \tilde{r}* - \theta(e) + \theta(e*)$, the Jacobian for the constant nominal-interest regime (at the steady-growth path) becomes

$$\tilde{J}(u, e) = \begin{Bmatrix} u[h_\pi \pi_u - \sigma f & u\{h_\pi(\pi_e - \pi_{\tilde{r}}\theta') + h_e \\ - u\sigma(f_u + f_\pi \pi_u)] & - u\sigma[f_\pi(\pi_e - \pi_{\tilde{r}}\theta') + f_{\tilde{r}}\theta']\} \\ eh_\pi \pi_u & e[h_\pi(\pi_e - \pi_{\tilde{r}}\theta') + h_e] \end{Bmatrix} \tag{a7.5}$$

and

$$\text{Tr}(\tilde{J}) = \text{Tr}(J) - eh_\pi \pi_{\tilde{r}}\theta' \tag{a7.6}$$

where $\text{Tr}(J)$ is the trace of the Jacobian for the regime with a constant real interest rate (corresponding to $\theta' = 0$). Since e, h_π and θ' are all positive it follows that $\text{Tr}(\check{J})$ is larger (smaller) than $\text{Tr}(J)$ when the investment effect dominates (is dominated by) the saving effect.

CHAPTER 8

Distributional questions in neo-Marxian and post-Keynesian theory

8.1 INTRODUCTION

Class conflict is the central concept in neo-Marxian distribution theory. Workers strive to increase wages, capitalists wish to raise profitability, and the distributive outcome depends on the relative strength of the two parties in the class struggle. The strength of the working class is seen as inversely related to the size of the reserve army of labour while capitalists are influenced by the level of demand relative to their total productive capacity.

A theory of this kind can be formalised as follows:

$$\left(\frac{w}{p}\right)' = \chi(e); \quad \chi' > 0 \tag{8.1}$$

$$\pi' = \zeta(u); \quad \zeta' > 0 \tag{8.2}$$

where $(w/p)'$ and π' denote the real wage and profit targets of workers and capitalists respectively.

Real wages and the share of profits are definitionally related,

$$\pi = 1 - \frac{\lambda w}{p} \tag{8.3}$$

and – given the stock of capital and the size of the total work-force ($\underline{L}$) – there is also a link between employment and the rate of utilisation,

$$e = \frac{L}{\underline{L}} = \frac{L}{Y}\frac{Y}{K}\frac{K}{\underline{L}} = \lambda u \sigma \frac{K}{\underline{L}} \tag{8.4}$$

If the target shares are to be realised, $\pi' = \pi$ and $(w/p)' = w/p$, then equations (8.1)–(8.4) determine $(u, e, w/p, \pi) = [u*, e*, (w/p)*, \pi*]$ conditionally on the predetermined variable $K/\underline{L}$, and this determination is quite *independent of conditions in the product market*. The addition of Keynesian saving and investment functions would therefore produce an overdeterminate and inconsistent system: if $S/Y = s(u, \pi, e)$ and $I/Y = f(u, \pi)$ then the Keynesian equilibrium condition $I = S$ will not in general be satisfied by the solution to (8.1)–(8.4).

This problem of overdeterminacy has recently been discussed extensively by Marglin (1984a) and Sawyer (1986). Marglin concentrates on steady-growth issues and assumes (i) that the capitalist part of the economy can draw on labour supplies from other sectors and (ii) that the rate of utilisation is exogenously given. In terms of equations (8.1) and (8.2) he assumes that $\chi' = 0$ and that $\zeta(u) = \pm \infty$ for $u \lesssim u*$. The labour supply is thus infinitely elastic at some exogenously given wage rate, $(w/p*)$, and the rate of employment drops out of the system. The neo-Marxian solution values to this special case of the system are confronted with a Keynesian equilibrium condition, and overdeterminacy results.

Sawyer, considers a number of different models and concludes that 'conflict over income shares leads to the view that, at least over the medium to long term, it is the interaction of price and wage formation which sets the level of economic activity . . . The use of both a conflict approach and aggregate demand considerations leads to a problem of overdeterminacy' (Sawyer, 1986, pp. 39–40). But how robust is this conclusion? What are the implications of any such overdeterminacy for the integration of Marxian and Keynesian theory and what is the relation between this analysis and the theory in chapters 3–7?

8.2 TARGET SHARES

The terminology surrounding equation (8.1) may be different, but the target-wage equation is strikingly similar to a normal upward-sloping neoclassical labour-supply curve. The most obvious difference is that a neoclassical supply function relates the labour supply to the real-wage rate while in (8.1) the equation has been turned around. This causal reversal reflects important differences in the underlying perception of how the economy functions. Neoclassical economists refer to individual maximising behaviour and specify the labour supply as a function of the real-wage rate faced by individual members of the labour force. The neo-Marxian formulation in (8.1)–(8.4), in contrast, is cast in terms of conflict, power and classes, and wage rates are determined by the factors which govern the relative strength of workers and capitalists.

The neo-Marxian interpretation of the relation between wages and employment thus differs from neoclassical interpretations but in a purely algebraic sense this difference in causal structure is irrelevant: the neoclassical and neo-Marxian formulations are algebraically equivalent. Given the difference in the underlying vision, this equivalence is puzzling and leads one to question whether in fact (8.1)–(8.4) is a reasonable representation of the neo-Marxian view. The answer is no: the concept of a stable and time-invariant functional relation between the employment rate (utilisation rate) and the real-wage rate (the share of profits) sits awkwardly with a conflict approach. A neoclassical utility-maximising individual may balance the disutility of work against the real-wage rate, but the neo-Marxian vision is different.

Class conflict over distribution suggests that workers may feel solidarity with fellow workers and have definite views on a fair distribution of income between workers. But workers must reject the legitimacy of profits as a claim on income if the term class conflict is to have any real meaning. As far as workers are concerned the only fair level of profits is no profits. Workers may not be in a position to eliminate profits completely but they will always *attempt* to raise the level of real wages. The ability to achieve a rise in real wages will depend on the balance of power: when capitalists have the upper hand, real wages may decline in spite of the attempt by workers to raise wages, and, even when workers are strong, the increase in wages will be a gradual process – there may be a series of increasing short-run real-wage targets but workers' ultimate wage target is a wage share of unity.

Analogously, firms will always aim to squeeze real wages. The individual firm may be wary of reducing its own wage offers relative to wages in other firms since relative wages and changes in wage rates may influence the attitudes of workers toward the firm. The extent, however, to which these attitudes are translated into behavioural changes – e.g. industrial unrest, increasing labour turnover and diminished work effort – will depend on the strength of workers *vis-à-vis* the firm. The desire and ability of firms to reduce wages will therefore also depend on the balance of power in the class struggle.

A conflict approach may thus lead one to expect that variables like the rates of employment and utilisation play a part in determining the distribution of income, but it makes little sense to specify two independent target equations as in (8.1) and (8.2). The target of workers is to eliminate profits, and the aim of firms is to reduce wage costs as much as possible (to minimise efficiency wages). These targets are incompatible and, furthermore, it is the actual outcome – and not the targets themselves – which is determined by the relative strength of the classes.

Relative strength will depend on the power of workers *vis-à-vis* capitalists in the labour market as well as on the ability of capitalists to pass on money-wage increases in the form of higher prices. The rates of employment and capital utilisation therefore both play a part and the *outcome* of the distributive struggle can be represented by

$$[\lambda(1 - \pi) =] \frac{w}{p} = \Xi(e, u); \quad \Xi_e > 0, \ \Xi_u < 0 \tag{8.5}$$

Equation (8.5) replaces the two target equations (8.1) and (8.2). *Relative* strength as determined by (e, u) now determines real wages and the share of profits rather than labour-market conditions (e) determining real wages and product-market conditions (u) determining the share of profits.

The substitution of (8.5) for (8.1) and (8.2) may not appear very important. In fact equation (8.5) retains many similarities with neoclassical theory: as a special case of (8.5) we have $w/p = \Xi(e/u) = \Xi(K/\underline{L})$ and the idea that real wages may depend on the ratio of the capital stock to the total labour force would not come as a surprise to neoclassical economists. However, the revised system (8.3)–(8.5) contains four variables and only three equations. We have abandoned two independent target equations – corresponding to neoclassical supply and demand equations – and added a single equation describing the outcome of the distributive struggle as a function of variables determining the relative strength of the parties. This change has introduced an extra degree of freedom: the level of activity in the economy can now be determined by Keynesian saving and investment functions, and the overdeterminacy has disappeared.

This argument does not fully explain the overdeterminacy in Marglin's system. His neo-Marxian model contains a single equation describing the distributional outcome, and this equation, $w/p = (w/p)*$, is a special case of (8.5). The cause of overdeterminacy in Marglin's synthesis of Marx and Keynes thus is slightly different. It arises from the introduction of *two* distinct investment functions. With a given saving function and a given distribution of income, a Keynesian equilibrium is obtained through variations in the level of economic activity, i.e. in the utilisation rate, u. Marglin, however, assumes that $u = \bar{u}$ is exogenous. Since he is concerned with steady growth this assumption is not necessarily 'un-Keynesian'. In the long run, investment is induced and the steady-growth investment function may, as shown in chapter 5, take the form $u = u*$. An inconsistency, however, is inevitable if the requirement of a constant u is combined with the introduction of a second investment function, $I/K = f(\pi)$.

In conclusion, a neo-Marxian determination of distribution through class conflict can be combined with Keynesian aggregate-demand considerations without any overdeterminacy. A neoclassical labour-market equilibrium, on the other hand, leaves no room for Keynesian demand, and if the neo-Marxian theory is phrased in terms of two independent target equations (supply and demand equations) then the combined Keynesian-cum-Marxian system will be overdetermined. But, in contrast to neoclassical maximisation from which separate supply and demand functions emerge naturally, a conflict approach does not suggest the simultaneous achievement of two independently determined target shares: workers and capitalists *always* aim to increase their respective income shares. The outcome depends on relative strength and can be described through a single equation which includes all the variables affecting the position of the two classes.

8.3 AN ALTERNATIVE SPECIFICATION

Equation (8.5) is one possible representation of a conflict approach, but it is not the only one, and it may not even be the most reasonable. The relative strength of the classes is, by assumption, determined by the rates of employment and utilisation but if, say, the configuration of these variables is such that the relative advantage lies with workers then why don't they keep on squeezing profits until wages make up total income? Unless the relative strength of the working class depends inversely on the share of wages, one would expect the share of wages to converge to unity (zero) if the balance of power favours workers (capitalists). This argument suggests the following alternative formulation of the conflict approach:

$$\hat{w} - \hat{p} = \varXi(e, u) \tag{8.6}$$

A specification of neo-Marxian conflict theory along these lines is a central element in Goodwin's formulation of Marx's theory of cyclical accumulation. The difference is that Goodwin takes the utilisation rate, u, to be exogenously given, and, since Goodwin analysed a cyclical growth path rather than a steady state, a constant utilisation rate cannot be interpreted as a Keynesian investment function. The exogeneity of u, however, eliminates a degree of freedom, and the imposition of Keynesian saving and investment functions would cause Goodwin's system to be overdetermined. If, instead, u is maintained as a free variable, (8.3), (8.4) and (8.6) allow for a Keynesian determination of the level of activity.

8.4 INFLATION

Marglin (1984a, chapter 20, pp. 488–9) appears to advocate an overdeterminate synthesis of Marx and Keynes. At first sight this is surprising: consistency would seem a necessary condition for the successful integration of neo-Marxian distribution theory and Keynesian effective-demand theory, and in fact Marglin's synthesis does not violate the consistency requirement. In order to overcome the inconsistency, he introduces the rate of inflation as an additional variable and assumes that investment and/or the real-wage rate depends on the rate of inflation. Thus, it is argued that, although the rate of inflation is constant in steady growth and the rise in prices will be expected, workers may not be able to 'translate their inflationary expectations into wage claims' (p. 514).

It does not, however, seem obvious why the power of workers should be affected by a rate of inflation which is constant and fully foreseen. Furthermore, the argument implies that Marglin's own original specification of the neo-Marxian model has been incomplete and needs to be amended. As a theory of long-term inflation, Marglin's formulation thus does not seem fully convincing in its present form (see also Nell, 1985).

Inflation is also at the centre of the analysis in Rowthorn (1977), and Rowthorn presents his argument in terms of a model which in some respects resembles the one given by (8.1)–(8.4). He argues that the rate of employment determines a 'negotiated' real-wage rate as in (8.1) and that, analogously with (8.2), firms have a 'target profit share' which depends on product-market conditions as reflected in the rate of utilisation.[1] The equilibrium shares defined by equations (8.1) and (8.2), however, need not always be compatible. On the contrary, an 'aspiration gap' is said to exist if the sum of these two equilibrium shares exceeds (or falls short of) unity, and the size of the aspiration gap will, Rowthorn argues, determine the rate of unanticipated inflation. Unanticipated price increases in turn allow realised income shares to deviate from their equilibrium values and thus serve to reconcile a neo-Marxian distribution theory with a Keynesian determination of output and employment.

Unlike Marglin, however, Rowthorn explicitly denies the possibility that unanticipated inflation may perform this role in steady growth. In Rowthorn's model, Keynesian factors may influence the determination of output and employment in the short run, but the actual and anticipated inflation rates must coincide in steady growth. Effective demand thus cannot play an independent role in the long run. Instead, aggregate demand must itself adapt to ensure a combination of employment and utilisation which eliminates the aspiration gap. This adaptation, Rowthorn argues, takes place through induced changes in monetary and fiscal policy.

In Rowthorn's model, the long-run values of output and employment are thus determined exclusively by a neo-Marxian distribution system, i.e. by the solution to equations (8.1)–(8.4) with $w/p = (w/p)'$ and $\pi = \pi'$. From a Keynesian perspective this aspect of the analysis seems questionable, and the argument in section 8.2 suggests that other scenarios are indeed possible.

---

[1] Rowthorn (1977) casts his wage equation in terms of a 'negotiated wage share' rather than a real-wage rate. Given the simplifying assumption of constant labour productivity, however, the two specifications are equivalent. Rowthorn, furthermore, considers the

Effective demand may play a role in the long run if the distribution of income is determined by the net balance of forces as in (8.5). This specification implies that the distributive outcome may be unchanged if *both* workers and capital become stronger.[2] The increased strength of both parties may, however, have other effects: the intensity of the distributive struggle may increase and, as a symptom of this increase, one would expect to see a rise in the rate of inflation. The rate of inflation thus would also find a place within this alternative approach.

8.5 THEORIES OF MONOPOLY CAPITAL

One criticism of any synthesis of Marx and Keynes which includes equations like (8.3)–(8.5) concerns the ability of workers to influence the share of wages directly. In a closed monetary economy, workers may achieve some control over money-wage rates, but, unless firms' mark-up factor is reduced, there will be no change in real wages. In a synthesis of Marx and Keynes, the distributional equations (8.5) or (8.6) are therefore best interpreted along Kaleckian lines: the proximate determinant of distribution is the mark-up or, in Kalecki's terminology, the degree of monopoly.[3]

Kalecki's theory of the degree of monopoly has been criticised as being either tautological or, alternatively, a special case of neoclassical distribution theory. The criticism, however, is false. The theory expresses a conflict approach to distribution: distribution is not determined by supply and demand in the labour market but by the balance of power between the classes, and, just as neoclassical economists need to specify the determinants of supply and demand, so Kaleckians must provide a theory for the determination of the balance of class power and its influence on the mark-up.

In equations (8.5) and (8.6) the rates of employment and utilisation both influence the degree of monopoly, but, although Kalecki did mention the possible influence of both these factors on the mark-up, his main emphasis was on secular changes in the competitive environment and in the strength of working-class organisations (e.g. Kalecki, 1971b). His argument in

[1] influence of taxes and foreign trade, and these factors have been ignored in the present formulation.

[2] Rowthorn's short-run analysis of the *ex post* distributive outcome shares this property. Realised income shares are below (above) the target/negotiated shares when the aspiration gap is positive (negative), and reduced-form equations for realised income shares can be derived. These equations take the general form specified in (8.5): the realised share of wages becomes a function of both the rate of employment and capital utilisation.

[3] It is therefore slightly misleading to adopt the real-wage rate as a dependent variable, but using (8.3) the equations could be rephrased to give the mark-up as a function of the rates of employment and utilisation.

favour of a direct influence of workers' strength on the mark-up has been considered already and, as shown in section 3.10, this argument is not fully convincing in the context of a closed economy. But what about changes in the competitive environment?

The view that capitalism has moved toward ever-increasing monopolisation is deeply ingrained in radical economics, most prominently so in the theories of monopoly capital. The main concern of these theories has been the macroeconomic implications of increased concentration.[4] It is argued that increasing concentration has led to a rise in the average economy-wide mark-up factor and that this rise in the degree of monopoly can explain observed trends in utilisation rates, profitability and growth.[5]

Between the 1950s and the early 1980s most advanced OECD countries experienced a decline in profitability, and from the late 1960s there has also been a fall in growth rates and the utilisation of capital. Can these trends be explained by a rise in the degree of monopoly? The observed decline has a secular character, and if the economy fluctuates around a steady-growth path then an analysis of the effects of changes in the degree of monopoly on the steady-growth path may help to answer this question.

Following Kalecki, writers in the monopoly-capital tradition do not usually regard the availability of labour as a binding constraint on long-term development, and they explicitly reject the notion that long-term growth rates are governed by the natural rate. The model in chapters 4–6 thus does not appear to be an adequate representation of the monopoly-capital story. With the exception of the investment function, the elements of the basic monopoly-capital model are, however, uncontroversial.

The pricing equation is given by

$$p = mc \tag{8.7}$$

where m is the degree of monopoly, p is the price and c is marginal cost, the latter assumed equal to average variable cost. For simplicity, I shall assume that variable cost consists entirely of labour cost and that the

[4] Kalecki (1943), Steindl (1976; first published in 1952) and Baran and Sweezy (1966) are classic contributions to the monopoly-capital literature. Recent work includes Aaronovitch and Sawyer (1975), Cowling (1981, 1982), Rowthorn (1981), Sawyer (1982, 1985), Foster and Szlajfer (1984), Dutt (1984a, 1984b), Marglin (1984b), Taylor (1985), Amadeo (1986) and Pitelis (1987). The analysis in this and the following sections draws heavily on Auerbach and Skott (1988).
[5] See Cowling and Waterson (1976) for a formalisation of the effects of concentration on the average mark-up. One peculiarity of their argument is that apparently they fail to appreciate that concentration is itself endogenous in their model and that it is determined jointly with the average mark-up. The Cowling–Waterson model is discussed further in Auerbach and Skott (1985, 1988).

technical output–capital ratio is a given constant, σ. Furthermore, it is reasonable to suppose that total overhead cost is proportional to the capital stock, and all overheads can thus be included by a simple reinterpretation of the depreciation parameter δ. With these assumptions the rate of profits, $\pi u \sigma$, is given by

$$\pi u \sigma = \sigma u \, \frac{m-1}{m} - \delta \tag{8.8}$$

In the monopoly-capital literature, the saving function is usually of the simple classical variety,

$$\frac{S}{Y} = s_p \pi \tag{8.9}$$

and equilibrium in the product market requires that

$$S = I \tag{8.10}$$

In order to close the model one needs to specify an investment function. The exact specification of this function is, as argued in chapter 4, contentious but, along a steady-growth path, utilisation rates must be at the desired level. The precise specification of the desired utilisation, $u*$, derived in chapter 4 can be challenged, but, whatever the precise relation may be, an increase in the degree of monopoly cannot induce a change in desired utilisation which fully offsets the positive effect on the rate of profits: induced increases in the desired degree of excess capacity only make sense if the resultant rise in profit margins is sufficient to raise the profit rate. Otherwise firms would be better off if they did not try to defend the rise in the mark-up against erosion through new entry. A rise in the degree of monopoly must therefore raise the profit rate at the optimal rate of utilisation. Algebraically,

$$\sigma u* \, \pi* = \sigma u* \, \frac{m-1}{m} - \delta \tag{8.11}$$

and

$$\frac{\mathrm{d}(\sigma u* \, \pi*)}{\mathrm{d}m} = \frac{\sigma u*}{m^2} + \frac{\sigma(m-1)}{m} \, \frac{\mathrm{d}u*}{\mathrm{d}m} > 0 \tag{8.12}$$

Equations (8.11) and (8.12) are satisfied in steady growth, and an increase in the degree of monopoly will thus raise the steady-growth value of the rate of profits. Furthermore, the steady-growth rate is proportional to the rate of profits – equation (8.9) – so the rate of growth of output (and employment) must also go up. In other words, the monopoly-capital model of *steady growth* is inconsistent with the stylised facts which the theory was supposed to explain.[6]

Steady growth is not of course in itself a concern of Kalecki and the monopoly-capital tradition. Theories of monopoly capital, however, attempt to explain secular developments and not just short-run fluctuations, and any secular argument must take into account the induced character of long-run accumulation. The long-run average value of u will not deviate far from $u*$, and if u fluctuates around $\underline{u} \simeq u*$ then π and g will fluctuate around $\underline{\pi} \simeq \pi*$ and $g \simeq g*$. A secular profit squeeze and stagnation thus require that $\pi*$ and $g*$ decline.

The inconsistency between the theory of monopoly capital and the empirical evidence remains if the reservations regarding workers' direct influence on the mark-up are suspended and one allows the mark-up to depend on the rate of employment. A neo-Marxian conflict approach suggests that

$$m = m(e); \quad m' < 0 \tag{8.13}$$

With this specification, the rate of employment must be constant in steady growth and we may assume that the variability in m is large enough to ensure that growth does in fact take place at the natural rate (i.e. $g* = n$).

Increasing monopolisation causes the mark-up function to shift upwards, but in steady growth we have

$$n = \frac{S}{K} = \frac{I}{K} \tag{8.14}$$

If both I/K and S/K are determined by the share of profits and the utilisation rate then (8.14) determines the steady-growth values of both of these variables, and the steady-growth value of π is thus independent of the change in the competitive environment. Since.

$$\pi* = \frac{m(e*) - 1}{m(e*)} \tag{8.15}$$

it follows that an upward shift in $m(e)$ is associated with a rise in the steady-growth value of the rate of employment. This extension of the monopoly-capital model thus fails to reconcile increasing monopolisation with a fall in employment. On the contrary, it implies a rise in employment. The difference, compared with the simple monopoly-capital model,

---

[6] One may note that Kalecki's own writing is quite explicit on the positive relation between the degree of monopoly and the share of profits in income. As evidence of increasing monopolisation he pointed to a significant decline in the relative share of wages in income in US manufacturing between 1879 and 1937. See Auerbach and Skott (1988) for a detailed examination of Cowling's (1982) argument in favour of a monopoly-capital explanation of UK experience.

is that here it is the rate of employment rather than the rate of growth of output and employment which is positively related to the degree of monopolisation.

The intuitive explanation of this result is straightforward. In spite of the upward shift in the mark-up function, the actual mark-up must be kept at its (unchanged) equilibrium level, and this is accomplished through an increase in employment, which strengthens workers in the distributive struggle.

8.6 EFFECTS OF A RISING DEGREE OF MONOPOLY IN THE PRESENT THEORY

How robust is the positive relation between the degree of monopoly and the rate of growth (or the rate of employment)? The present theory – developed in chapters 4–6 – differs from the simple monopoly-capital model in several respects, and writers in the monopoly-capital tradition may feel unhappy about some aspects of the theory. Exactly as a result of these differences, however, the present theory lends some support to the view that a rise in the degree of monopoly may cause a decline in growth and profitability.

Class conflict enters the theory in two ways: it may affect the saving and/or investment function and, secondly, it influences the 'adjustment costs' of changes in output and employment and hence the output-expansion function.

Inflation effects (or real interest-rate effects) on investment and saving have been discussed extensively in chapter 7, and inflation may, as argued above, depend on the intensity of the class struggle. In addition to these inflation effects, class conflict may have a direct influence on the investment function. An increase in the strength or militancy of workers may damage the business climate and dampen animal spirits. It may also, however, induce firms to adopt techniques with a higher capital intensity. The net effect is therefore uncertain, but potentially the influence of class struggle on aggregate demand may equalise the warranted and natural growth rates even if the mark-up is exogenously given. If investment and saving depend on the rate of employment (the strength of workers) then so will the warranted growth rate (g_w), i.e.

$$g_w = g(e; \text{ mark-up, animal spirits} \dots) \tag{8.16}$$

A rate of employment, $e*$, may therefore exist such that $g(e*; \dots) = n$.

The warranted growth rate is positively related to the mark-up and, if long-run growth is given by the natural rate n, it follows that an increase in the mark-up will be associated with a rise (fall) in the employment rate if

$g_e < 0 \, (> 0)$. The net effect of the direct and indirect (inflation) influence of class conflict on the Keynesian demand equations is thus uncertain. In contrast, the second channel through which class conflict enters the theory provides a clearer answer and one which is favourable to the hypothesis that increasing monopolisation has deflationary effects.

Note first that the realised mark-up is no longer an exogenous variable when the assumption of instantaneous and costless adjustment is abandoned: the existence of adjustment costs implies a positive relation between the mark-up and the rate of growth. Arguably, however, a rise in the degree of monopoly can be represented by a fall in the conjectured elasticity of demand $1/\gamma$ (by a rise in γ): in the standard model of static short-run equilibrium the share of profits is equal to γ, and the mark-up is thus given by $m = \gamma/(1 - \gamma)$.

A rise in γ causes the output-expansion function, (5.3), to shift down, but the two other equations defining the steady-growth path, equations (5.15) and (5.16), are unaffected. Since (5.15) and (5.16) (and the condition $g_w = n$) determine $u*$ and $\pi*$, it follows that neither utilisation nor profitability will be affected by the change in γ. Employment, however, will change. The output-expansion function has shifted down and, since $\pi*$ is unchanged, a higher rate of unemployment is needed in order to generate growth at the natural rate. An increase in γ thus causes a fall in the rate of employment. And, if the equilibrium rate of employment falls, the growth rate of the economy must, by definition, be below the natural rate during a transitional period. Profitability is positively related to the rate of growth and would therefore also suffer during the transition.

Unlike the simple conflict hypothesis in section 8.5, the present theory can thus reconcile a rising degree of monopoly with the evidence of falling profitability. The reason is that here the profit share and the rate of employment are positively related: high employment and strong workers depress the business climate and cause a reduction in the rate of expansion of production and employment unless there is a compensating increase in the share of profits. The simple conflict theory, in contrast, does not analyse firms' production decisions explicitly. It simply assumes that, strengthened by a high rate of employment, workers may achieve higher real wages and that the employment rate and the share of profits are thus inversely related.

Figure 8.1 shows the positively sloped $\hat{e} = 0$ locus as given by the output-expansion function, and the equation (8.13) characterising the simple conflict theory yields the inverse relation between employment and profitability drawn in figure 8.2. A rise in γ, the elasticity of the inverse demand curve, shifts the $\hat{e} = 0$ locus upward in figure 8.1, and the (e, π) locus in figure 8.2 also shifts upward following a rise in the mark-up

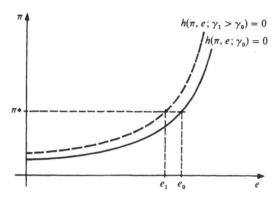

Figure 8.1: Effects on employment of a fall in the conjectured elasticity of demand (a rise in γ).

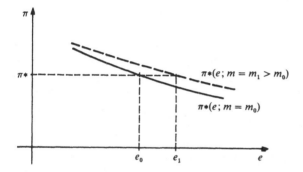

Figure 8.2: Effects on employment in the monopoly-capital model of a rise in the degree of monopoly.

function (8.13). Equilibrium in the product market requires an unchanged share of profits, and in figure 8.1 the rate of employment thus falls while in figure 8.2 it rises.

These results do not necessarily imply support for the view of increasing monopolisation as a cause of falling profitability. Note first that if the degree of monopoly is defined as the actual average mark-up then γ cannot be used as an indicator of the degree of monopoly. Furthermore, the effects of a rising value of γ are very similar to those arising from an increase in the strength and militancy of workers. An increase in workers' strength would also shift down the output-expansion function and cause a decline in the rate of employment along the steady-growth path (see section 5.7).

There is some evidence that workers in many countries have indeed become both stronger and more militant over much of the post-war period, and this change in militancy has played an important part in some explanations of the decline in profitability (e.g. Glyn and Sutcliffe, 1972; Bowles *et al.*, 1986).[7] One would therefore want to examine the direct evidence in favour of a rising degree of monopoly and the evidence is less compelling than it might appear at first sight.

There has been a strong tendency in both classical and neoclassical economics to analyse the capitalist firm in terms of the 'rational' entrepreneur operating within the 'black box' of the capitalist firm. As a result, changes in the techniques of business calculation and in the information available to decision-makers have been largely overlooked and developments in these areas have been of fundamental significance for the evolution of the competitive process.

A modern firm, swelling with profits, does not, like Andrew Carnegie, simply build another steel mill but may well enter into technically or geographically distant spheres where rates of return are higher. The modern multinational makes its 'cost-minimisation' calculations not, as firms did in former times with consideration of local wage rates, but on a world-wide basis. By these standards, what were formerly considered 'rational calculations' seem downright primitive. And, if the ability to make decisions on the basis of informed profit maximisation or other 'rational' criteria is restricted, then what does competition mean? Is an industry with many firms competitive if lack of information implies that no new entry takes place, even though all existing firms are highly profitable? The degree of competition cannot sensibly be adjudged without reference to the informational factors and the human infrastructure which determine the limits of 'rational decision-making'. In these areas enormous changes have taken place, changes which on balance tend to increase competitive pressures.

An additional and better-known objection to the view of increasing monopolisation concerns the delineation of markets. The monopoly-capitalist doctrine uses statistics showing long-term rises in market concentration as its central evidence of a decline in competition (Aaronovitch and Sawyer, 1975, chapters 4 and 5) but unless the relevant markets have remained constant over decades such measures may have a systematic bias.

Geographical expansion represents the most obvious area of change in the extent of markets, and the geographical expansion is in most cases associated with the growth of international trade. The standard response by monopoly-capital theorists to the increase in international trade has

---

[7] In contrast to the monopoly-capital school both Glyn and Sutcliffe (1972) and Bowles *et al.* (1986) argue that reductions in the profit share lead to lower growth rates.

been to argue that to a large extent imports are controlled by domestic monopolies. This is correct in some cases but, even if it is assumed that as much as one-quarter of all imports are 'controlled' by domestic companies, the usual conclusion suggesting a rising level of market concentration in Britain for the 1960s and 1970s is reversed (Utton and Morgan, 1983, chapter 2; see also Shepherd, 1982, for a discussion of the effects of imports on the US economy).

Taking into account foreign trade, it therefore seems hard to maintain the hypothesis of increasing market concentration. Furthermore, imports may cause the mark-up on *domestically produced* goods to fall even if the average profit–sales ratio has increased due to the control of imports by domestic monopolies. If, say, costs are lower in Germany and Ford replaces UK-produced cars by cheaper imports then the result will be higher profit margins and/or increased market share for Ford, but for domestic producers who retain production in the UK the effect will be a reduction in market shares and/or profitability.

In this context one should note, finally, that there are severe problems with the use of concentration data as an indicator of the level of competition. It is not obvious, for instance, why realised *ex post* levels of import penetration should be an appropriate measure of foreign competition. A market is an *ex ante* concept, one which dictates a sphere of *potential* competition, and it is no more legitimate to decide on the level of international incursion into a domestic market by measuring the level of imports than it would be to plot a demand curve for a product by looking at sales figures. If domestic firms react to the threat of increased foreign competition by lowering their prices, then no actual imports may be recorded. If, on the other hand, domestic firms maintain uncompetitive prices (associated with previous profit margins and applied to the given domestic unit labour costs) then import penetration will be rising as foreign competitors move in. The fact that the UK car industry suffered a large decline in profitability before import penetration by foreign firms became significant cannot (as suggested by Cowling, 1982, pp. 141–2) be taken as evidence that increasing international competition played no part in the decline of profitability. An alternative interpretation emphasising the importance of international competition is possible: the UK car industry was faced with the choice between defending its home market by lowering profit margins or retaining margins and letting in foreign competition. It responded initially by lowering profit margins, but, as these became perilously low, the fight to keep out competitors had to be conceded. BMC, for instance, only managed to hold on to its market share in the 1950s and 1960s through keen pricing of its small cars, the Morris Minor and the Mini, which were sold in highly competitive markets (the

VW Beetle, Citroën 2CV, Renault 4 and Fiat 500 being among the competitors). Although output and sales expanded rapidly during the period, this was achieved at the cost of very low profitability (see Williams *et al.*, 1983).

These considerations suggest that, although there has been a growing predominance of large firms in most national economies, the level of competition may well have had an underlying tendency to *increase* under capitalism (see Auerbach (1988)).

8.7 INFLATION AND UNEMPLOYMENT

One issue still requires elaboration. It has been assumed in earlier chapters that the Phillips curve takes the simple form

$$\hat{w} = \theta(e) \tag{8.17}$$

and that a constant rate of inflation will thus be associated with any given rate of employment. If the Phillips curve is augmented by the addition of an expectational term

$$\hat{w} = \theta(e) + \mu \hat{p}^e \tag{8.18}$$

then this property may no longer hold. Along a steady-growth path it is reasonable to assume $\hat{p}^e = \hat{p}$ and a constant profit share implies that $\hat{p} = \hat{w}$. If $\mu = 1$ then (8.18) therefore defines a unique steady-growth solution for the rate of employment, $e = **$.[8] In the regime with a fixed real interest rate, however, the steady-growth path has been determined without any reference to inflation and the formation of money wages, and only by chance, it would seem, will $e**$ be equal to the steady-growth value, $e*$, determined by (5.3), (5.15), (5.16) and (5.18a).

This problem is similar to the problem of overdeterminacy. It only arises, however, if the Phillips curve and the output-expansion function are specified independently of each other[9] and, in fact, the two relations are interdependent: they both reflect the power and militancy of workers.

To see this interdependence, consider the case where the two solutions for the rate of employment are equal initially, $e* = e**$, and assume that there is then a shift in the Phillips curve and a reduction in $e**$. Wage

---

[8] Similarly, the inclusion of a target real wage as in equation (8.1) will determine the steady-growth value of employment as a function of the profit share.

[9] Even if the Phillips curve and the output-expansion function are given independently, the problem could be overcome if saving and investment decisions are affected by changes in the rate of inflation. These possible effects have been discussed in section 8.6 above. The introduction of a government sector, furthermore, would allow the possibility of induced policy reactions as suggested by Rowthorn (1977).

aspirations have risen, but in the fixed real interest-rate regime workers have no direct influence on distribution. The result is accelerating wage inflation but constant real wages. Groups of workers will experience temporary gains and losses unless the wage-bargaining process is perfectly synchronised, but the average real wage remains constant.

Workers' frustration at this lack of success can have two effects. There may be disillusionment and defeat as workers readjust their wage target and the shift in the Phillips curve is reversed. Alternatively, the frustration will lead to industrial unrest affecting the social relations of production. The output-expansion function then shifts downward and causes a decline in the steady-growth value of $e*$. This process of adjustment comes to an end when the equality between $e*$ and $e**$ has been restored. In other words, if the Phillips curve takes the form (8.18) with $\mu = 1$ then a sustained shift in this curve must cause the output-expansion function to shift too. Workers' strength and militancy are major determinants of both the Phillips curve and the output-expansion function, and the resulting interdependency between the two relations implies that one or both of the relations will be shifting over time unless $e* = e**$.

Finally, it should be noted that if $\mu = 1$ then a Phillips curve of the form (8.18) defines a unique NAIRU (non-accelerating inflation rate of unemployment) and that in this case the discussion in section 5.8 of the nature of unemployment requires modification.

The NAIRU is determined by workers' strength and militancy and thus in neoclassical parlance by attitudes and preferences. It follows that this specification of the Phillips curve may be incompatible with the existence of a steady-growth path with involuntary unemployment in Keynes's sense. Unemployment cannot, however, be characterised as voluntary either. From a neo-Marxian perspective the terms voluntary and involuntary unemployment lose their meaning. The economic system needs unemployment as a means of disciplining workers. But this need does not make unemployment voluntary unless the legitimacy of capitalist relations of production is taken for granted. Class struggle is an expression of conflict over precisely this premise. Keynesian market failures can be an important argument against *laissez-faire* capitalism but conflict would exist even if markets had always worked smoothly. Inequalities of income and wealth as well as of opportunities, power and influence do not depend on Keynesian demand failures. Nor will conflict over the organisation of the work process inside the factory disappear as soon as the effective-demand problem is solved. Unemployment thus is not voluntary even in the case where (8.18) applies and $\mu = 1$.

8.8 SUMMARY AND CONCLUSIONS

In this chapter I have argued that neo-Marxian theories of distribution and inflation can be combined with a Keynesian determination of the level of economic activity. A conflict approach suggests that the wage and profit claims from workers and capitalists are incompatible and that the distributional outcome is determined by the *relative* strength of classes. The absolute strength of the classes, on the other hand, may influence the intensity of the class struggle and the rate of inflation.

The problems of overdeterminacy discussed by Sawyer (1986) are caused by the introduction of two separate equations for the target income shares of workers and capital rather than one equation specifying the distributional outcome as a function of the net balance of power. In the case of Marglin (1984a) the overdeterminacy derives from the imposition of two different investment functions.

In the context of a closed monetary economy the neo-Marxian distribution mechanism is best interpreted in a Kaleckian way: the proximate determinant of distribution is the mark-up. However, the argument that workers have a direct influence on the mark-up is unconvincing. Furthermore, if the mark-up varies inversely with the rate of employment (the strength of workers) then an increase in the degree of monopolisation will be associated with a rise in employment. This result contradicts the claims of the monopoly-capital tradition: stagnation cannot be explained by increasing monopolisation.

The theory in chapters 3–6 provides a different integration of Marx and Keynes. Instead of a dubious direct effect on distribution the theory suggests that class conflict enters in two distinct ways. The intensity of class conflict (and in particular the strength of workers and the rate of inflation) affects the saving and investment functions. Secondly, the strength and militancy of workers influence firms' production decisions: changes in output and employment are neither costless nor instantaneous and the shape and position of the adjustment-cost function depends on the strength and militancy of workers. This integration of Marx and Keynes differs from standard monopoly-capital models but because of these differences, paradoxically, the theory provides some support for the view that an increase in monopolisation may be deflationary. It is unclear, however, whether in fact there has been a secular decline in the degree of competition, and the trend decline in employment and profitability between the late 1950s and early 1980s is probably better explained by an increase in the strength and militancy of workers.

CHAPTER 9

Final remarks

9.1 KEYNESIANS, MONETARISTS AND THE REAL WORLD

Fluctuations in employment and economic activity characterise all capitalist economies. Are these fluctuations caused by exogenous shocks in, for instance, technology or the money supply? Alternatively, will the economy generate fluctuations endogenously even in the absence of external shocks? Many different answers have been given and the majority view has changed considerably over time.

Keynesian economics dominated the 1950s and 1960s, but at a theoretical level Keynes's ideas have always been met with scepticism. The main criticism of the Keynesian system has been the alleged lack of theoretical foundations. In comparison with Arrow–Debreu theories of general equilibrium, the macroeconomic relations of Keynesian economics have been deemed *ad hoc*, and already by the mid-1960s the search for microeconomic foundations was well under way.

Parallel to these developments in economic theory came the Vietnam war and 1968 marked the beginning of industrial and political militancy in Europe. The breakdown of the Bretton Woods system, the Yom Kippur war and the oil shock followed in the early 1970s. These events had significant economic repercussions, but the world-wide radicalisation of youth movements and workers alike found no place in the Keynesian system. The Keynesians of the day had accepted the methodological individualism of their neoclassical and monetarist counterparts. Class conflict was alien to their economic theories and, as inflation spiralled, the Keynesians could only observe that the Phillips curve appeared to be shifting in unpredictable ways.

The empirical weakness of Keynesian economics in this area was seized upon by the monetarists. The Phillips curve, they argued, shifts because workers revise their expectations concerning future prices in the light of past inflation. The breakdown of the Phillips curve was thus interpreted as a vindication of 'rational economic man' and as proof that Keynesian theory had failed to identify structures that remain invariant over time: Keynesian economics lacked theoretical foundations in optimising behaviour.

This combination of empirical shortcomings in the explanation of inflation and a latent unease over microeconomic foundations caused the demise of Keynesian economics. In economic theory, the sharpening of class conflict in the late 1960s and the emergence of mass unemployment in the 1970s and 1980s have been associated with the affirmation of faith in the efficacy of markets and in the methodological necessity of an economic theory based on individual rationality.

It is indubitable that changing expectations influence wage-bargaining. But the inclusion of such effects has not produced a stable Phillips curve. Today even those economists who accept the existence of a 'natural rate of unemployment' debate the causes of shifts in this rate, and the expecta- tional effects on wage formation cannot explain the rapid acceleration in inflation from the late 1960s onwards. Many orthodox economists there- fore add proxies for 'militancy' to their wage equations. Newell and Symons (1987), for instance, include a dummy variable for 1969–76 'to account for the worldwide increased labour militancy over this period' (p. 581), and this variable proves to be highly significant statistically. Vari- ables of this kind, however, are *ad hoc* intrusions in models of individual optimisation: a change in militancy – a sudden and synchronised change in the behaviour of myriads of individual workers – is a curious phenomenon in models based on exogenous preferences and methodological individual- ism. Marxian economics, in contrast, has always emphasised the import- ance of workers' militancy and class conflict.

In this book I have shown how Keynesian and Marxian insights can be combined in a coherent theory of the capitalist economy. Furthermore, the theory presented here overcomes the standard neoclassical criticism of Keynesian and Marxian theory: prices are flexible, the output–capital ratio is allowed to vary endogenously in the long run, financial factors are analy- sed explicitly, and firms base their production and investment decisions on profit maximisation. The analysis has been mathematically rigorous and the level of descriptive realism much higher than is to be found in most current theoretical work, whether 'new classical' or 'new Keynesian'.

I have analysed three types of agents: firms, households and banks. Firms operate under conditions of imperfect competition. They decide the rates of production, employment and investment, and these decisions are derived from profit maximisation at the microeconomic level. The theory thus presents an integrated micro–macro story. Households hold financial assets (including equity in firms) and their saving decisions are modelled in terms of desired relations between income flows and asset stocks. They also supply labour and have a direct influence on nominal wage rates as well as on the social relations of production: the behaviour of workers in the production process affects the 'business climate' and the production decisions of firms. Banks, finally, set interest rates on bank loans and deposits.

The interaction between the behaviour of these three types of agents in four markets (goods, labour, money, securities) has been analysed in different time frames and it has been shown that:

1 Keynesian effective demand plays a critical role in the determination of both the distribution of income and the rate of employment, and although workers are able to influence money-wage rates such changes may affect neither real-wage rates nor the level of demand.

2 Under plausible conditions, a steady-growth path exists and the steady-growth rate is equal to the growth rate of the labour force. Harrod's first problem – the inequality between warranted and natural growth rates – thus does not arise. But the warranted rate does not adjust to the natural rate through variations in the output–capital ratio as in neoclassical theories. Instead, the equalisation comes about via a Marxian conflict mechanism. The rate of unemployment – the size of the reserve army of labour – affects the strength of workers in the conflict with capital, and this relation ensures that high employment rates have negative feedback effects on firms' production and employment decisions.

3 The steady-growth value of the rate of employment is influenced by Keynesian and Marxian factors (e.g. animal spirits and militancy) as well as by other parameters in the model. In contrast to the predictions of neoclassical theories, firms' financing decisions, for instance, affect the steady-growth path.

4 In spite of perfectly flexible prices, the steady-growth path is likely to be (locally asymptotically) unstable. In essence, the cause of instability is a Harrodian interaction of multiplier and accelerator effects.

5 Monotonic divergence from the steady-growth path is averted by the stabilising influence of the reserve army of labour: high (low) rates of employment lead to a strong (weak) working class and this reduces (raises) the growth rate of output chosen by firms.

6 The dynamic behaviour of the economy is sensitive to changes in monetary regimes, and an active monetary policy can – at least in principle – secure the stability of the steady-growth path.

9.2 LIMITATIONS OF THE THEORY

Many refinements of the theory presented in this book are possible, and some important limitations of the framework have already surfaced in chapter 8. In the discussion of competition in that chapter, I have argued that, contrary to the claims of theories of monopoly capital, the evolution of capitalist economies may well have been characterised by increasing competition. In order to decide the question, however, one must look carefully at international aspects: increasing internationalisation implies that it is no longer possible to view any individual national economy – not even the US – as a self-contained closed economy. The only closed economy is the world economy.

What is at issue here is not just the need to introduce additional institutional detail in order to make the theory more 'realistic'. The geographical dimension is of central importance in discussions of growth and cycles. It is difficult to think of any important questions concerning long-term growth which do not involve spatial aspects in an essential way. One may be concerned about world-wide movements in growth rates and in employment, but the huge disparities in living standards make it almost meaningless to conduct an argument in terms of averages. Differences in growth rates and in income levels between different countries and regions are arguably of far greater importance than the average level and growth of income.

Marxists often refer to the 'law of uneven development', and as a purely empirical regularity there is an abundance of evidence to support this 'law'. The relative decline of Britain, the meteoric rise of Japan and the gradual erosion of US predominance in the post-war period are but prominent examples. But it is hardly satisfactory to 'explain' international instability simply as the result of a law of uneven development. The underlying reasons behind the law need to be understood, and one cannot even begin to explore these issues within the confines of a closed-economy model.

Orthodox neoclassical models of growth and international trade suggest a gradual equalisation of factor incomes between different regions and countries. The empirical evidence does not confirm this expectation. The UK represents one striking anomaly, and in general there is little evidence of a negative correlation between the levels and rates of growth of per capita income. Samples which are chosen such that all countries in the sample have similar income levels at the end of the period will show a spurious correlation, but unbiased samples of nations with similar characteristics at the start of the period present a different picture. De Long (1987), for instance, has analysed data for 1870–1979 and concludes that the 'data do not show convergence on any but the most optimistic reading. They do not support the claim that those nations that should have been able to rapidly assimilate industrial technology have all converged ... The forces making for "convergence" even among industrial nations appear little stronger than the forces making for "divergence"' (pp. 8–9).

One may choose to ascribe the lack of convergence to the effects of exogenous shocks or, more generally, to the influence of non-economic factors, but it seems more promising to examine the possibility that endogenous economic forces contribute to the observed unevenness in both real income and growth. The existence of increasing returns is here an obvious candidate. Although an assumption of convex production possibility sets is almost universal in economic theory, this assumption appears to be based on analytical convenience rather than empirical evidence.

Increasing returns are sometimes observable at the level of the individual firm, but this is probably not the most important form of increasing returns. The existence of external increasing returns and interdependencies between the division of labour and the extent of the market have been recognised since Adam Smith. Furthermore, dynamic increasing returns must also be taken into account. Although often conceived of in a narrow technical sense as 'learning by doing', dynamic increasing returns may encompass wider social aspects such as endogenous changes in industrial relations or in attitudes to work and risk-taking (Myrdal, 1957).

In the present theory increasing returns could have been included analogously with the analysis of diminishing returns in section 6.6. In a one-sector model without spatial disaggregation the introduction of increasing returns makes little difference to the qualitative behaviour of the economy. In a spatially disaggregated model, however, increasing returns can be a powerful source of divergence. I have discussed some of the issues and presented a rudimentary model of the process of divergence in Skott (1985a). But it is no more than a first sketch, and much more work needs to be done.

The closed-economy framework adopted in this book, however, will be directly relevant to some issues, and the analysis of a spatially aggregated economy may also guard against a number of simple mistakes. Thus, a fall in money wages may be a possible route to expansion in any single country. But if money wages were to fall in all countries then the closed-economy model would be more appropriate and, as shown in chapter 5, the results can then be very different. The analysis of a spatially aggregated economy, finally, may be a necessary step before approaching the more difficult questions of uneven development. These latter questions arguably present the greatest challenge to contemporary economics.

Bibliography

Aaronovitch, S. and M. Sawyer (1975) *Big Business*. London and Basingstoke: Macmillan.

Amadeo, E. J. (1986) 'Notes on capacity utilisation, distribution and accumulation'. *Contributions to Political Economy*, 5, pp. 83–94.

Arestis, P. and G. Hadjimatheou (1982) *Introducing Macroeconomic Modelling – an Econometric Study of the UK*. London and Basingstoke: Macmillan.

Asimakopulos, A. (1983) 'Kalecki and Keynes on finance, investment and saving'. *Cambridge Journal of Economics*, 7, pp. 221–33.

Auerbach, P. (1988) *Competition*. Oxford: Basil Blackwell.

Auerbach, P. and P. Skott (1985) 'Concentration and profits once again: the failure of the Cournot solution'. Working Paper 85–04, University College London.

   (1988) 'Concentration, competition and distribution'. *International Review of Applied Economics*, 2, pp. 42–61.

Baran, P. and P. Sweezy (1966) *Monopoly Capital*. Harmondsworth: Penguin.

Barro, R. and H. Grossman (1976) *Money, Employment and Inflation*. Cambridge: Cambridge University Press.

Baumol, W. J. (1959) *Business Behaviour, Value and Growth*. New York: Macmillan.

   (1977) 'Say's (at least) eight laws, or what Say and James Mill may really have meant'. *Economica*, 44, pp. 145–62.

Benassy, J. P. (1975) 'Neo-Keynesian disequilibrium theory in a monetary economy'. *Review of Economic Studies*, 42, pp. 503–23.

Black, J. (1962) 'The technical progress function and the production function'. *Economica*, 29, pp. 166–70.

Bliss, C. J. (1975) *Capital Theory and the Distribution of Income*. Amsterdam: North Holland.

Bowles, S. (1985) 'The production process in a competitive economy: Walrasian, Neo-Hobbesian and Marxian models'. *American Economic Review*, 75, pp. 16–36.

Bowles, S., D. M. Gordon and T. E. Weisskopf (1986) 'Power and profits: the social structure of accumulation and the profitability of the postwar US economy'. *Review of Radical Political Economics*, 18, pp. 132–67.

Cagan, P. (1956) 'The monetary dynamics of hyperinflation'. In M. Friedman (ed.) *Studies in the Quantity Theory of Money*. Chicago: University of Chicago Press.

Carsberg, B. and A. Hope (1976) *Business Investment Decisions under Inflation –*

Theory and Practice. London: Institute of Chartered Accountants in England and Wales.

Champernowne, D. G. (1971) 'The stability of Kaldor's 1957 model'. *Review of Economic Studies*, 38, pp. 47–62.

Chang, W. W. and D. J. Smyth (1971) 'The existence and persistence of cycles in a non-linear model: Kaldor's 1940 model re-examined'. *Review of Economic Studies*, 38, pp. 37–44.

Chick, V. (1983) *Macroeconomics After Keynes*. Oxford: Philip Allan.

(1986) 'The evolution of the banking system and the theory of saving, investment and interest'. *Economies et Sociétés, Cahiers de l'ISMSA Série Monnaie et Production*, no. 3.

Costabile, L. and R. E. Rowthorn (1985) 'Malthus's theory of wages and growth'. *Economic Journal*, 95, pp. 418–37.

Cowling, K. (1981) 'Oligopoly, distribution and the rate of profit'. *European Economic Review*, 15, pp. 195–224.

(1982) *Monopoly Capitalism*. London and Basingstoke: Macmillan.

Cowling, K. and M. Waterson (1976) 'Price cost margins and market structure'. *Economica*, 43, pp. 267–74.

Dana, R. A. and P. Malgrange (1984) 'The dynamics of a discrete version of a growth cycle model'. In J. P. Ancot (ed.) *Analysing the Structure of Econometric Models*. Amsterdam: M. Nijhof.

Davidson, P. (1986) 'Finance, funding, saving and investment'. *Journal of Post Keynesian Economics*, 9, pp. 101–10.

De Long, J. Bradford (1987) 'Have productivity levels converged?'. NBER Working Paper no. 2419. Cambridge, MA: National Bureau of Economic Research.

Desai, M. (1973) 'Growth cycles and inflation in a model of the class struggle'. *Journal of Economic Theory*, 6, pp. 527–45.

Desai, M. and M. Pemberton (1981) 'A note on the Goodwin model'. Mimeo.

Desai, M. and G. Weber (1987) 'Money, inflation and unemployment: an econometric model of the Keynes effect'. Discussion Paper A.59, Demeic Econometrics Programme, London School of Economics.

Dutt, A. K. (1984a) 'Stagnation, income distribution and monopoly power'. *Cambridge Journal of Economics*, 8, no. 1, pp. 24–41.

(1984b) 'Competition, monopoly power and the prices of production'. Discussion Paper no. 44, Florida International University.

Eichner, A. (1976) *The Megacorp and Oligopoly*. Cambridge: Cambridge University Press.

Eichner, A. and J. Kregel (1975) 'An essay on post-Keynesian theory: a new paradigm in economics'. *Journal of Economic Literature*, 13, pp. 1293–314.

Eisner, R. and R. H. Strotz (1963) 'Determinants of business investment'. In *Commission on Money and Credit: Impact of Monetary Policy*. Englewood Cliffs, NJ: Prentice-Hall, pp. 60–138.

Fay, J. A. and J. L. Medoff (1985) 'Labor and output over the business cycle: some direct evidence'. *American Economic Review*, 75, pp. 638–55.

Fazi, E. and N. Salvadori (1981) 'The existence of a two-class economy in the Kaldor model of growth and distribution'. *Kyklos*, 34, pp. 582–92.

(1985) 'The existence of a two-class economy in a general Cambridge model of growth and distribution'. *Cambridge Journal of Economics*, 9, pp. 155–64.

Foster, J. B. and H. Szlajfer (eds.) (1984) *The Faltering Economy: the Problem of*

Accumulation under Monopoly Capitalism. New York: Monthly Review Press.

Friedman, M. (1968) 'The role of monetary policy'. *American Economic Review*, 58, no. 1, pp. 1–17.

Glyn, A. and R. B. Sutcliffe (1972) *British Workers and the Profits Squeeze.* Harmondsworth: Penguin.

Goodwin, R. M. (1967) 'A growth cycle'. In C. H. Feinstein (ed.) *Socialism, Capitalism and Growth.* Cambridge: Cambridge University Press.

Goodwin, R. M., M. Krüger and A. Vercelli (eds.) (1984) *Non-linear Models of Fluctuating Growth.* Berlin: Springer.

Gould, J. P. (1968) 'Adjustment costs in the theory of investment of the firm'. *Review of Economic Studies*, 35, pp. 47–55.

Grandmont, J.-M. (1985) 'On endogenous competitive business cycles'. *Econometrica*, 53, pp. 995–1046.

Groth, C. (1981) 'Cyklisk kapitalakkumulation'. Memo no. 101, University of Copenhagen.

(1988) 'IS–LM dynamics and the hypothesis of combined adaptive-forward-looking expectations'. In P. Flaschel and M. Krüger (eds.) *Recent Approaches to Economic Dynamics.* Frankfurt-on-Main: Peter Lang Verlag.

Grubb, D. (1986) 'Topics in the Phillips curve'. *Economic Journal*, 96, pp. 55–79.

Hahn, F. H. (1972) *The Share of Wages in National Income.* London: Weidenfeld and Nicolson.

(1973) *On the Notion of Equilibrium in Economics.* Cambridge: Cambridge University Press.

(1984) 'In praise of economic theory'. Jevons Memorial Lecture, University College London.

Hahnel, R. and H. Sherman (1982) 'The rate of profit over the business cycle'. *Cambridge Journal of Economics*, 6, pp. 185–94.

Hale, J. K. (1969) *Ordinary Differential Equations.* New York: Wiley Interscience.

Hall, R. and C. Hitch (1939) 'Price theory and business behaviour'. *Oxford Economic Papers*, 2, pp. 12–45.

Harcourt, G. C. (1972) *Some Cambridge Controversies in the Theory of Capital.* Cambridge: Cambridge University Press.

Harcourt, G. C. and P. Kenyon (1976) 'Pricing and the investment decision'. *Kyklos*, 29, pp. 449–77.

Harrod, R. (1936) *The Trade Cycle: an Essay.* Oxford: Oxford University Press.

(1939) 'An essay in dynamic theory'. *Economic Journal*, 49, pp. 14–33.

(1973) *Economic Dynamics.* London and Basingstoke: Macmillan.

Hicks, J. R. (1950) *A Contribution to the Theory of the Trade Cycle.* Oxford: Oxford University Press.

(1965) *Capital and Growth.* Oxford: Oxford University Press.

Jones, H. (1975) *Modern Theories of Economic Growth.* London: Nelson and Sons.

Kahn, R. (1977) 'Malinvaud on Keynes'. *Cambridge Journal of Economics*, 1, pp. 375–88.

Kaldor, N. (1940) 'A model of the trade cycle'. *Economic Journal*, 50, pp. 78–92.

(1951) 'Mr. Hicks on the trade cycle'. *Economic Journal*, 61, pp. 833–47.

(1954) 'The relation of economic growth and cyclical fluctuations'. *Economic Journal*, 64, pp. 53–71.

(1956) 'Alternative theories of distribution'. *Review of Economic Studies*, 23, pp. 83–100.

(1957) 'A model of economic growth'. *Economic Journal*, 67, pp. 591–624.

(1959) 'Economic growth and the problem of inflation – parts 1 and 2'. *Economica*, 26, pp. 212–26 and 287–98.

(1961) 'Capital accumulation and economic growth'. In F. A. Lutz and D. C. Hague (eds.) *The Theory of Capital*. New York: Macmillan.

(1966) 'Marginal productivity and the macroeconomic theories of distribution'. *Review of Economic Studies*, 33, pp. 309–19.

(1971) 'A comment'. *Review of Economic Studies*, 38, pp. 45–6.

(1972) 'The irrelevance of equilibrium economics'. *Economic Journal*, 82, pp. 1237–55.

(1982) *The Scourge of Monetarism*. Oxford: Oxford University Press.

Kaldor, N. and J. A. Mirrlees (1962) 'A new model of economic growth'. *Review of Economic Studies*, 29, pp. 174–92.

Kalecki, M. (1943) *Studies in Economic Dynamics*. London: Allen and Unwin.

(1954) *Theory of Economic Dynamics*. London: Allen and Unwin.

(1968) 'Trend and the business cycle'. *Economic Journal*, 78, pp. 263–76.

(1971a) *Selected Essays on the Dynamics of the Capitalist Economy*. Cambridge: Cambridge University Press.

(1971b) 'Class struggle and the distribution of national income'. *Kyklos*, 24, pp. 1–11.

Keynes, J. M. (1930) *A Treatise on Money*. London and Basingstoke: Macmillan.

(1936) *The General Theory of Employment, Interest and Money*. London and Basingstoke: Macmillan.

(1973) *Collected Writings*, vol. 14. London and Basingstoke: Macmillan.

Kornai, J. (1971) *Anti-equilibrium*. Amsterdam: North-Holland.

Kregel, J. A. (1984–5) 'Constraints on the expansion of output and employment: real or monetary'. *Journal of Post Keynesian Economics*, 7, pp. 139–52.

(1986) 'A note on finance, liquidity, saving and investment'. *Journal of Post Keynesian Economics*, 9, pp. 91–100.

Kuznets, S. (1971) *Economic Growth of Nations*. Cambridge, MA: Belknap Press.

Leijonhufvud, A. (1968) *On Keynesian Economics and the Economics of Keynes*. Oxford: Oxford University Press.

(1986) 'Whatever happened to Keynesian economics?'. Paper delivered at Nobel Conference XII: 'The Legacy of Keynes', Gustavus Adolphus College, Saint Peter, Minnesota.

Lucas, R. E. (1967) 'Adjustment costs and the theory of supply'. *Journal of Political Economy*, 75, pp. 321–34.

(1981) *Studies in Business Cycle Theory*. Oxford: Basil Blackwell.

Marglin, S. A. (1984a) *Growth, Distribution and Prices*. Cambridge, MA: Harvard University Press.

(1984b) 'Growth, distribution, and inflation: a centennial synthesis'. *Cambridge Journal of Economics*, 8, pp. 115–44.

Marris, R. (1964) *The Economic Theory of 'Managerial' Capitalism*. London: Macmillan.

Marx, K. (1976) *Capital* Harmondsworth: Penguin.

Meade, J. (1965) 'The outcome of the Pasinetti process: a note'. *Economic Journal*, 76, pp. 161–6.

Moore, B. J. (1984) 'Unpacking the post Keynesian black box: wages, bank lending and the money supply'. *Thames Papers in Political Economy*, Spring.

Morishima, M. (1984) 'The good and bad uses of mathematics: with special reference to general equilibrium analysis'. In G. Routh and P. J. D. Wiles (eds.) *Economics in Disarray*. Oxford: Basil Blackwell.

Myrdal, G. (1957) *Economic Theory and Underdeveloped Regions*. London: Duckworth.

Nell, E. (1985) 'Jean-Baptiste Marglin: a comment on "Growth, Distribution and Inflation"'. *Cambridge Journal of Economics*, 9, pp. 173–8.

Newell, A. and J. S. V. Symons (1987) 'Corporatism, *laissez-faire* and unemployment'. *European Economic Review*, 31, no. 3, pp. 567–601.

Nickell, S. J. (1978) *The Investment Decision of Firms*. Cambridge: Cambridge University Press.

    (1987) 'Why is wage inflation in Britain so high?'. *Oxford Bulletin of Economics and Statistics*, 49, pp. 103–28.

Olech, C. (1963) 'On the global stability of an autonomous system on the plane'. In *Contributions to Differential Equations*, vol. 1. New York: John Wiley and Sons.

Pasinetti, L. L. (1962) 'Rate of profit and income distribution in relation to the rate of economic growth'. *Review of Economic Studies*, 29, pp. 267–79.

    (1966) 'New results in an old framework: comment on Samuelson and Modigliani'. *Review of Economic Studies*, 33, pp. 303–6.

Peel, D. A. and J. S. Metcalfe (1979) 'Divergent expectations and the dynamic stability of some simple macroeconomic models'. *Economic Journal*, 89, pp. 789–98.

Pitelis, C. (1987) *Corporate Capital: Control, Ownership, Saving and Crisis*. Cambridge: Cambridge University Press.

Richardson, D. R. (1986) 'Asimakopulos on Kalecki and Keynes on finance, investment and saving'. *Cambridge Journal of Economics*, 10, pp. 191–8.

Robinson, J. (1962) *Economic Philosophy*. London and Basingstoke: Macmillan.

    (1966) 'Comment on Samuelson and Modigliani'. *Review of Economic Studies*, 33, pp. 307–8.

    (1974) 'History versus equilibrium'. *Thames Papers in Political Economy*, Autumn.

    (1978) *Contributions to Modern Economics*. Oxford: Blackwell.

Rowthorn, B. (1977) 'Conflict, inflation and money'. *Cambridge Journal of Economics*, 1, pp. 215–39.

    (1981) 'Demand, real wages and economic growth'. *Thames Papers in Political Economy*, Autumn.

Samuelson, P. A. (1964) 'A brief survey of post-Keynesian developments'. In R. L. Lekachman (ed.) *Keynes' General Theory*. London and Basingstoke: Macmillan.

Samuelson, P. A. and F. Modigliani (1966) 'The Pasinetti paradox in neoclassical and more general models'. *Review of Economic Studies*, 33, pp. 269–301.

Sawyer, M. (1982) *Macro-economics in Question*. Brighton: Wheatsheaf.

    (1985) *The Economics of Michal Kalecki*. London and Basingstoke: Macmillan.

    (1986) 'Conflict over aggregate demand in post Keynesian economics: the problem of over-determinacy'. Mimeo.

Say, J.-B. (1844) *A Treatise on Political Economy: or the Production, Distribution and Consumption of Wealth*. Translated from the fourth French edition by C. R. Prinsep. Philadelphia: Grigg and Eliot.

Semmler, W. (1986) 'On nonlinear theories of economic cycles and the persistence of business cycles'. *Mathematical Social Sciences*, 12, pp. 47–76.

Sen, A. K. (1979) 'Rational fools: a critique of the behavioural foundations of economic theory'. In F. H. Hahn and M. Hollis (eds.) *Philosophy and Economic Theory*. Oxford: Oxford University Press.

Shah, A. and M. Desai (1981) 'Growth cycles with induced technical change'. *Economic Journal*, 91, pp. 1006–10.

Shepherd, W. (1982) 'Causes of increased competition in the U.S. economy 1939–1980'. *Review of Economics and Statistics*, 64, no. 4, pp. 613–26.

Skott, P. (1981) 'On the "Kaldorian" saving function'. *Kyklos*, 34, pp. 563–81.

(1983) 'An essay on Keynes and general equilibrium theory'. *Thames Papers in Political Economy*, Summer.

(1985a) 'Vicious circles and cumulative causation'. *Thames Papers in Political Economy*, Summer.

(1985b) 'Some observations on Keynes, Say's law and the quantity theory'. Working Paper 85–05, University College London.

(1986) 'On general equilibrium theory, rationality and the costs of spurious generality'. *British Review of Economic Issues*, 8, pp. 29–50.

(1988a) 'Finance, accumulation and the choice of technique'. *Cambridge Journal of Economics*, 12, pp. 339–54.

(1988b) 'Dynamics of a Keynesian economy under different monetary regimes'. In P. Flaschel and M. Krüger (eds.) *Recent Approaches to Dynamic Economics*. Frankfurt-on-Main: Peter Lang Verlag.

(1989a) 'Effective demand, class struggle and cyclical growth'. *International Economic Review*, 30, pp. 231–47.

(1989b) *Kaldor's Growth and Distribution Theory*. Frankfurt-on-Main: Peter Lang Verlag.

Solow, R. M. (1956) 'A contribution to the theory of economic growth'. *Quarterly Journal of Economics*, 70, pp. 65–94.

Spence, M. (1977) 'Entry, investment and oligopolistic pricing'. *Bell Journal of Economics*, 8, pp. 534–44.

Steindl, J. (1976) *Maturity and Stagnation in American Capitalism*. New York: Monthly Review Press. (First published in 1952.)

Swan, T. W. (1956) 'Economic growth and capital accumulation'. *The Economic Record*, 32, pp. 334–61.

Taylor, L. (1983) *Structuralist Macroeconomics*. New York: Basic Books.

(1985) 'A stagnationist model of economic growth'. *Cambridge Journal of Economics*, 9, pp. 383–403.

Tobin, J. (1960) 'Towards a *general* Kaldorian theory of distribution'. *Review of Economic Studies*, 27, pp. 119–20.

Torre, V. (1977) 'Existence of limit cycles and control in complete Keynesian system by theory of bifurcation'. *Econometrica*, 45, pp. 1457–66.

Utton, M. and E. Morgan (1983) *Concentration and Foreign Trade*. Cambridge: Cambridge University Press.

van der Ploeg, F. (1983) 'Economic growth and conflict over the distribution of income'. *Journal of Economic Dynamics and Control*, 6, pp. 253–79.

Varian, H. R. (1979) 'Catastrophe theory and the business cycle'. *Economic Inquiry*, 17, pp. 14–28.

Wadhwani, S. (1987) 'The effects of inflation and real wages on employment'. *Economica*, 54, pp. 21–40.

Weintraub, E. R. (1979) *Microfoundations*. Cambridge: Cambridge University Press.

Williams, K., J. Williams and D. Thomas (1983) *Why Are the British Bad at Manufacturing*. London: Routledge and Kegan Paul.
Wolfstetter, E. (1982) 'Fiscal policy and the classical growth cycle'. *Zeitschrift für Nationalökonomie*, 42, pp. 375–93.
Wood, A. (1975) *A Theory of Profits*. Cambridge: Cambridge University Press.

Index